The Technology of Video and Audio Streaming

Second Edition

10/2007

The Technology of Video and Audio Streaming

Second Edition

David Austerberry

ELSEVIER

AMSTERDAM • BOSTON • HEIDELBERG • LONDON
NEW YORK • OXFORD • PARIS • SAN DIEGO
SAN FRANCISCO • SINGAPORE • SYDNEY • TOKYO

Focal Press is an imprint of Elsevier

Focal Press

Focal Press
is An imprint of Elsevier.

200 Wheeler Road, Burlington, MA 01803, USA
Linacre House, Jordan Hill, Oxford OX2 8DP, UK

 Recognizing the importance of preserving what has been written, Elsevier prints its books on acid-free paper whenever possible.

Library of Congress Cataloging-in-Publication Data
Austerberry, David.
    The technology of video and audio streaming / David Austerberry. – 2nd ed.
        p.   cm.
    Includes bibliographical references and index.
    ISBN 0-240-80580-1
    1. Streaming technology (Telecommunications)   2. Digital video.   3. Sound – Recording and reproducing – Digital techniques.   I. Title.
    TK5105.386 .A97 2004
    006.7'876 – dc22

                                                                    2004017485

British Library Cataloguing-in-Publication Data
A catalogue record for this book is available from the British Library.

ISBN: 0240805801

For information on all Focal Press publications visit our website at
www.books.elsevier.com

04 05 06 07 08 09   10 9 8 7 6 5 4 3 2 1

Printed in the United States of America

Contents

Preface

The first edition of this book came about because I had made a career move from television to streaming media. Although it was still video, streaming seemed like a different world. The two camps, television and IT, had evolved separately. It was not just the technology. It was the work practices, the jargon – everything was different. I soon found that the two sides often misunderstood each other, and I had to learn the other's point of view. What I missed was a top-down view of the technologies. I knew I could get deep technical information about encoding, setting up servers, distribution networks. But for the business decisions about what to purchase I did not need such detail – I wanted the big picture. I found out the hard way by doing all the research. It was just one more step to turn that information into a book.

As with any technology, the book became outdated. Companies closed down or were bought out. The industry has consolidated into fewer leading suppliers, but what a potential purchaser of systems needs are stable companies that are going to be around for support and upgrades.

The second edition brings the information up to date, especially in the areas of MPEG-4, Windows Media, Real, and Apple QuickTime.

Much has happened since I wrote the first edition of this book. There has been an expansion across the board in the availability of network bandwidth. The price of fiber circuits is decreasing. Within corporate networks, it is becoming normal to link network switches with fiber. Gigabit Ethernet is replacing 10baseT. In many countries, the local loop is being unbundled. This gives the consumer a choice of ADSL providers. They may also have the option of data over cable from the local cable television network. All this competition is driving down prices.

As third-generation wireless networks are rolled out, it becomes feasible to view video from mobile appliances. These new developments are freeing the use of streaming technology from just the PC platform. Although the PC has many advantages as a rich media terminal, the advent of other channels is increasing its acceptance by corporations.

There are still many hurdles. Potentially, streaming over IP offers cable television networks a means to deliver video on demand. One problem is that there is an installed base of legacy set-top boxes with no support for video over IP. Another problem is the cost of the media servers.

What will all this universal access to video-on-demand mean? Since the dawn of television, video has been accepted as a great communicator. The ability of a viewer to choose what and when they want to watch has presented many new opportunities. For government, it is now possible for the public to watch proceedings and committees. Combined with e-mail, this provides the platform to offer 'open government.' The training providers were early adopters of streaming, which transformed the possibilities for distance learning by the addition of video. The lecturers now had a face and a voice.

For the corporation it adds another channel to their communications to staff, to investors, and for public relations. Advertisers are beginning to try the medium. A naturally conservative bunch, they have been wary of any technological barriers between them and the consumer. The general acceptance of media plug-ins to the Web browser now makes the potential audience very large. The content delivery networks can stream reliable video to the consumer. The advertisers can add the medium to existing channels as a new way to reach what is often a very specific demographic group.

This edition adds more information on MPEG-4. When I wrote the first edition, many of the MPEG-4 standards were still in development. In the intervening period the advanced video codec (AVC), also known as H.264, has been developed, and through 2004 will be released in many encoding products. Microsoft has made many improvements to Windows Media, with version 9 offering very efficient encoding for video from thumbnail size up to high-definition television. Microsoft also submitted the codec to the SMPTE (Society of Motion Picture and Television Engineers) for standardization as VC-9. Windows Media Player 10 adds new facilities for discovering online content.

The potential user of streaming has a choice of codecs, with MPEG-4 and Windows Media both offering performance and facilities undreamt of ten years ago. I would like to thank Envivio and their UK reseller, Offstump, for help with information on MPEG-4 applications, with a special mention for Kevin Steele. Jason Chow at TWIinteractive gave me a thorough run-down on the Interactive Content Factory, an innovative application that leverages the power of streaming.

David Austerberry, June 2004

Acknowledgments

The original idea for a book stemmed from a meeting with Jennifer Welham of Focal Press at a papers session during an annual conference of the National Association of Broadcasters. I would like to thank Philip O'Ferrall for suggesting streaming media as a good subject for a book; we were building an ASP to provide streaming facilities. I received great assistance from Colin Birch at Tyrell Corporation, and would like to thank Joe Apted at ClipStream (a VTR company) for the views of an encoding shop manager. I am especially grateful to Gavin Starks for his assistance and for reading through my draft copy.

The web sites of RealNetworks, Microsoft, and Apple have provided much background reading on the three main architectures.

While I was undertaking the research for this book I found so many dead links on the Web – many startups in the streaming business have closed down or have been acquired by other companies. I wanted to keep the links and references up to date in this fast-changing business, so rather than printing links in the text, all the references for this book are to be found on the associated web site at www.davidausterberry.com/streaming.html.

Section 1

Basics

1 Introduction

Streaming media is an exciting addition to the rich media producers' toolbox. Just as the cinema and radio were ousted by television as the primary mass communication medium, streaming is set to transform the World Wide Web. The original text-based standards of the Web have been stretched far beyond the original functionality of the core protocols to incorporate images and animation, yet video and audio are accepted as the most natural way to communicate. Through the experience of television, we now have come to expect video to be the primary vehicle for the dissemination of knowledge and entertainment. This has driven the continuing developments that now allow video to be delivered over the Internet as a live stream.

Streaming has been heralded by many as an alternative delivery channel to conventional radio and television – video over IP. But that is a narrow view; streaming can be at its most compelling when its special strengths are exploited. As part of an interactive rich media presentation it becomes a whole new communication channel that can compete in its own right with print, radio, television, and the text-based Web.

500 years of print development

It took 500 years from the time Gutenberg introduced the printing press to reach the electronic book of today. In the short period of the last 10 years, we have moved from the textual web page to rich media. Some of the main components of the illuminated manuscript still exist in the web page. The illustrated drop-capital (called an *historiated initial*) and the floral borders or marginalia have been replaced by the GIF image. The illustrations, engravings, and half-tones of the print medium are now JPEG images. But the elements of the web page are not that different from the books of 1500.

We can thank Tim Berners-Lee for the development of the hypertext markup language (HTML) that has exploded into a whole new way of communicating.

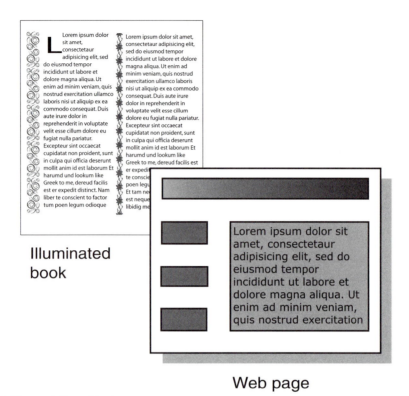

Illuminated
book

Web page

Figure 1.1 The evolution of text on a page.

Most businesses today place great reliance on a company web site to provide information about their products and services, along with a host of corporate information and possibly file downloads. Soon after its inception, the Web was exploited as a medium that could be used to sell products and services. But if the sales department wanted to give a presentation to a customer, the only ways open to them were either face-to-face or through the medium of television.

100 years of the moving image

The moving image, by contrast, has been around for only 100 years. Since the development of cinematography in the 1890s by the Lumière brothers and Edison, the movie has become part of our general culture and entertainment. Fifty years later the television was introduced to the public, bringing moving images into the home. Film and television textual content has always been simple, limited to a few lines of text, a lower third, and a logo. The low vertical

Figure 1.2 Representation of cable TV news.

resolution of standard definition television does not allow the use of small character heights. Some cable television news stations are transmitting a more web-like design. The main video program is squeezed back and additional content is displayed in sidebars and banners. Interactivity with the viewer, however, is lacking. Television can support a limited interactivity: voting by responding to a short list of different choices, and on-screen navigation.

The Web meets television

Rich media combines the Web, interactive multimedia, and television in an exciting new medium in its own right. The multimedia CD-ROM has been with us for some time, and is very popular for training applications with interactive navigation around a seamless combination of graphics, video, and audio. The programs were always physically distributed on CD-ROM, and now on DVD. Unfortunately the MPEG-1 files were much too large for streaming. Advances in audio and video compression now make it possible for such files to be distributed in real-time over the Web.

Macromedia's Flash vector graphics are a stepping-stone on the evolution from hypertext to rich media. The web designers and developers used a great deal of creativity and innovative scripting to make some very dynamic, interactive web sites using Flash. With Flash MX2004 these sites now can include true

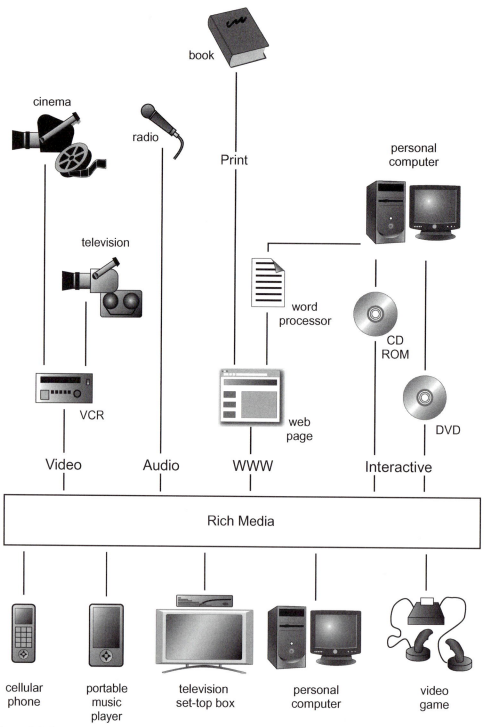

Figure 1.3 Evolution from diverse media to a new generation of integrated media.

streaming video and audio embedded in the animation. So by combining the production methods of the multimedia disk with the skills of the web developer, a whole new way to communicate ideas has been created.

Convergence

The media are converging – there is a blurring of the edges between the traditional divides of mass communication. Print now has e-books, and the newspapers have their own web sites carrying background to the stories and access to the archives. The television set-top box can be used to surf the Web, send e-mail, or interact with the program and commercials. Now a web site may have embedded video and audio.

New technologies have emerged, notably MPEG-4 and the third-generation wireless standards. MPEG-4 has taken a leap forward as a platform for rich media. You can now synchronize three-dimensional and synthetic content with regular video and images in an interactive presentation. For the creative artist it is a whole new toolbox.

The new wireless devices can display pictures and video as well as text and graphics. The screens can be as large as 320 × 240 pixels, and in full color. The bandwidth may be much lower than the hundreds of kilobits that can be downloaded to a PC through a cable modem or an ADSL connection, but much is possible for the innovative content creator.

This convergence has raised many challenges. How to contain production costs? How to manage content? How to integrate different creative disciplines? Can content be repurposed for other media by cost-effective processes? The technologies themselves present issues. How do you create content for the tiny screen on a wireless device and for high-definition television?

What is streaming?

The terms streaming media and webcasting often are used synonymously. In this book I refer to webcasting as the equivalent of television broadcasting, but delivered over the Web. Live or prerecorded content is streamed to a schedule and pushed out to the viewer. The alternative is on-demand delivery, where the user pulls down the content, often interactively.

Webcasting embraces both streaming and file download. Streamed media is delivered direct from the source to the player in real-time. This is a continuous process, with no intermediate storage of the media clip. In many ways this is much like conventional television. Similarly, if the content has been stored for on-demand delivery, it is delivered at a controlled rate to the display in real-time as if it were live. Contrast this with much of the MP3 music delivery, where the file is downloaded in its entirety to the local disk drive before playback, a process called download-and-play.

True streaming could be considered a subset of webcasting. But streaming does not have to use the Web; streams can be delivered through wireless networks or over private intranets. So streaming and webcasting overlap and coexist.

Streaming media has been around for 70 years. The conventional television that we grew up with would be called streaming media if it were invented today. The original television systems delivered live pictures from the camera, via the distribution network, to the home receiver. In the 1950s, Ampex developed a means of storing the picture streams: the videotape recorder. This gave broadcasters the option of live broadcast (streaming), or playing prerecorded programs from tape. The television receiver has no storage or buffering; the picture is displayed synchronized to the emissions from the transmitter. Television normally is transmitted over a fixed bandwidth connection with a high quality of service (QoS).

Today, streaming media is taken to mean digitally encoded files delivered over the World Wide Web to PCs, or *IP broadcasting*. Whereas television has a one-way channel to the viewer, Internet Protocol (IP) delivery has a bidirectional connection between the media source and the viewer. This allows a more interactive connection that can enable facilities just not possible with conventional television.

The first of these new facilities is that content can be provided on demand. This often has been promised for conventional television, but has not yet proved to be financially viable. Streaming also differs from television in that the media source (the server) can adapt to cope with varying availability of bandwidth. The goal is to deliver the best picture possible under the prevailing network conditions.

A normal unicast stream over IP uses a one-to-one connection between the server and the client (the media player). Scheduled streaming also can be multicast, where a single IP stream is served to the network. The routers deliver the same stream to all the viewers that have requested the content. This allows great savings in the utilization of corporate networks for applications like live briefings or training sessions. As a single stream is viewed by all, it cannot be used for on-demand delivery.

Like subscription television, streaming media can offer conditional access to content using digital rights management. This can be used wherever the owner of the content wants to control who can view; for example, for reasons of corporate confidentiality, or for entertainment, to ensure that the viewer has paid for the content.

What is real-time?

Streaming often is referred to as real-time; this is a somewhat vague term. It implies viewing an event as it happens. Typical television systems have latency; it may be milliseconds, but with highly compressed codecs the latency can be some seconds. The primary factor that makes a stream real-time is that there is no intermediate storage of the data packets. There may be some short buffers, like frame stores in the decoder, but the signal essentially streams all the way from the camera to the player. Streamed media is not stored on the local disk in the client machine, unless a download specifically is requested (and allowed).

Just because streaming is real-time does not mean it has to be live. Pre-recorded files also can be delivered in real-time. The server delivers the packets to the network at a rate that matches the correct video playback speed.

Applications

Wherever electronic communication is used, the applications for streaming are endless. Streaming can be delivered as a complete video package of linear programming, as a subscription service, or as pay-per-view (PPV). It can form part of an interactive web site or it can be a tool in its own right, for video preview and film dailies. Some applications are:

- Internet broadcasting (corporate communications)
- Education (viewing lectures and distance learning)
- Web-based channels (IP-TV, Internet radio)
- Video-on-demand (VOD)
- Music distribution (music on-demand)
- Internet and intranet browsing of content (asset management)

The big advantage of streaming over television is the exploitation of IP Connectivity – a ubiquitous medium. How many office workers have a television on their desk and a hookup to the cable television system?

Europe and the United States

Over the years the United States and Europe have adopted different standards that impact upon this book. The first is the television standards, with the United States adopting a 525-line/30-frame format versus the European standard of 625 lines/ 25 frames per second. The other is the different telecommunications standards, with the Bell hierarchy in the United States giving a base broadband rate of 1.5 Mbit/s (T-1), and the 2 Mbit/s (E-1) of the Europe Telecommunications Standards Institute (ETSI). It is relatively easy to convert from one to another, so the differing standards are not an obstacle to international media delivery.

The production team

Much like web design, streaming media production requires a multidisciplinary team. A web site requires content authors, graphic designers, and web developers. The site also needs IT staff to run the servers and security systems.

To utilize streaming you will have to add the video production team to this group of people. This is the same as a television production team, but the videographer should understand the limitations of the medium. Streaming media players are not high-definition television.

If you are producing rich media, many of the skills should already be present in your web team. These include the design skills plus the ability to write the SMIL and TIME scripts used to synchronize the many elements of an interactive production. So, with luck, you may not need to add to your web production team to incorporate streaming.

How this book is organized

This book is divided into three sections. The first is a background to telecommunications and audio/video compression. The second section contains the core chapters on streaming. The final section covers associated technologies and some applications for streaming media.

The book is not intended to replace the operation and installation manuals provided by the vendors of streaming architectures. Those will give much more detail on the specifics of setting up their products.

Summary

Streaming media presents the professional communicator with a whole new way to deliver information, messages, and entertainment. By leveraging the Internet, distribution costs can be much lower than the traditional media.

The successful webcaster will need to assemble a multiskilled and creative team to produce high-quality streaming media content. The Web audience is unforgiving, so content has to be compelling to receive worthwhile viewing figures that will give a return on the investment in streaming.

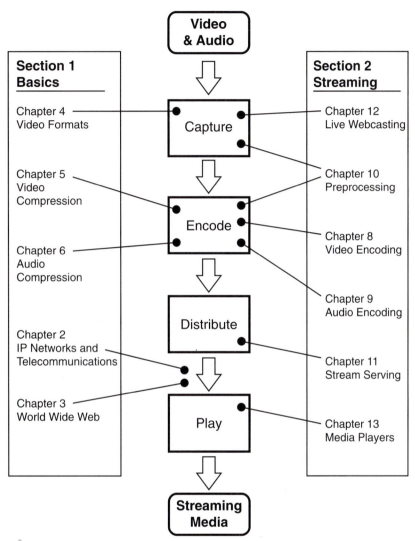

Figure 1.4 The chapter content.

The development of streaming has benefited from a very wide range of disciplines. We can thank the neurophysiologists for the research in understanding the psychoacoustics of human hearing that has been so vital to the design of audio compression algorithms. Similar work has led to advances in video compression. The information technology engineers constantly are improving content delivery within the framework of the existing Web infrastructure. We must not forget the creativity of the multimedia developer in exploiting the technologies to produce visually stimulating content. And a final word for Napster;

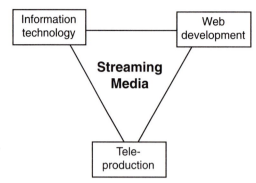

Figure 1.5 The production team.

peer-to-peer distribution has driven the need to deploy digital rights management systems to protect the intellectual property of the content creators and owners.

Streaming technology is very fast-moving. New versions of codecs are released every year. New technologies obsolete the incumbent, so any streaming content creation and management system must be designed to be flexible and extensible. Some of the newer applications like mobile and wireless are likely to be more stable. The phone manufacturers prefer fixed standards to ensure reliable operation and low manufacturing cost.

Perhaps the greatest advance that benefits the content creator is the recent emergence of tools to aid the production processes. Just as the word processor brought basic DTP to every desktop, these tools will allow the small business and corporate user to deploy streaming without the need to outsource. The streaming production shop will be freed to concentrate on the more creative content creation.

2 IP networks and telecommunications

Introduction

Why is a network drawn as a cloud? Is it because most are unaware of the processes happening as data tranverses the network?

In all but the smallest of enterprises, the IT department maintains the computer network infrastructure. How many of us are concerned with what happens beyond the RJ-45 jack on the wall? It says a lot for computer networks that we often forget the network is there. We haul files across the world at the click of a mouse, and they arrive seconds later.

With video media, things are different; we place many more demands on the network. So it helps to understand a little more about the data network, and the telecommunications infrastructure that underpins it.

The first thing that is different about the delivery of multimedia streams is that usually they do not use the universal TCP/IP (Transport Control Protocol over Internet Protocol). Second, the media files are very large compared with the average e-mail message or web page. Third, delivery in real-time is a prerequisite for smooth playback of video and audio.

A new set of network protocols has been developed to support multimedia streaming. As an example, advances in Internet protocols now support *multicasting*, where one media stream serves hundreds or thousands of players. This is a handy facility for optimizing network resources if you want to webcast live to large audiences.

The media files are streamed over the general telecommunications network. Again, this is something we rarely think about, unless your company wants a new telephone switch. Communications channels become an issue as soon as you start to encode. The codec (compression/decompression) configuration menu will offer a number of compression choices: dial-up modem, dual-ISDN, DSL, T-1. So it helps to understand the pipes through which the media is delivered. Streaming is not like the web page where the content arrives after a short delay, and how it reached the browser is of little concern to the user. With streaming the intervening network has a major impact on the delivered quality of the video and audio.

Most streaming files are delivered over a data network. For internal corporate communications it may be the local network or, for an enterprise with widely dispersed sites, a wide-area network. For business-to-business and consumer streaming, the Internet is a likely carrier. The Internet has become ubiquitous for data communications, from simple e-mail to complex electronic commerce applications. The Internet needs a physical layer, the fiber and copper that carry the data. For this we turn to the telcos. It may be your incumbent telephony supplier, or one of the new wideband fiber networks. In all probability, an end-to-end Internet connection will use a combination of many carriers and networks.

This chapter gives an overview of the connections that carry the stream. The first section is about data networks. The second is about telecommunications, with the focus on the last mile to your browser. This final link includes the two popular broadband consumer products: DSL and the cable modem.

Network layers

The concept of interconnected networking, or the Internet, has its origins in the quest by the U.S. military to connect research institutions over a packet-switched network. In the 1970s the U.S. Department of Defense DARPA project developed the multilayer model of network protocols that evolved into today's Internet. The International Standards Organization later augmented the communication protocols, which evolved into the Open Systems Interface model (the ISO OSI). The Internet does not wholly adhere to the open systems interface; Figure 2.1 shows the relationship, but note that the principles are similar. Later protocols do adhere more closely to the ISO seven-layer model.

The DARPA model defined four layers:

- Network access layer
- Internet layer
- Host-to-host layer
- Process layer

The network access layer includes a number of protocols that deliver the data over the physical network (the copper and fiber). The protocol chosen depends upon the type of physical network. The Internet layer delivers the data packets from the source to the destination address. It masks the network technology in use from other layers. The host-to-host layer handles the connection rendezvous and manages the data flow. The process layer is for the implementation of the user application, like e-mail and file transfer.

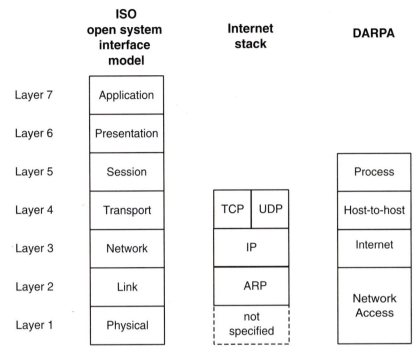

Figure 2.1 Multilayer network model.

Internet Protocol

Internet Protocol is the main network (layer 3) communication protocol. The other protocols at layer 3 are used for control of the network routers to set up the connections. IP has a drawback, however; it is an unreliable delivery system.

- There is variable network latency.
- The packets can arrive in a different order from transmission.
- Packets can be lost.

These potential problems are corrected by the higher layer protocols and applications. The most well-known protocol is at the transport layer, Transport Control Protocol (TCP). This is used together with Internet Protocol – the ubiquitous TCP/IP. One of the great strengths of TCP is its reliability. The built-in error protection of TCP makes it an excellent protocol for the delivery of general purpose data, but the way this is implemented proves to be a disadvantage for streaming applications. TCP sequences the data bytes with a forwarding acknowledgement number that indicates to the destination the next byte the source expects to receive. If bytes are not acknowledged within a specified time period they are retransmitted. This feature of TCP allows devices to detect lost packets and request a retransmission. The repeated transmission will add to the communication latency, but that is not normally an issue with data exchange. TCP also provides flow control of the data. With audio and video, the viewer requires a continuous stream to view the source in real-time. Retransmission of data is going to add delays; retransmission also uses up bandwidth in the data channel. Ultimately, high levels of network transmission errors will empty the receive buffer in the media player. The interruption to the stream will ultimately will lead to interruptions to the video playback. The alternative is to ignore lost packets. This may cause loss or distortion of a single video frame, but that is a transient event that will be ignored by the viewer. So for real-time applications, timely delivery is more important than error-free transmission.

User Datagram Protocol (UDP)

Streaming needs a transmission protocol that can ignore data errors. Such a protocol is the User Datagram Protocol (UDP). It is used as a transport proto-

Table 2.1 TCP versus UDP

TCP	UDP
Connection oriented	Connectionless
Reliable	Unreliable
Controls data flow	No flow control

Table 2.2 Popular Internet Applications and Their Underlying Transport Protocols

Application	Application-layer Protocol	Typical Transport Protocol
E-mail	SMTP	TCP
Remote terminal access	Telnet	TCP
Web	HTTP	TCP
File transfer	FTP	TCP
Remote file server	NFS	UDP
Streaming media	RTSP or proprietary	UDP
Voice-over IP	Proprietary	UDP
Network management	SNMP	UDP
Routing protocol	RIP	UDP
Name translation	DNS	UDP

col for several application-layer protocols, notably the Network File System (NFS), Simple Network Management Protocol (SNMP), and the Domain Name System (DNS). UDP has neither the error correction nor the flow control of TCP, so this task has to be handled by an application at a higher layer in the stack. It does, however, carry a checksum of the payload data. The media players can often mask video data errors.

IP version 6

Most of the Internet uses IP version 4. This protocol has been around since 1981, but is showing its age as use of the Internet has spiraled. It now has many shortcomings, so IP version 6 is offering to solve many of the problem issues. The first problem is lack of addresses. As more and more users connect to the Internet, version 4 addresses are going to run out. The use of always-on broadband connections means that the dynamic sharing of IP addresses (used with dial-up modems) can no longer be used to advantage. One solution to better utilization of the existing address ranges is to move from the fixed number groups of the A, B, and C classes to classless addressing or CIDR (classless inter-domain routing). The class D addresses reserved for multicast are particularly limited in number. If multicasting is to be exploited to save network congestion, many more addresses will be needed. IP version 6 solves the address space issue by increasing from 32-bit address space to 128 bits. This gives 6×10^{23} IP addresses per square meter of the Earth's surface. This may seem to be a ridiculous overkill, but it allows far more freedom for multi-level hierarchies of address allocation. This is the same as telephone numbers, with the hierarchy of area codes. The big advantage of this hierarchy is that the tables in the network routers can be simplified, so the fine-grain routing need only be done at the destination router.

Many other improvements have been incorporated into the version 6 protocol, including a simplified packet header, again to improve router throughput.

The advantages specific to streaming will be two-fold: the increased address space and the opportunity to manage quality of service (QoS). One header field is the traffic flow identification, which will allow routers to distinguish real-time data from mail and file transfer (FTP).

MPEG-4 potentially could take advantage of this packet priority. The scalable coding option provides a baseline low-resolution image, with helper packets to add detail to an image for higher resolution, albeit requiring a higher bandwidth. The low-resolution image could be allocated a higher priority than the high-resolution helper signals. So if the network becomes congested the resolution degrades gracefully as packets are dropped, rather than the stalling that we see with conventional codecs.

Routers compliant with IP version 6 support multicasting as a standard facility.

Real-time protocols

A number of different protocols have been developed to facilitate real-time streaming of multimedia content. Streaming means that the mean frame rate of the video viewed at the player is dictated by the transmitted frame rate. The delivery rate has to be controlled so that the video data arrives just before it is required for display on the player. The associated audio track or tracks must also remain synchronized to the video. IP data transmission is not a synchronous process and delivery is by best effort. To achieve synchronism, timing references have to be embedded in the stream.

Table 2.3 Summary of Protocols Used for Multimedia Sessions

Abbreviation	Title	Notes	RFC number
RSVP	Resource Reservation Protocol	Protocol specification	2205
	RSVP applicability statement	Guide to deployment	2208
	Message processing rules		2209
RTCP	Real-Time Control Protocol	Part of RTP	1889
RTSP	Real-Time Streaming Protocol		2326
RTP	Real-Time Protocol		1889
SDP	Session Description Protocol		2327
UDP	User Datagram Protocol		768

The Internet Engineering Task Force issues Request For Comment documents (RFC) that become the de facto protocols.

Intimately linked to real-time delivery is the quality of service (QoS). To ensure the reliable delivery of packets, the network bandwidth would have to be reserved for the stream. This generally is not the case with the Internet. One protocol that allows resources to be reserved by a client is Resource Reservation Protocol (RSVP). It allows the client to negotiate with routers in the path for bandwidth, but does not actually deliver the data. RSVP is not widely supported.

Transport protocol for real-time applications (RTP)

Real-Time Protocol (RTP) is a transport protocol that was developed for streaming data. RTP includes extra data fields not present in TCP. It provides a time-stamp and sequence number to facilitate the data transport timing, and allows control of the media server so that the video stream is served at the correct rate for real-time display. The media player then uses these RTP fields to assemble the received packets into the correct order and playback rate.

Sequence number The value of this 16-bit number increments by one for each packet. It is used by the player to detect packet loss and then to sequence the packets in the correct order. The initial number for a stream session is chosen at random.

Timestamp This is a sampling instance derived from a reference clock to allow for synchronization and jitter calculations. It is monotonic and linear in time.

Source identifiers CSRC is a unique identifier for the synchronization of the RTP stream. One or more CSRCs exist when the RTP stream is carrying information for multiple media sources. This could be the case for a video mix between two sources or for embedded content.

RTP usually runs on UDP, and uses its multiplexing and checksum features. Note that RTP does not provide any control of the quality of service or reservation of network resources.

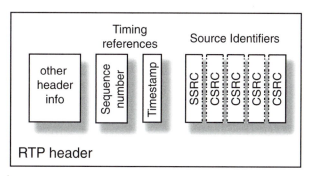

Figure 2.2 RTP header.

Proprietary private data formats also are used for data transport between the media server and the browser client. An example is RealNetworks Real Data Transport (RDT).

Real-Time Control Protocol (RTCP)

RTCP is used in conjunction with RTP. It gives feedback to each participant in an RTP session that can be used to control the session. The messages include reception reports, including number of packets lost and jitter statistics (early or late arrivals). This information potentially can be used by higher layer applications to modify the transmission. For example, the bit rate of a stream could be changed to counter network congestion. Some RTCP messages relate to control of a video conference with multiple participants.

Session Description Protocol (SDP)

SDP is a media description format intended for describing multimedia sessions, including video-conferencing. It includes session announcement and session invitation.

Real-Time Streaming Protocol (RTSP)

The Real-Time Streaming Protocol is an application-level protocol for the control of real-time multimedia data. RTSP provides an extensible framework rather than a protocol. It allows interactive, VCR-like control of the playback: Play, Pause, and so on. A streaming server also can react to network congestion, changing the media bandwidth to suit the available capacity.

RTSP was developed intentionally to be similar in syntax and operation to HTTP version 1.1. It does differ in several important aspects, however. With RTSP both client and server can issue requests during interaction – with HTTP the client always issues the requests (for documents). RTSP has to retain the state of a session, whereas HTTP is stateless.

RTSP supports the use of RTP as the underlying data delivery protocol. The protocol is intended to give a means of choosing the optimum delivery channel to a client. Some corporate firewalls will not pass UDP. The streaming server has to offer a choice of delivery protocols – UDP, multicast UDP, and TCP – to suit different clients.

RTSP is not the only streaming control protocol. Real's precursor, Progressive Networks, used a proprietary protocol before RTSP was developed.

MMS

The Microsoft Media Server (MMS) is Microsoft's proprietary control protocol. MMS handles client interaction – the controls like Play or Stop. MMS uses TCP as the delivery layer. The media data can be transmitted separately over UDP or TCP.

SMPTE time code

RTSP uses Society of Motion Picture and Television Engineers (SMPTE) time code as a time reference for video frames. Note that RTP uses a different time reference, the Network Time Protocol (NTP), which is based on universal time (UTC). RTP uses the middle 32 bits of the NTP 64-bit fixed-point number to represent the time. The high 16 bits of the 32-bit NTP fraction are used to represent subsecond timing – this gives a resolution of about 15 μs, or about one quarter of a television line.

Multicasting

Suppose the CEO of an enterprise wants to stream an address to all the staff. Let us say there are 500 staff at headquarters on the West coast, 1,000 personnel work at the South coast plant, and another 500 at the East coast offices. The normal way to transmit an Internet presentation is to set up a one-to-one

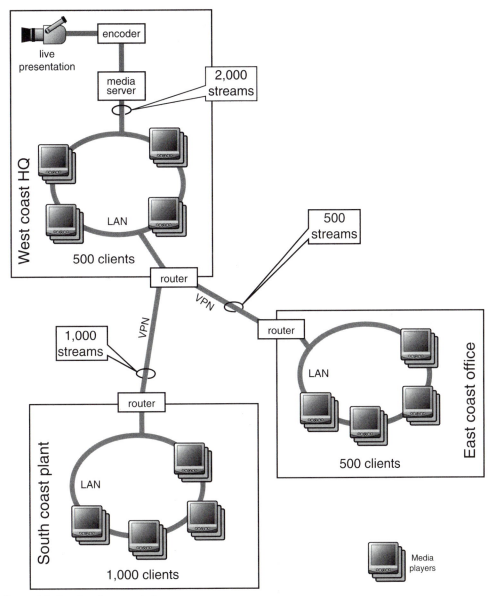

Figure 2.3 A unicast presentation.

connection for each media player client. This is called *unicasting*. In this example you would have to transmit 500 + 1,000 + 500 (= 2,000) separate content streams.

The webcaster can look with envy at the television broadcaster. With one transmitter and one tower the broadcaster can reach every resident living within his or her service area. In a metropolitan area he or she can reach an audience of several million people. As a webcaster you have to provide server resource for each viewer, plus the bandwidth of the Internet has to be sufficient to carry all the streams that you want to serve.

Multicasting offers an alternative to conventional streaming or unicasting. A single stream is served to the Internet as a multicast. All the viewers then can attach to the same stream. The client initiates a multicast; the server just delivers the stream to the network. Further viewers just attach to the same stream. The server has no knowledge of where the stream is going, unlike the normal TCP client–server handshaking interactions of an Internet connection. A client will be made aware of a multicast by some out-of-band channel; it could be by e-mail or through publicity on a web site. The viewer then requests the multicast at the appropriate date and time. An alternative is to use the session announcement protocol.

Note that you can broadcast to a network, but it is not like a television broadcast. It is used by network administrators for control messages, and does not propagate beyond the local subnet.

Multicasting sounds like a very efficient solution to the resource problems of delivering a webcast to very large audiences. But there are catches. First, it can be used only for live or simulated live webcasting. You lose the interactivity of on-demand streaming. The second drawback is that many older network routers do not support multicasting. There are ways around this: Multicast streams can be tunneled through legacy plant, and the multicast enabled backbone (MBone) can be used. Many of the problems have restricted its use to corporate networks (intranets). Large public webcasts have had to resort to conventional splitting and caching to guarantee delivery to all potential clients.

Note that multicasting is not limited to streaming; it also can be used for general data delivery (like database upgrades across a dispersed enterprise, or for video conferencing).

Multicast address allocation

Most IP addresses that are classless (CIDR) fall into Class C. If you work for a very large corporation or government department, then you may use the Class A and B address spaces. Multicasting uses a reserved set of IP addresses in Class D, ranging from 224.0.0.0 to 239.255.255.255. To make public Internet multicasts you will need a unique address. Although some addresses are permanently allocated to hosts, they are usually transient and allocated for a single

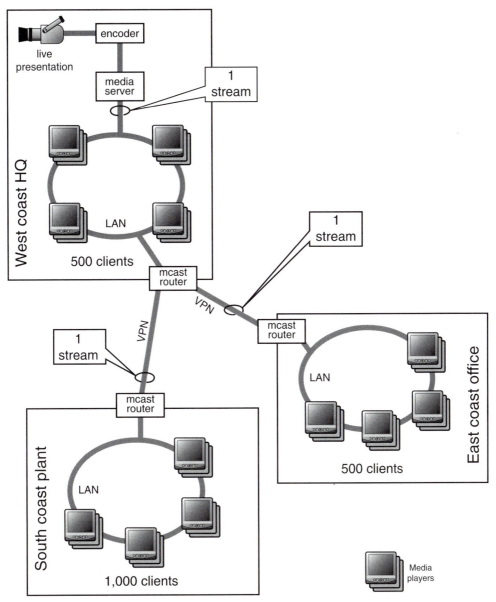

Figure 2.4 Multicast presentation.

multicast event. There is a proposal to dynamically allocate the host group addresses, much like the dynamic allocation of client IP addresses. The permanent addresses have to be registered with the Internet Assigned Numbers Authority (IANA), or the designated proxy organization for your country (like the RIPENCC in Europe). There has been a certain amount of chaos in this area, and it is not unknown for an address not to be unique. Hopefully the upgrades to IP version 6 will help to solve that problem by making far more addresses available.

IGMP

Most of the complexity of a multicast lies with the routing, not with the server and the client. Instead of the server sending individual packets to each client, a single packet is transmitted to a multicast group. This group is allocated a single IP address.

The primary mechanism for controlling the delivery of the datagram to multiple destinations is the Internet Group-Membership Protocol (IGMP). It is a session-layer protocol used by the client to join and leave a multicast. A multicast-enabled router uses this session information to set up the route from the server to the client. The router will forward multicast datagrams only if regular IGMP messages are received from downstream clients (typically at intervals of about 60 seconds). Several routing options have been developed for multicast routing:

- Protocol Independent Multicast (PIM)
- Distance-Vector Multicast Routing Protocol (DVMRP)
- Core-based tree (CBT)
- Multicast Open Shortest Path First (MOSPF)

There are two ways of multicast routing: dense mode and sparse mode.

Sparse and dense routing

Dense mode floods the network then prunes back the unused branches. This assumes that the viewers of the multicast are densely distributed through the network, which could be the case for corporate communications over an intranet. It requires a generous bandwidth. DVMRP, MOSPF, and PIM dense mode are all such protocols. The reach of dense routing trees is limited by the time-to-live parameter (TTL). The value of TTL is decreased by one each time a datagram passes through a router; once it reaches zero, the router will discard the packets. This can be used to restrict the range of the multicast that potentially could propagate through the entire Internet. TTL is measured in seconds and usually is set to a default value of 64.

The other type of multicast routing is sparse mode, which is used for applications where the clients are dispersed, possibly geographically, over a wide

Table 2.4 Time-to-Live Initial Values

Scope	TTL
Local area	16
National high-bandwidth sites	32
National sites	48
Continental sites	64
Intercontinental high-bandwidth sites	128
Worldwide coverage	192

area of the network. In such a case the dense-mode flooding would cause unnecessary congestion on the network.

The core-based tree (CBT) uses a core router to construct a distribution tree. Edge routers send requests to join the tree, and then a branch is set up. Network traffic will concentrate around the core, which can cause problems with congestion.

MBone

The multicast-enabled backbone project (MBone) was set up in 1992 to enable the IETF (Internet Engineering Task Force) meetings to set up audioconferencing to communicate with remote delegates. In 1994, the MBone was used to multicast a Rolling Stones concert to the public.

The term is used more now to refer to the general multicast-enabled backbone. This piggybacks onto the general unicast Internet backbone. The multicast datagrams are encapsulated as unicast packets and tunnel through unicast networks.

Telecommunications

Telecommunications networks originally were set up for telephony, but more than half the traffic is now data. The packet-switched networks used for data and telephony traffic also can be used to carry the Internet. The circuits are constructed in a hierarchy of bit rates designed to carry multiple voice circuits, with the basic unit being 64 kbit/s. Data is carried in a compatible form.

T-1 and E-1

If you ever have tried encoding multimedia content, you will have seen T-1 on the menu. T-1 is the basic digital carrier used in North America. It transmits data at 1.5 Mbit/s in the DS-1 (digital signal) format. The European equivalent is E-1 at 2 Mbit/s.

U.S. and international standards

There are two main telecommunications standards: ANSI, used in North America and parts of the Pacific Rim, and the ITU-T standards, used in the rest of the world. The ANSI hierarchy is based on a digital signal (DS0) of 64 kbit/s.

Plesiochronous Digital Hierarchy (PDH)

The early digital trunk circuits multiplexed a large number of voice circuits into a single high data-rate channel. The systems at the remote ends were not absolutely locked together; instead, each runs off a local reference clock. These clocks were classed as *plesiochronous*; *plesio* is a Latin term derived from the Greek meaning *near*, so plesiochronous refers to clocks that are in near synchronism. The early data circuits were asynchronous; the clocks were derived from simple crystal oscillators, which could vary from the nominal by a few parts per million. Large receive buffers are used to manage the data flows. In PDH networks, to cope with terminal equipment running on slightly different clocks, extra bits are stuffed into the data stream. This bit stuffing ensures that a slower receiver can keep up with the real payload rate by simply dropping the extra bits.

To extract a single voice circuit from a DS3, the channel has to be demultiplexed back to DS1 channels. To build trunk circuits in rings around a country, each city passed would have to demultiplex and remultiplex the data stream to extract a few voice circuits.

Synchronous networks (SONET)

To avoid the multiplexing issues and the overheads of bit stuffing, highly synchronous networks were developed. By referencing terminal equipment to a single cesium standard clock, the synchronism could be ensured to a high degree of accuracy.

The standard uses a byte-interleaved multiplexing scheme. The payload data is held in a fixed structure of frames. At a network terminal the signals can be added or dropped from the data stream, without the need to process the other traffic.

It is rather like a conveyor belt carrying fixed size containers at a regular spacing. As the belt passes a city, you take away the containers you want, and drop new ones into gaps. The other containers pass unhindered.

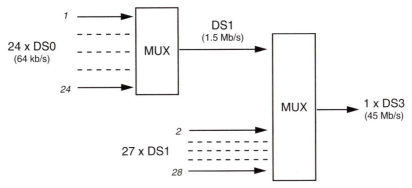

Figure 2.5 Voice circuit multiplexing.

Table 2.5 Plesiochronous Digital Hierarchies

	ITU-T standard			*ANSI standard*	
Signal	*Data rate*	*Channels*	*Signal*	*Data rate*	*Channels*
			DS0	64 kbit/s	
E1	2.048 Mbit/s		DS1	1.544 Mbit/s	24 × DS0
E2	8.45 Mbit/s	4 × E1	DS2	6.3 Mbit/s	96 × DS0
E3	34 Mbit/s	16 × E1	DS3	45 Mbit/s	28 × DS1
E4	144 Mbit/s	64 × E1			

The Synchronous Optical Network (SONET) is a subset of the Synchronous Digital Hierarchy (SDH), an ITU-T standard. The SDH standard can accommodate both ITU and ANSI PDH signals.

Frame relay

So far I have been describing voice circuits. When a voice circuit is set up you reserve a bandwidth slot for the duration of the call. If none is available you get a busy tone. The requirements for data are different. The reserved bandwidth is not as important as ensuring the delivery. Data can use the spare capacity as voice traffic changes up and down; data packets can be dispatched as capacity is available.

Frame relay is a standard for packet-switched networks that operate at layer 2 – the data link layer of the OSI model. A bidirectional virtual circuit is set up over the network between the two communicating devices. Variable-length data packets are then routed over this virtual circuit. A number of virtual circuits can

Table 2.6 Synchronous Digital Hierarchies

Data rate	SDH		SONET	
	Signal	Capacity	Signal	Capacity
51.84 Mbit/s	STM-0	21 × E1	STS-1, OC-1	28 × DS1 or 1 × DS3
155 Mbit/s	STM-1	63 × E1 or 1 × E4	STS-3, OC-3	84 × DS1 or 3 × DS3
622 Mbit/s	STM-4	252 × E1 or 4 × E4	STS-12, OC-12	336 × DS1 or 12 × DS3
2.48 Gbit/s	STM-16	1008 × E1 or 16 × E4	STS-48, OC-48	1344 × DS1 or 48 × DS3

share a physical link; the link bandwidth is shared dynamically, giving much more efficient use of the link.

This is called opportunistic bandwidth. Because there is now a queue of data awaiting available bandwidth, quality of service becomes an issue. The advantage is that the toll rates can be lower than the reserved bandwidth of a voice circuit.

ATM

Asynchronous Transfer Mode (ATM) was developed for high-speed packet transport over optical networks like SONET. ATM uses small fixed-size data cells rather than the large packets of frame relay. Each cell is 53 bytes long, with a payload of 48 bytes. These small cells are more suited to voice and multimedia traffic, where low latencies are demanded.

Both permanent and switched (PVC and SVC) virtual circuits can be set up. The cell header carries the virtual channel and virtual path identifier that are used to identify connections within the network. ATM is linked to other network layers by the ATM Adaptation Layer (AAL). The packets are given one of five categories of priority by traffic class:

1. Constant bit rate
2. Real-time variable bit rate
3. Non-real-time bit rate
4. Available bit rate
5. Unspecified bandwidth or 'best effort'

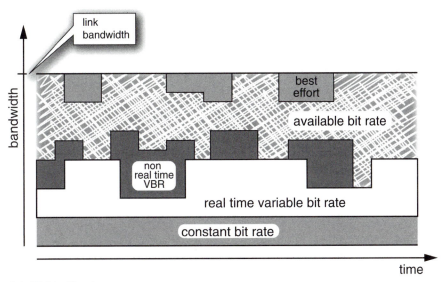

Figure 2.6 ATM traffic classes.

Constant bit rate has the best QoS, with low cell jitter. It can be used for broadcast video contribution circuits, possibly a 34 Mbit/s data stream. The variable bit rate real-time can be used for standard voice circuits. IP traffic usually is allocated the unspecified bandwidth.

Some characteristics that make ATM particularly attractive for television distribution are the choice of uni- or bidirectional links; the two-way links can be asymmetric.

As network traffic increases, the bandwidths grow to the point where optical switching becomes the only cost-effective way to handle the very high data rates of the network backbones. So the electronic processing of SONET and SDH will fall by the wayside. The move now is to an all-optical infrastructure called photonic networking.

Photonic networking

As IP becomes the standard for data exchange, and voice-over IP becomes more used, the overhead of the ATM traffic engineering becomes more of a hindrance.

Proposals to run IP directly over the Dense-Wave Division Multiplexed (DWDM) photonic network would greatly simplify the routing of traffic by stripping out two layers, ATM and SONET. To introduce this new concept, the capability of IP routing would have to be extended.

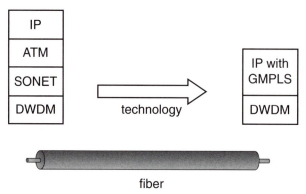

fiber

Figure 2.7 The technology migration to photonic routing.

Generalized Multiprotocol Label Switching (GMPLS)

Most of the telecommunications networks have evolved to carry voice traffic and general data packets. Neither of these models is really suited to the streaming of multimedia. IP routing has evolved to use label switching, which can improve the efficiency of network communications. MPLS is a potential technology that can improve the QoS of content delivery, by allowing traffic engineering of packet routing.

Generalized MPLS extends this capability to cover legacy ATM and SONET terminal equipment plus the new optical cross-connects, so that potentially IP can be transmitted directly over DWDM.

The local loop

There is a wide choice of connections to the Internet, split into the lower cost services for the consumer and higher capacity services for corporate systems.

Services tailored to the domestic consumer, for reasons of cost, usually use existing connections. Virtually all homes have a copper pair from the telephone company, and many in metropolitan areas have a coaxial connection to the local cable television system. Both of these connections can be used to carry Internet data alongside the existing services.

Wireless also offers connectivity, sometimes as a hybrid with a telephone back-channel.

The enterprise user

A corporate user with tens or hundreds of users will require a higher bandwidth and more reliable connection to the Internet. Traditional connections like a T-1 or E-1 circuit can provide a starting point, or T-3/E-3 where a higher capacity is required. Once a corporation moves to the use of streaming on a large scale, T-1/E-1 is unlikely to serve more than a handful of users. If you want to webcast, then outgoing capacity could be an issue. Serious consideration should be given to capacity planning. Will staff be allowed to watch streams from the public Internet, or will access be limited to the corporate intranet? Is streaming to be unicast or will multicast also be used?

Options for small businesses

Many small businesses have leased ISDN lines for telephony and data. These also can be used for connection to the Internet, but the capacity is limited for multimedia streaming to a single client. Alternatives include xDSL and T-1/E-1.

Consumer connections

Cost is the primary concern here, and usually takes precedence over the quality of service. Whereas business lines usually offer a guaranteed service, residential users are often provided with variable-rate access. At periods of high demand, network congestion increases and the service throttles back. Streaming media codecs incorporate design features to cope with these variable bandwidth conditions.

ISDN

The Integrated Subscriber Digital Network (ISDN) is a service offered by telcos that enables voice, data, and multimedia to be carried over a single line to the central office or exchange. ISDN often is introduced to a business just for voice and fax services. It has also been generally adopted for the delivery of large data files in the desktop publishing environment. Video-conferencing systems can use ISDN for H320 or H323 connections. When streaming media first rolled out, ISDN seemed a natural vehicle to deliver content.

The basic service (basic rate interface or BRI) carries two bidirectional 64 kbit/s channels over two twisted pairs. The primary rate has a higher capacity of 23 or 30 channels. A separate data channel carries control information.

The data rate of the BRI is more than sufficient for streaming audio, but for video is considered barely adequate. Note that the BRI includes two channels, which if used together can give a download of 128 kbit/s. This often is seen on streaming encoder configurations as dual ISDN. ISDN offers a guaranteed data rate, unlike a dial-up modem, where a 56 kbit/s throughput is the maximum achievable, and lower rates are normal, especially over long or noisy lines.

Table 2.7 ISDN Bit Rates

	Geographical area	B-channels 64 kbit/s	Data channel	Total data rate
BRI		2	1 × 16 kbit/s	192 kbit/s
PRI	N. America, Japan	23	1 × 64 kbit/s	1.544 Mbit/s
	Europe and rest of world	30	1 × 64 kbit/s	2.048 Mbit/s

Leveraging existing copper

The local telcos have a ready-made delivery pipe for media streams, the plain old telephone line. Copper pairs have virtually 100 percent penetration to the home, so are an attractive carrier for content. The first use has been dial-up modems over an analog speech channel.

Dial-up modems

The use of an analog modem over a voice circuit is not really an option for the reception of video streaming unless the pictures are thumbnail size. However, it can be successfully used for streaming audio, where the bandwidth requirement is more modest.

The dial-up modem uses an analog voice circuit to the central office (CO); this is limited to a maximum speed of 56 kbit/s. In practice the best that can be achieved is more likely to be 40 kbit/s. Bear this in mind when you are encoding content. A 56 kbit/s data stream will not pass through a dial-up circuit. A lower aggregate rate has to be chosen, for example Real recommends 34 kbit/s.

Much research effort has been devoted to exploiting the existing copper pair used by the analog telephone circuit. Although ISDN to the home has been successful in some countries (notably Germany), it is by no means in universal use. One drawback is that the bandwidth available (128 kbit/s) is insufficient for value-added services like video-on-demand (VOD).

The digital subscriber line (DSL)

ISDN could be considered the first digital subscriber line, but the focus now is on delivering higher data rates over the same copper pair used for the analog voice circuit, the plain old telephony service (POTS). This gives the bandwidth necessary for applications like streaming, but at a lower cost from the traditional ISDN/T1 provision.

HDSL

The first development was the high bit-rate digital subscriber line (HDSL). It uses the same four-level phase amplitude modulation as ISDN (referred to as 2B1Q). By applying more sophisticated DSP technology and by using a wider bandwidth, HDSL can achieve the same, symmetric rates as T1 or E1 (1.5 or 2 Mbit/s) over a range of 12,000 ft using two pairs of 24 a.w.g. wire (3 km of 0.5 mm). This range is the Carrier Serving Area (CSA); that is, the area served by the local exchange carrier or telco (in the USA the RBOC), often using Digital Loop Carrier (DLC) technology.

In many areas HDSL has replaced the original T-1, which required repeaters every few hundred yards. In Europe a variant of HDSL uses a single pair, but cannot achieve the same range. This is not a problem in countries like Germany and Italy, where the local loop tends to be shorter.

All the HDSL systems are loop powered (no local power requirement at the subscriber end) and they use the analog voice band for data.

ADSL

Asymmetric DSL or ADSL is designed to allow the plain old telephone service (POTS) to be used at the same time as the digital service. This means that the line still can be used for voice or fax while data transfer is taking place. Frequency division multiplexing is used to separate the channels. The data occupies the spectrum from 25 kHz up to over 1 MHz, leaving the low-frequency baseband clear for the POTS.

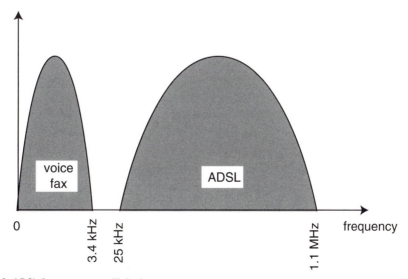

Figure 2.8 ADSL frequency multiplexing.

The downstream data capacity is much higher than upstream, hence the descriptor *asymmetric*. Typical maximum downstream rates range from 1.5 up to 8 Mbit/s, and upstream up to 1 Mbit/s. The actual performance varies from supplier to supplier, and upon the local propagation conditions.

ADSL is good for large file downloads and receiving streaming files. The drawback is that the client can transmit data only at a lower rate (maybe 300 kbit/s), so it is not going to be suitable for a home webcasting station. For such applications the HDSL connection is a better option, albeit at higher cost. The ADSL splitter is a passive device, so the telephone service will still operate normally, even when the modem is not powered.

Rate-adaptive DSL

Rate-adaptive DSL is an option where full specification DSL is not possible. The data rate adapts to the propagation conditions. The bandwidth is not guaranteed, but depends upon the distance from the CO.

G.lite

A key factor in providing low-cost ADSL circuits is to avoid a truck roll for the installation. G.lite was developed from full specification ADSL (called g.dmt) as a system that could be installed simply by the consumer. G.lite does not require the installation of a splitter, so it often is referred to as *splitterless*. Many consumer systems do not give very good results with splitterless systems. The solution is the use of a low-cost filter in the line to each device.

Other DSL standards

You may come across a number of other abbreviations related to DSL:

Symmetric DSL (SDSL or SHDSL) This new development gives equal up and down bandwidths and offers a lower cost alternative for E1/T1 lines. It is popular with business users with servers that need a higher upstream bandwidth that ADSL offers.

MSDL (moderate speed DSL) Does not achieve CSA range at T-1 rates but can satisfactorily offer lower rates (512 or 384 kbit/s), so still holds advantages over an analog modem or ISDN.

VDSL (very high speed DSL) Used for a final short-distance copper link from fiber to the curb (FTTC) systems. It can achieve T-3 data rates (45 Mbit/s) over 1,000 ft.

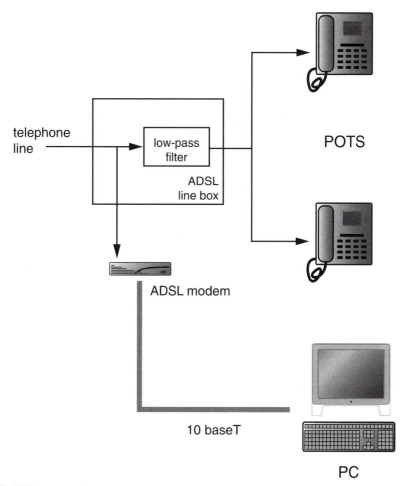

Figure 2.9 ADSL connections.

Cable modems

Cable TV is the other connection in many homes. Cable operators are updating older coaxial cable systems to provide wideband fiber networks, with coax for the final link to the home. Spare capacity can be utilized to provide Internet access alongside conventional television channels. This is referred to as data over cable (DOC).

The cable modem can be a PCI card fitted in the PC, or an external modem hooked up with Ethernet or USB. The modem uses one of the video channels for the downstream (head-end to consumer) connection. Between 27 and 56 Mbit/s of data can be carried over a single channel with a bandwidth of

6–8 MHz. This data is not for just one consumer but is shared between users on a node, much like an Ethernet network. The digital cable networks use Quadrature Amplitude Modulation (QAM). The upstream (consumer to head-end) channel uses the free spectrum under the video channels (5–24 MHz), with a bandwidth about 2 MHz and a data rate of 3 Mbit/s. QPSK or QAM modulation is used. Again, it is a shared channel.

The telcos often make a point of saying that there is only one user on an ADSL line, so there are no issues of network contention. They cite this as an issue with cable systems. But the phone company most likely will hook up the ADSL termination equipment with an Ethernet, which also has a finite capacity. So treat these claims with care. How many cable modems are sharing a node, and how many ADSL modems share the Ethernet bandwidth?

Satellite

ADSL is fine if you live near the telco central office, cable modems are great if your neighborhood has cable television. If you live in rural areas, you will have to look elsewhere for broadband provision. The alternative to a copper or fiber connection is a microwave connection. This could be from a satellite or MMDS.

Very small aperture satellite antennae (VSAT) offer one-way and two-way links to the Internet. In North America the DirecTV satellites offer a data service called DirecWay. A similar service is offered in Europe by the Astra satellites.

Mobile

The alternative to the constraints of copper or fiber is to use wireless communication, through cellular networks covering large territories or local area networks often called Wi–Fi.

Third-generation wireless networks

The International Telecommunications Union (ITU) has developed a set of standards for a third generation of wireless networks that can provide IP connectivity to mobile devices.

The second-generation digital cell phones (analog being the first generation) were limited to about 14 kbit/s data rate, clearly inadequate for video streaming. The new third-generation wireless networks (3G) offer the potential of data rates from around 300 kbit/s for somebody walking or in a moving vehicle, up to 2.4 Mbit/s for a stationary terminal. The phone operators are offering a wide range of video services, from streaming entertainment and sport, to video conferencing and videophone applications. The connection is 'always-on,' so can be used like a conventional copper/fiber network connection.

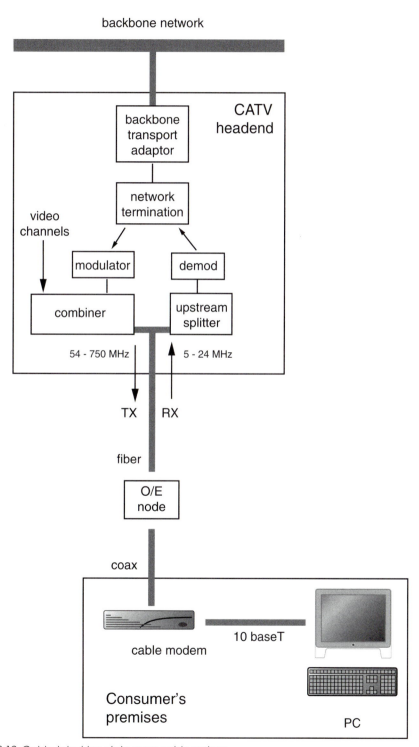

Figure 2.10 Cable television data over cable system.

Wi-Fi or IEEE 802.11

The alternative to the 3G networks is Wi-Fi (wireless fidelity) local area networks. There are a number of wireless networking standards including the IEEE 802.11 family. To aid consumers, the Wi-Fi Alliance (WECA) certifies appliances to be interoperable regardless of the manufacturer as long as they are using the same version of the IEEE standards. There are three main standards: 802.11a, b, and g.

Table 2.8 IEEE 802.11 Standards

	Data rate	Carrier frequency band	No. of channels
IEEE802.11a	54 Mbit/s	5 GHz	8
IEEE802.11b	11 Mbit/s	2.4 GHz	14
IEEE802.11g	54 Mbit/s	2.4 GHz	14

The range of the wireless networks is short, up to a maximum of 100 meters, but that is more than adequate to flood your local coffee bar with wireless connectivity to the Internet.

The 2.4-GHz band can be congested, as it is shared with a number of cordless appliances, phones, and Bluetooth devices, plus microwave ovens.

Always-on and client security

The domestic user of the Internet with a cable modem or DSL connection that stays permanently connected to the network is at a higher risk of attack by hackers than the user of a dial-up circuit who is connected only for short periods of time.

As a consequence the user with permanent connection will have to take greater security precautions with software and/or hardware firewalls. The wireless networks come with integral encryption to make snooping more difficult.

Summary

It is a demonstration of the flexibility of the OSI layer model of network communications that a system developed for the transfer of text and data files has been stretched to carry real-time multimedia. That is not to say everything is dandy. Anyone who has watched streams will know it is not always an enriching experience. Stalling video and distorted audio do not make for good viewing.

Yet if we watch the same file when downloaded to a local disk, the quality is remarkably good.

The problem lies with a number of bottlenecks between the origin of the content and the player. These may be between the origin and the first Internet point-of-presence, across the backbone, or the last mile to the viewer (the local loop).

As broadband access extends to the home, the problems with the local loop should be solved, but there are still issues with network congestion and the costs of edge serving. Traffic will only increase; there are other demands beyond streaming and rich media – voice-over IP and video-conferencing are two expanding markets.

Multicasting can help ease the demands on the servers and the network for live or scheduled (simulated live) webcasts. Interactive applications, like distance learning, still provide many challenges, not the least stemming from their demands for low round-trip delays.

For the mobile user or remote communities, fixed wireless and satellite offer alternatives to copper and fiber. Wireless is now widely used with mobile devices, the laptop, and the cell phone. Only time will tell if the spectrum can cope with demand.

3 The World Wide Web

Introduction

This chapter starts with a brief overview of the World Wide Web and web sites, and then describes some of the key elements of a web page. This chapter covers the enhancements that have been added to web pages to add dynamic and graphical content: animated GIFs, dynamic HTML, and Flash vector graphics.

The Web, for many people, has become synonymous with the Internet. The use of the Web has become ubiquitous, from the cyber-café in a backpackers' hostel to high bandwidth corporate intranets. But universal adoption of the web browser as the user interface, for many, has masked the fact that the Internet provides the communication fabric; the Web refers to the linked pages of content. The Web is only one of the several applications that use the Internet. The earlier applications popular in the academic community include gopher, TELNET, and FTP. Streaming media came along later, and also is delivered over the Internet. However, streaming is intimately linked to the Web. Web pages often embed the pointers to streaming media, and the media player itself can be embedded in a conventional web page, so that video appears alongside the text and still images. The Internet is just one delivery channel; streaming can be delivered to a set-top box for display on a television or via cellular radio to hand-held wireless devices.

The original Web was text based. Great strides have been made by the more creative web designers to create dynamic sites without using streaming video. Vector graphics are great for many web applications, but they are clearly not suitable for many of the applications for which streaming is used. The corporate quarterly call to stockholders is not going to look too good with a cartoon CEO.

Thin clients and the web browser

In the old mainframe computing days, the client was usually a VDU running a basic Teletype emulation. The PC led to the development of distributed computing, but carried with it a maintenance nightmare for the IT department. To upgrade one application can involve visiting every PC across the enterprise. Remote administration is making this easier, but deployment is by no means universal. Users have a bad habit of installing their own applications, even games. When the PC crashes, IT then has to come and fix it. Again there are ways and means of preventing such behavior. In the 1990s, IT departments searching for solutions to these and other problems made moves to return to a more centralized model. In this model a web browser replaces the VDU, albeit with far more facilities.

The database and the application server (the business logic) are presented through web pages on a web server. This migration makes it much easier for a corporation to use streaming, as the core infrastructure of web servers already exists. You may need to upgrade the network infrastructure to handle the wider bandwidths, but the web-enabled client workstations are ready to go.

This same model has been adopted for general informational web sites. Rather than serving the conventional static HTML pages, the application server creates dynamic content on the fly, interacting with input from the browser.

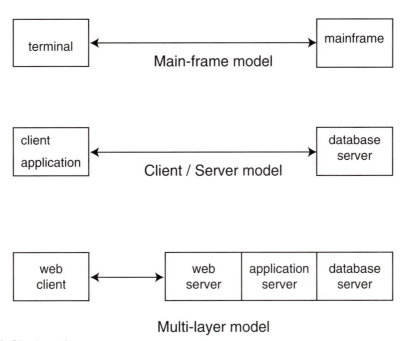

Figure 3.1 Clients and servers.

The web browser is becoming the de facto thin client. So it has become the primary application for access to the Internet and corporate application servers (via an intranet). So, although a stand-alone media player can request files directly from the content server and play stand-alone, the players most often are embedded in the web client. This close association is also best suited to rich media content, where text, video, and images are presented as a synchronized multimedia experience.

Some basic background knowledge of the Web, therefore, is required to understand fully the deployment of streaming media. Most enterprises already will have either a house web project team or an external agency maintaining a text site, so this chapter is an aid to interfacing with that team.

WWW

The World Wide Web is the generic name for all the web pages that can be accessed via the Internet. The Web derives its name from the web-like structure constructed by the links between web pages.

At the heart lies the HyperText Markup Language (HTML) used to author the pages of a web site. Hypertext is electronic text that has cross-links within the document and between documents.

HyperText Markup Language (HTML)

HTML is a language developed to describe how text, graphics, and other information are formatted into documents, and how those documents are organized and linked together. The files contain only text – images and media files are referenced by links. An HTML page does not have to be a web page; HTML pages can be used just like word processor files, and never uploaded to a web server, just retrieved from disk, locally or over a network, and rendered by the browser.

An HTML page has a basic structure of a *header* and the *body* (which contains the content). The layout instructions are referred to as *tags*.

HTML is written in plain text, so it can be authored using a basic word processor or text editor. The HTML standard has developed through several versions, with support for graphics and creative layout improving with each new release. The final version was HTML 4.0. HTML has outlived its usefulness, having grown in an ad hoc manner from its original design aim to enable the exchange and linking of text documents. Future revisions are to be as an application of XML (eXtensible Markup Language), the first implementation being XHTML 1.0. This will ease the development of more complex multimedia applications.

Examples of other tag sets include Synchronized Multimedia Integration Language (SMIL) and Scalable Vector Graphics (SVG).

XML

The eXtensible Markup Language (XML) is a structured set of rules for defining data. With XML you can separate structure and content from the presentation. So a file could be displayed on a web browser, much like HTML, but also on a wireless device or a television set-top box. The content then can be rendered to suit the display device.

XML is not just for delivering documents to displays – it can be used for generic data exchange between applications. Because XML is extensible, it can be used for yet to be developed applications, unlike HTML, which is now set in stone.

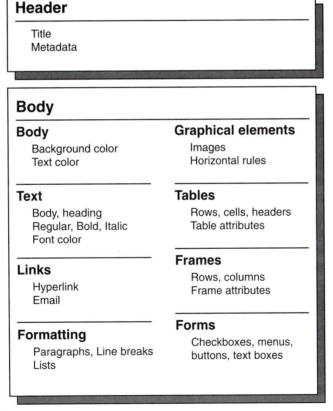

Header

Title
Metadata

Body

Body
Background color
Text color

Graphical elements
Images
Horizontal rules

Text
Body, heading
Regular, Bold, Italic
Font color

Tables
Rows, cells, headers
Table attributes

Links
Hyperlink
Email

Frames
Rows, columns
Frame attributes

Formatting
Paragraphs, Line breaks
Lists

Forms
Checkboxes, menus,
buttons, text boxes

Figure 3.2 HTML tags.

HyperText Transport Protocol (HTTP)

HTTP was developed for the delivery of HTML files. It is used for application-level communication between the browser and the web server in distributed, collaborative, hypermedia information systems. The communications consist of requests and responses.

The headers indicate the purpose of a request. The message uses the Uniform Resource Identifier (URI), in the form of the familiar URL or name (URN) to indicate the resource. In the response, MIME-like information describes the format of the data to be transferred.

HTTP also is used as a generic protocol for communication between user agents and proxies or gateways to other Internet systems. This includes those supported by the RTSP, SMTP, and FTP protocols. In this way, HTTP allows basic access level to multimedia content sourced from a diverse range of applications.

This protocol is important for streaming, because it is used for the web pages that link to the content, and it is often the only choice for a communication protocol in simple network installations. Some company firewalls prevent access to regular streaming media using real-time protocols, so HTTP is the only option for the delivery of media streams.

It is an application-layer protocol, commonly used over a TCP/IP connection. It is a stateless protocol; that means each command is executed in isolation, with no knowledge of preceding commands. Cookies are used as a way around this so that web servers more intelligently can serve content to a browser by storing state information in the cookie.

This may be viewed as a disadvantage of HTTP, but it has great benefits. Because the protocol is stateless and connectionless, the web server is relieved of the overhead of maintaining a connection to the browser. This characteristic leaves the resources of the server free to handle many, many users simultaneously.

Web graphics

A basic web browser will render HTML files into a screen image. Text is sent as a straight ASCII-like format; the font properties are sent separately as tags and rendered by the browser to give the appropriate display. Text formatting codes give positional information for the text, and enable the author to use other devices like tables and forms.

The source files for bit-mapped images are potentially very large, which leads to long download times – unpopular with users. There are two ways around this: line art can be sent as the very compact GIF and continuous-tone images can be compressed using the JPEG standard.

Graphic Interchange Format (GIF)

CompuServe released the original GIF format in 1987 as a means of encoding raster graphic images into a compact file. Normally it is used for the placement of line art on web pages; it is not suitable for continuous-tone images. In 1989 the format was extended to include support for transparency and interlace (GIF89a). GIFs allowed web designers to liven up the rather dull text-only pages with graphic elements. The GIF format supports indexed color images with a maximum of 256 different colors. It uses the LZW algorithm for lossless compression.

Portable Network Graphics (PNG)

GIF is a copyright of CompuServe (AOL) and distributed under a royalty-free license for general use across the web. PNG was developed as an alternative open format, with additional features. It had limited support from the earlier browsers, so had a slow acceptance by web designers. It uses lossless compression, and can encode grayscale or color images, up to 24 bits per pixel. It carries an alpha channel to define the transparency.

JPEG

The Joint Photographic Experts Group developed this extremely popular format for lossy compression of raster images. It has proved to be the forerunner for the techniques of video compression. JPEG compression is used for continuous-tone images, like photographs. It can be used for any image, but line art would exhibit artifacts at the high compression settings that give an equivalent small file size that a GIF image would give for line art.

Bit maps and vectors

There are two ways of coding an image: as a bit map or as vector graphics. The bit map is the familiar rectangular grid or raster of picture elements (pixels).

Table 3.1 HTML Graphic Formats

	Line art	Photos	Colors	Transparency	Compression	Animation
GIF	Y		8-bit	Y	Lossless	Y
PNG	Y		24-bit	Y	Lossless	N
JPEG		Y	24-bit	N	Lossy	N

Each pixel carries brightness and color values. The alternative representation is vector graphics. Objects are described by geometric characteristics, so an object could be made up of lines and curves. It could be a shape, a circle, or a square, each filled with a specific color.

Vector graphic images are resolution independent. To display vector graphics, they are rendered to a bit map by the graphics adaptor. Similarly a raster image processor in a printer will convert the image to a regular grid of dots.

Vectors are more suited to line artwork, clipart, or cartoons, whereas bit maps are used for continuous-tone objects, like natural video and photographs.

Animating pages

Animation is a halfway house to streaming, with the big advantage that well-designed animations use far less bandwidth than video streams. Macromedia's Flash animated vector graphics typify such animation – not to ignore the fact that Flash file downloads can be lengthy through 28k or 56k modems.

There are three main ways to animate: a GIF object can be animated; DHTML allows objects to move and reveal; Flash is a step up, allowing fully animated and interactive graphic sequences.

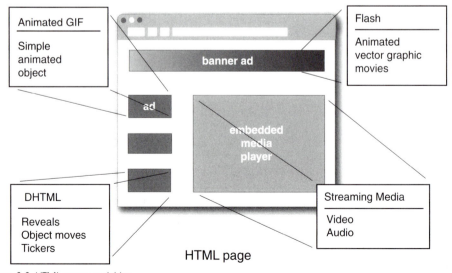

Figure 3.3 HTML page add-ins.

Animated GIFs

A number of GIFs can be played in rapid sequence, much like a cartoon flip-book, to produce a basic animation. It is suited only to short clips of a few seconds. It is much used on web pages as an attention seeker, like a flashing neon sign. The animated GIF is being replaced with Flash animation because of the vast capabilities of the format.

Dynamic HTML

A straight HTML page is static; once it has been downloaded it sits there until you select a new link and another page is downloaded. Dynamic HTML or DHTML allows the content of a page to change after it has been loaded. Typically it is used for hidden menus that appear when the mouse passes over a button. It also can be used to move objects around the screen along a programmed path. Pages can be periodically refreshed; this is used for news tickers on web pages.

DHTML is a mix of technologies. The core is the Document Object Model (DOM). The DOM allows changes to be made to cascading style sheets and to basic HTML. The changes are made with client-side scripts using JavaScript or VBScript.

Flash

Flash is an animated vector-graphic format that offers the advantages of dynamic graphics, without the large file sizes required by true video. It requires a plug-in to the web browser to play back the files. The player can be downloaded free of charge from the Macromedia web site.

Shockwave and Flash player comparison

Macromedia offers two web players: Shockwave and Flash, each with a distinct purpose. The Flash player is used for fast-loading front-end web applications such as user interaction, interactive online advertising, and short- to medium-form animation. The Shockwave player is used for long-form content. It is popular for games, and for interactive multimedia product demonstrations and training. The Shockwave player also will play Flash content.

Note that the Flash content is delivered in Shockwave file format (.SWF). Shockwave content is authored specifically on Macromedia Director, whereas Flash files can be generated by many applications (not just Macromedia).

Proprietary tools

It often is said that you can lay out a web page with a basic text editor like Microsoft Notepad. To improve productivity, especially with the more creative sites, a number of specialized products can be used. These high-level tools let you concentrate on the design and content creation, rather than the mechanics of HTML.

Web page editing Macromedia *Dreamweaver* and Adobe *GoLive*.

Web animation Macromedia *Director* and *Flash MX*.

Plug-ins

Apart from the basic graphic formats supported by web browsers, other formats are viewed with a software application that plugs into the browser – a *plug-in*. There is marked reluctance by users to install plug-ins. It may be that a corporate IT department does not want the maintenance issues. The public is suspicious, associating plug-ins with backdoors to their hard drive, possibly introducing viruses, and compromising confidentiality with unseen reporting to remote web servers.

   For this reason it is unwise to step outside the most popular plug-ins if you want the widest audience for your web site. Many users have Flash, Shockwave, QuickTime, Real, and Windows Media. Other plug-ins have not achieved the same level of market penetration; select them with care.

Web servers

At its most basic, the web server delivers a file in answer to a request from a browser.

- The user asks for a page using a URL.
- The web server maps the URL to a filename.
- The server reads the file from disk.
- The server transmits the HTML file to the browser using HTTP.

The web server has to handle many hundreds or thousands of connections concurrently. To handle this high processing load a combination of multiprocessing and multithreading is used. Communication between the browser and server uses HyperText Transport Protocol (HTTP) over a TCP/IP connection. The first

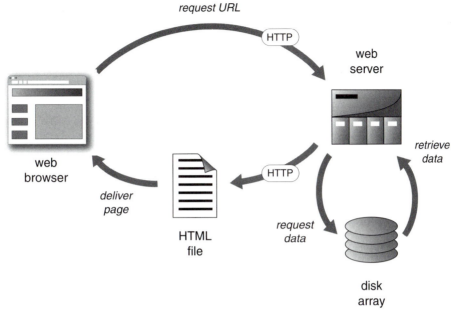

Figure 3.4 Requesting an HTML page.

version of HTTP required a separate TCP connection to be negotiated for each browser request. So a page with many graphic elements needed a TCP connection to be set up for each element. HTTP 1.1 now maintains a persistent TCP connection during an HTTP session; this cuts down the communications overheads.

Content types, MIME

If the file is a web page, it will be HTML format, but the page may also have embedded graphics or media files. To instruct the browser how to handle these files correctly, the media content type is specified in the header using the Multipurpose Internet Mail Extension, or MIME (RFC 1521). MIME types include audio, image, text, and video. Subtypes beginning with /x- are private values, and require a proprietary application to view. The type 'message' is used for mail. The browser has several options for handling the file:

- The browser can handle the file internally.
- The browser can call a plug-in.
- The browser can pass the file to another application.
- The browser can download the file to disk.

The browser preferences define how each MIME type is handled. Table 3.2 gives typical examples.

Server farms

If your web site handles large traffic volumes, one server is unlikely to cope with the demand. Several servers can be deployed to share the load. Special hardware or software balances the load of browser connections across the servers. Similar load balancers also are used with streaming media. Servers are sometimes split by content – one cluster for text, one for images, and one for video files.

Tuning

A web server usually is tuned to optimize I/O connections, as the processor load is low. Contrast this with an application server that is probably tuned for high processor utilization. The tuning requirements vary from site to site; it depends on factors like the balance of static to dynamic content, and whether security, like SSL, is used. The streaming media server also will require tuning, but to satisfy a different set of requirements. The streaming files are much larger, and require continuous transfer. An on-demand server will require wide interconnections from the disk array.

Table 3.2 MIME Types

Description	Extension	MIME type/subtype	Handling
Hypertext	htm, html	text/html	View with browser
Image	jpg, jpeg, jpe	image/jpeg	View with browser
GIF Image	gif	image/gif	View with browser
MP3 audio file	mp3	audio/x-mpeg	Listen with player
Real Media file	rm	application/vnd.rn-reamedia	View with plug-in or post-process with player
Windows Media	wmv	video/x-ms-wmv	View with plug-in or post-process with layer

Summary

The web has evolved a great deal since Berners-Lee developed the concepts of linked and cross-referenced text documents while working at CERN. Under the auspices of W3C, XML now offers an extensible and flexible set of formats that can be used for the delivery of multimedia content, not just to web browsers, but also to TV set-top boxes, cell phones, and PDAs. As part of this rationalization HTML is evolving into the XML-compatible XHTML.

The HTML standards have developed into a format that can support innovative and high standards of graphic design. The main element that is missing is natural video and audio – streaming media.

The web server lies at the heart of access to streaming media content. The video content often is embedded in a web page and the links announcing content normally are placed in pages. For a content delivery system with a low level of streaming traffic, this same web server may be used to source the media files. But for any system of size, the advantages of using a separate streaming server are compelling.

4 Video formats

Introduction

Before video can be streamed it must go through several processing stages. Streaming video starts with a television camera, which may be combined with other cameras in a switcher. Alternatively, the signal is recorded for later editing. The second stage is to convert the video to a computer file format, an operation called *capture* or *ingest*. Finally, it can be processed by the streaming encoder.

There are many similarities between television and computer video, but there are minor differences in the standards and formats that are relevant to capture. This chapter gives an overview of the broadcast television standards for the reader who may be more familiar with computer formats like AVI and Quick-Time. This chapter also covers the many tape formats you will encounter, and the different interconnections that can be used between the tape deck and the encoding workstation.

Although we live in a digital world, there is still much legacy analog equipment in use in video production. We must not forget that the majority of television viewers still watch an analog transmission, and the changeover to digital reception may not happen until 2010, varying from country to country. The pioneers in digital transmission have been the satellite operators, where the driving force for the deployment of digital transmission (using the MPEG-2 standard) has been ability to transmit four to six times the number of channels within a given transponder bandwidth. An overview has to start in the analog domain.

Essentially, television is the reproduction of a moving two-dimensional image by the transmission of a regular sequence of color frames or *rasters*. Each frame is transmitted as horizontal lines with synchronizing information. Television started as a monochrome system, with color added later. The color information was interleaved into the luminance channel without requiring any additional bandwidth. How this was achieved is a precursor to modern compression techniques.

Analog television uses several techniques to lower the bandwidth requirements without causing unacceptable visual artifacts. Some of these artifacts today may be considered as obvious distortions, but remember that the engineering compromises were made half a century ago, and were implemented with a handful of vacuum tubes. The methods used include scan interlace, color space conversion, and chrominance band limiting.

Scanning

The scene captured by the camera lens is projected onto a planar sensor. The early tube cameras scanned the light-sensitive sensor layer in lines, generating a varying voltage proportional to the incident light. Analog television is specified in terms of lines and frames, rather than the regular pixel grids familiar to computer users. There are two picture dimensions for standard definition television, the NTSC system used in North America, and the PAL and SECAM systems used in Europe and Asia. The NTSC system was developed from an earlier monochrome standard: RS-170.

Table 4.1 Analog picture resolutions

	Line duration (µS)	Picture height (line)	Line rate (Hz)	Frame rate (Hz)	Active picture area	
					Width (µS)	Height (lines)
RS-170		525	15,750	30		486
NTSC	63.49	525	15,734.26	29.96	720	486
PAL, SECAM	64	625	15,625	25	52	576

The transmitted signal includes vertical and horizontal blanking intervals, used for synchronization of the receiver and to allow flyback time of a scanning electron beam in the CRT display. As a consequence the signal is split into the active picture area and synchronization information.

The brightness values of each pixel are read from top left to bottom right, always reading left to right. Why not alternate the direction of the scan from line to line, a serpentine scan? That would remove the need for the line flyback in the CRT. Unfortunately any nonlinearity in the scan drivers would mean misalignment of left-to-right lines relative to the right-to-left.

Interlaced scan

The developers of television had many problems to grapple with, not least the difficulty of driving the scans at high writing speed, and the limited transmission bandwidth that was then possible. To give a display without apparent flicker, it had long been known from the motion picture industry that the frame rate had to be greater than 48 per second. Although movies are shot at 24 frames per second, the projector displays each frame twice. It was not possible for the early television receiver to display each frame twice – that would have needed a picture store. Such developments had to wait for affordable digital memory.

The compromise was to transmit a frame as two halves or fields – one field of the even lines, one of the odd lines. Thus the transmitted signal is a 250- or 300-line picture, but the final display has 500 or 600 lines. This is called an interlaced scan, as opposed to a simple top-to-bottom scan, called progressive, that computer video graphic adaptors use. To avoid a line-by-line flicker, the phosphors used in the CRT continue to emit light after the stimulation by the electron beam. The persistence time for the light output to decay is chosen to maintain emission until the next writing cycle. Interlaced scans had another great benefit; the bandwidth required for transmission was halved.

Drawbacks of interlaced scanning

Interlacing gave a very acceptable picture when the source of pictures was the television camera. The combination of the modulation transfer factor of the taking lens (which acts as a low-pass spatial filter) and the finite scanning beam size of the early tube camera meant that picture detail was filtered of high-frequency vertical detail, giving a natural anti-aliasing.

Once computer graphics equipment was introduced, it became possible (if there was no vertical filtering) to generate very hard vertical brightness transitions. These did produce visible flicker on horizontal edges at the frame refresh rate (25 or 30 Hz). The workaround was for the character generator manufacturers to apply spatial filters to the original image. These softened the edges and lowered the incidence of visible flicker. This vertical filtering means that in practice an interlaced scan has a lower vertical resolution than a progressive scan.

The second drawback is that television postproduction uses many special effects that transform the scene geometry (squeezes and zooms). These have to be processed as a complete picture of the odd and the even fields. After the mathematical transforms, the new frame then has to be converted back to the two interlaced fields.

Frame rates

Video equipment is sold in two standards, 25 or 30 frames per second. These are a hangover from the early days of television. The receivers had poor power supply regulation, so line-related hum was evident throughout the processing.

Interlaced scan
Analog lines

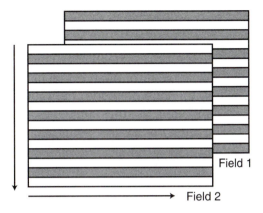

Field 1

Field 2

Interlaced scan
Pixel grid

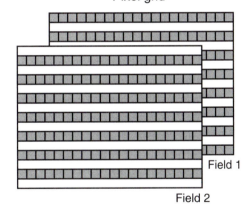

Field 1

Field 2

Progressive scan
Pixel grid

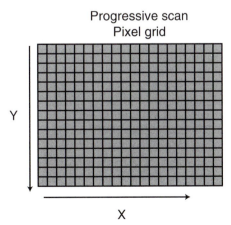

Y

X

Figure 4.1 Progressive and interlaced scanning.

To avoid 'hum bars' scrolling through the picture, the field rate was chosen to be the same as the power line frequency, 50 Hz in Europe and 60 Hz in the United States. This was not a big issue until international program exchange started; but by then the standards were entrenched.

In all probability all your production can be done in one standard. The problem arises if you want to edit together material shot at two different frame rates; for example, a program shot at the headquarters in the United States and an insert shot in a European office. The best way around this is to have the foreign tape converted to the standard that you use for editing. It is best to go for a high-quality conversion; it should be motion compensated. A low-quality conversion will exhibit motion artifacts, juddering, or softness around moving objects. These artifacts will give your streaming encoder a hard time, and lower the final streaming video quality.

If you have the opportunity to plan ahead, it is best to shoot an entire production in one format.

Color space conversion

Human vision has two types of sensor: the rods, sensitive to light level; and the cones, sensitive to levels within three spectral bands – red, green, and blue (RGB). To give realistic color reproduction the television system is based on these three spectral bands or primary colors. A requirement of the original NTSC

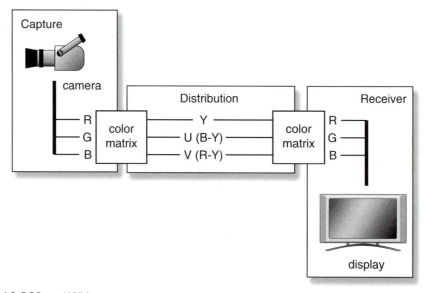

Figure 4.2 RGB and YUV.

system was backward compatibility of the legacy monochrome system. To that end the RGB color space is mapped to a luminance signal (used by a monochrome receiver) and two color difference or chrominance signals. By a reverse matrix process, the original RGB signals then can be derived by the color receiver.

The luminance component is called Y or luma, the color components R-Y (or V) and B-Y (or U). The user of bit map imaging programs like Photoshop will be familiar with different color spaces.

Table 4.2 Color spaces

Designation	Name	Notes
RGB	Red, Green, Blue	The native format
CYMK	Cyan, Yellow, Magenta, Black	For color printing
HSB	Hue, Saturation, Brightness	Related to human perception
L-a-b	Luminance, a (green to red) and b (blue to yellow)	The CIE model

Color television is most similar to the CIE (Commission Internationale d'Eclairage) model of color with a luminance and two color-related components.

Additive and subtractive color

The computer color displays use the additive system of color to represent the different hues we perceive. The light emitted by red, green, and blue pixels add to give the wanted color. All three together add to give white light. Contrast this with subtractive systems, like color printing. Here the ink or pigment subtracts or absorbs part of the visible spectrum to give the desired color. The pigments are the secondary colors cyan, yellow, and magenta. The three together at maximum density subtract all light, and so appear black.

Chrominance band limiting

When NTSC was developed, it was known that the human eye perceives color detail at a lower acuity than luminance detail. This meant that the color channels could be transmitted at a lower resolution than the luminance signal without an apparent loss of picture detail. In the NTSC system the two chroma channels, I and Q, are limited to bandwidths of 1.3 MHz and 400 kHz, respectively. Contrast this with the luminance bandwidth of 4.2 MHz. The PAL system has slightly larger bandwidths, 5 or 5.5 MHz for luminance, and symmetrical bandwidths of 1.5 MHz for the U and V color channels.

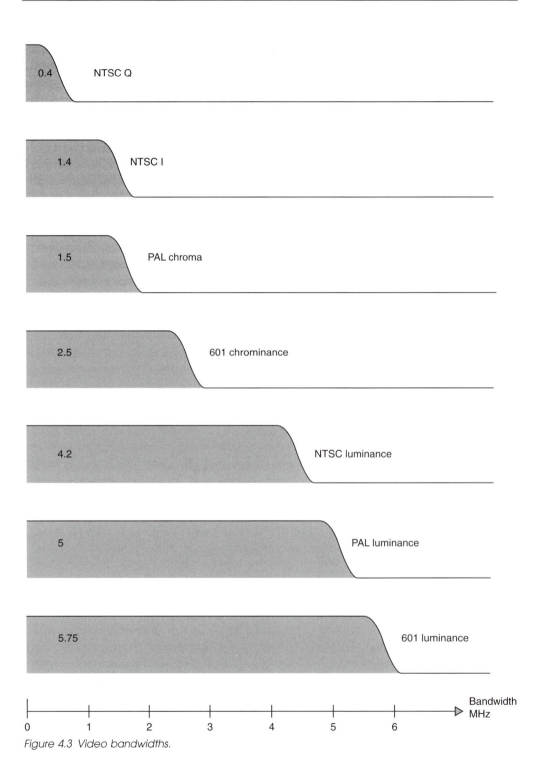

Figure 4.3 Video bandwidths.

This limitation of chroma detail has proved acceptable for final distribution of television programming, but the more demanding requirements of postproduction require more detail. A good example is chroma key or blue-screen compositing. If PAL or NTSC sources are used, the chroma mattes (or keys) have very soft edges, too soft to produce a realistic composite scene.

Component and composite

Although your workstation has three cables carrying RGB to the display monitor (and possibly a sync channel), such an interconnection is feasible for only a short distance of a few meters. For general distribution the three color components have to be combined to a single channel. The NTSC developers had open to them a number of possible modulation schemes to carry the color information within the existing bandwidth of the monochrome system. They opted for quadrature amplitude modulation of the two color components onto a subcarrier. This is not the only possible method; the SECAM team later adopted frequency modulation of the color components. Frequency modulation offered potential advantages for videotape recording and RF propagation.

The advent of digital processing opened up the possibility of many other systems. One short-lived analog standard used time-division multiplexing of the three components, with temporal compression of each component – this was called Multiplexed Analog Component or MAC.

The advances in multiplexing really began with the adoption of digital distribution. A number of proprietary bit-parallel schemes existed for short-range

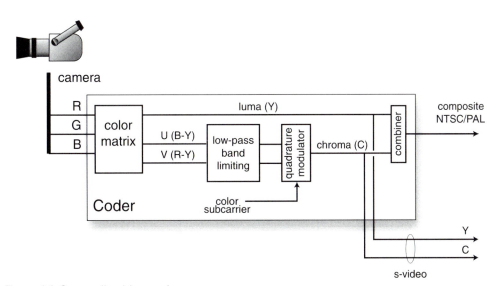

Figure 4.4 Composite video coder.

interconnection of computer graphics equipment, but it was long recognized that a cost-effective solution had to use serial transmission so that standard coaxial cable and connectors could be used.

Drawbacks of analog composite

When analog composite video is encoded, the luminance and the modulated color components simply are added together. It is the job of the receiver to separate the color information. The simplest decoders exhibit two main artifacts. Cross-luminance is the interpretation of color information as luminance detail. This is visible as dot-crawl, or *hanging dots*, especially in areas of saturated color. The other effect is cross-color, where high-frequency luminance detail is interpreted as color. This is most commonly seen in patterned fabrics, like checked shirts and jackets; the fabric has a rainbow effect.

Many decoder designs have been developed to counteract these effects, primarily based on the comb filter. A comb filter very effectively can separate the interleaved frequency components of the luminance and chrominance information for static pictures. Unfortunately, if the subject is moving, this no longer holds true. To get around this, manufacturers can use a motion-adaptive filter. The other problem that arises is limited to low-cost VCRs. The playback signal has timing jitter, so it is not possible for a comb filter to separate the two components effectively.

S-Video

S-Video is a workaround, to avoid the cross-luminance and cross-color artifacts of the composite system and the playback jitter problems that prevent the use of comb decoders. It uses the same quadrature amplitude modulation system, but carries the chrominance component as a separate circuit. It requires two coaxial cables so is suited only to short-range local interconnections.

Digital composite

Digital composite was another short-lived, but very successful, standard. It acted as a stepping-stone from analog composite to digital component. It was developed as a spin-off from the D-2 digital composite tape format. Digital composite simply sampled the analog composite waveform at four times subcarrier. D-2 offered the advantages of digital recording (error correction, cloned copies) in an analog composite environment.

If you used analog recording you were limited in the number of generations of tape copies before picture degradation became unacceptable, somewhere around four generations. This constraint limited the use of complex multilayered visual effects in postproduction.

Digital component coding

A number of proprietary digital formats evolved for special effects and computer graphics equipment. These early developers established some of the ground rules that could support realistic pictures:

- Three color channels
- Eight bits per channel
- Around 700 pixels per television line

601

The standard ITU-R BT601, to give its full designation, has proved to be a solid foundation for much of the later developments in digital video technology. 601 was intended for program production, so it offered a high picture quality, with sufficient resolution for special effects. One specific example is chroma-keying or matting. This is where the talent is shot in front of a blue or green screen. In postproduction the colored screen is replaced with another picture. Much loved by weathermen, it also has many applications for the corporate and training productions that may well be encoded for streaming.

Sampling

Much as the NTSC standard uses band limiting for the I and Q color components, the 601 standard also exploits the feature of the human visual system that color is perceived at a lower acuity. The color information is sampled at a lower spatial resolution than the luminance. There are several schemes, but the 601 standard uses half the sampling frequency. Early digital systems used four times color subcarrier as the sampling rate. The luminance signal is close to this frequency, hence $4 \times$ sampling. The chrominance channels are sampled at half this, so the nomenclature for the YUV sample is 4:2:2. The vertical resolution for luminance and chrominance is the same. If chrominance is sampled every other line, we arrive at symmetric color sample spatial scaling. This is called 4:2:0 sampling, and was adopted for MPEG-1 and later used for MPEG-2 MP@ML. The alternative is to sample color at one-quarter the luminance rate, 4:1:1. This has been adopted for the DV format. The color resolution is still as good as

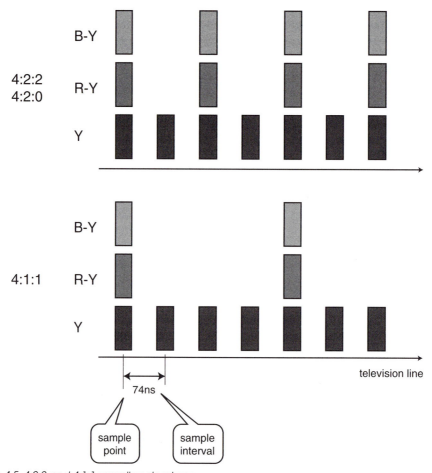

Figure 4.5 4:2:2 and 4:1:1 sampling structures.

analog composite, but is not suitable for high-quality chroma key matting operations.

Coding range

Computer video uses the full gamut of codes to specify colors: black has a value of zero, white is 255 (8-bit coding). Video uses a restricted range, giving headroom above white level and below black. If the original source is analog, this headroom avoids clipping of the video signal (in the case of DC offsets or analog-to-digital converter misalignment). So the actual range is from 16 to 235, a range of 220 values, as opposed to the 256 values of computer graphics. You can convert from one range to the other, but this will introduce rounding errors, so it should be applied with regard to the number of conversions.

Eight and 10 bits

The 601 standard originally specified 8-bit sample values. This proved insufficient for extensive video processing. For example, keying processes could cause visible banding on graduated tones. To ease this problem the standard was extended to support 10-bit samples, although many products support only 8-bit interfaces. The two least significant bits (of the 10) are truncated or rounded.

For streaming applications, 10-bit interfaces are a luxury, 8 bits are fine.

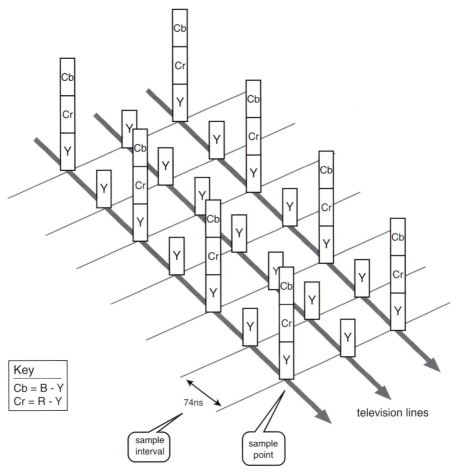

Figure 4.6 4:2:0 sampling structure.

Gamma

If you are used to creating graphics for computer video, you may well be familiar with the display gamma, 2.2 for Windows and 1.8 for Macintosh. Television has a fixed gamma, so all the receivers should be the same.

Scanning resolutions

There are two picture dimensions for standard definition television: the 525-line system used in North America and the 625-line system used in Europe and Asia.

Table 4.3 Digital Picture Resolutions

Line/field rates	Active picture area (pixels)		Total including sync interval (pixels)		Frame rate
	Width	Height	Width	Height	
525/60	720	486	864	525	29.96 Hz
625/60	720	576	864	625	25 Hz

Table 4.4 Computer Monitor Resolutions

Designation	Resolution	
VGA	640 × 480	Video graphics array
SVGA	800 × 600	Super video graphics array
XVGA, XGA	1024 × 768	Extended video graphics array
SXGA	1280 × 1024	Super XGA
UXGA	1600 × 1024	Ultra XGA

Computer displays use a plethora of scanning rates and screen resolutions. The frame rates vary from 60 Hz up to 120 Hz.

There are higher resolution displays, 1920 × 1200 for HDTV, plus specialist workstation displays with resolutions of 3840 × 2400 for demanding applications.

Square and rectangular pixels

Most computer paint programs use square pixels. That means a circle 10 pixels high is also 10 pixels wide. Digital television does not use square pixels. The horizontal resolution is chosen to have a sensible mathematical relationship to sampling frequencies, line rate, and frame rate. Simple geometry was not an overriding concern for the original analog systems. The television pixels depart from a square by about 10 percent; 525/60 is higher than wide by 11/10, 625/50 wider than high by 59/54. Later versions of Adobe Photoshop introduced the facility to use nonsquare pixels, so art can be exported directly to video applications.

Does it matter? Usually the scaling algorithms in the video codecs should convert from one aspect to another, so you should not have to worry about it – unless a circle is no longer circular by the time it is displayed on the player.

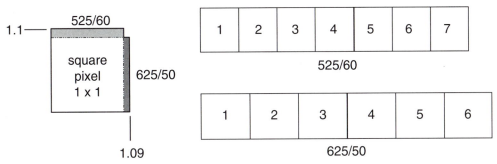

Figure 4.7 Pixel aspect ratios.

Videotape formats

The newcomer to video recording might well ask 'Why are there so many formats, and which should I use?' Videotape formats seem to grow with a geometric progression. They were developed originally as all-encompassing formats, but now are optimized for specific applications. Formats may be developed for the highest quality – for studio recording and high-definition work – or for the low-cost, low-weight demands of newsgathering and consumer camcorders. There have been about 100 formats developed over the last 50 years, but less than 20 have been successful in the marketplace. The SMPTE has standardized many of the tape formats, using letters for analog formats (type C) and numbers for the digital formats (D-1).

Many formats have evolved to give backward compatibility with legacy formats. This allows broadcasters to use the same deck to play back new digital recordings and archive analog recordings, saving cost and space (that several decks would occupy).

The enabling development for videotape recording was the flying head. This gave a fast enough writing speed to record the high frequencies of the video waveform, while retaining a low linear tape speed. Initially released in the transverse-scan quadruplex format by Ampex, it soon evolved into the helical scan system that video recorders use today.

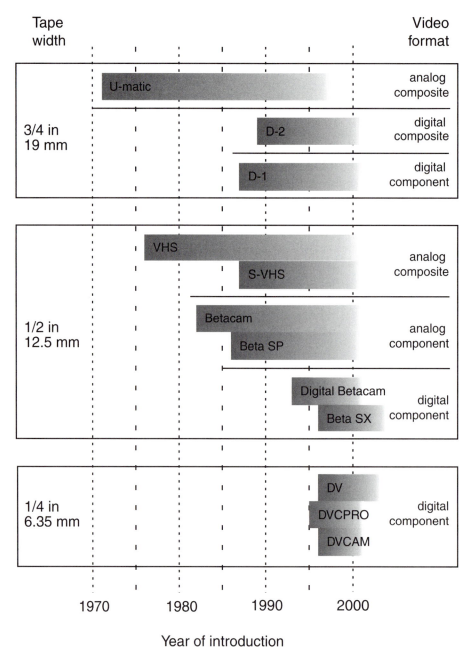

Figure 4.8 Evolution of videotape formats.

Analog formats

One-inch C-format

This was the most successful of the open-reel 1-inch formats, and was the work-horse of the edit bay until the production-quality cassette formats were developed. A consequence of its success is that much archive material recorded on this format is still lying in vaults. To use this for streaming content it is probably best to have it dubbed to a digital format and then encode from the digital copy.

U-matic

A consortium of JVC, Matsushita, and Sony developed the U-matic format in the late 1960s, originally as a domestic format. It soon was adopted for industrial and professional use, and also by television networks for early electronic newsgathering trials. Sony only ceased manufacture in 2000, so there is a lot of material out there in this format, especially corporate and industrial content.

The format used 19-mm tape, with color-under recording. It used a 110-mm diameter head drum rotating at 1,800 rpm. Contrast this with the DV recorder, which has a drum diameter of 21.7 mm turning at 9,000 rpm. There were several implementations, including hi-band and SP.

VHS

Dating from 1976, this has been the most successful tape format to date. It was developed for the domestic market for single-generation recordings. It does not offer acceptable multigeneration performance that is required for professional editing applications. As an analog format it does exhibit visible picture noise, an artifact that impairs the potential quality of streaming video. It is best avoided for capture of new material; you should opt for one of the DV formats.

S-VHS

This development of VHS offered improved record quality. It is noted for the adoption of the S-video interconnection, where the modulated chroma is kept separate from the luminance channel as opposed to being combined as is the case with composite video (NTSC, PAL).

Betacam and Beta SP

This format used compressed time division multiplexing of the R-Y and B-Y chroma channels, making it a true component recorder as opposed to the Y-C recorders previously available (U-matic records a single modulated chroma channel). Broadcasters rapidly adopted this for general production recording as well as ENG use. The SP version offered improved performance.

MII

Another 1/2-inch format, this time from Matsushita, MII used very similar design principles to Betacam. It replaced the largely unsuccessful M-format. Several major networks around the world adopted MII, which probably had the best performance of any analog format.

Digital formats

Digital formats split into composite and component.

Digital composite

D-2 was developed as a replacement for aging robotic cart machines that for 20 years played out television commercials 24 hours a day. Being a cassette format, it was easily handled by machinery rather than a human tape jockey. The digital format meant that tapes could be cloned as repeated plays caused tape wear. It was also used as a general-purpose replacement for the C-format open reel machine. Although a digital format, the recorder usually was used with analog plant.

D-3 was a Panasonic product, using 1/2-inch tape. It was used in a similar way to D-2, with analog composite interconnections.

Digital composite has largely been replaced by component VTRs, giving the many advantages of component processing.

Digital component

The first digital component VTR was D-1. This was the pioneering digital component format, much loved for film transfer and high-end commercial production. It does not use compression, and was designed to use the new BT601 sampling format. It uses 19-mm tape with 8-bit words per color channel. Panasonic later developed the D-5 format, using 1/2-inch tape, similar to the D-3 machines. It offered 10-bit recording of 270 Mbit/s video, or 8-bit for the little-used 16:9 360 Mbit/s format.

Most component formats now use 1/2- or 1/4-inch tape. The basic choice is between the Betacam derivates (1/2 inch) or the DV format (1/4 inch), although there are several other formats. Sony manufactures two 1/2-inch formats, Digital Betacam and IMX.

Digital Betacam

Digital Betacam is a general-purpose, high-quality digital recorder intended as a replacement for the Betacam SP analog format. It uses modest DCT compression, and can be considered essentially transparent. It is very popular for all forms of teleproduction, from field shooting to studio recording and editing.

IMX

IMX uses MPEG-2 recording at rates up to 50 Mbit/s. The coding is the studio profile with 4:2:2 sampling and I-frame–only compression.

Note that the digital Betacam is essentially a closed system with regular video interconnections. IMX can exchange video as the compressed data files, either to other VTRs or to disk recorders.

DV

DV is a group of different professional and consumer camcorder formats, all based on the DV 1/4-inch format cassette. The format specifies two tape cassette sizes, the standard for VTRs and the miniDV for camcorders. The compact size lends itself to the implementation of very small camcorders, the so-called palmcorders. The DV format samples video at 4:1:1 (525/60) or 4:2:0 (625/50), then uses DCT intraframe coding with a 5:1 reduction in data; this gives a final data rate of 25 Mbit/s for standard definition pictures. It often is referred to as DV25 compression. It has two digital stereo audio channels. The normal tape stock is metal evaporated.

When broadcasters expressed interest in these compact and lightweight DV camcorders, Panasonic and Sony developed two new formats based on the DV tape, and achieved a better performance (the DVCPRO and the DVCAM, respectively). Panasonic also offered enhanced professional formats, including 50 Mbit/s recording (DVCPRO-50). This uses 4:2:2 sampling and milder compression (3.3:1).

Most manufacturers have adopted the IEEE 1394 interface as the general port on their products to allow users to download the DV compressed files to the video editing system in the native format, as an alternative to regular video interconnects.

DV comes in several flavors from different manufacturers:

DV The original consumer format, also known as DVC.

DVCPRO (SMPTE D-7) A high-quality format from Panasonic, much liked for professional field use. Uses nearly twice the linear tape speed of the consumer versions and uses the more reliable metal particle tape. This improves performance in editing applications and lowers the bit error rate. It is also available in a 50 Mbit/s version.

DVCAM This is the Sony professional format based on the DV cassette. Like DVCPRO it uses a higher linear tape speed and it uses metal particle tape.

There are many other formats; a few of the more common ones are:

D-5 Uses a similar transport to the D-3 digital composite recorder, but offers 10-bit 4:2:2 component recording. The video signal is not compressed so it is popular for high-end uses in postproduction. A development of the D-5 formats allows high definition video to be recoded, albeit with mild compression. The HD-D5 has become a popular format for program interchange.

D-9 (Digital-S) Uses a metal particle tape in a VHS footprint cassette. D-9 decks potentially can play back VHS, S-VHS, and Digital-S tapes.

Table 4.5 Analog Tape Formats

	Format	Tape width	Max. playing time	Composition
Analog composite	C-format	1 in	94 mins	Ferric oxide
	U-Matic	3/4 in	60 mins	Ferric oxide
	U-Matic SP	3/4 in	60 mins	Metal particle
Analog component	Betacam	1/2 in	300 mins	Ferro-chrome
	Betacam SP	1/2 in	90 mins	Metal particle
	MII	1/2 in	90 mins	Metal

Video compression

The compression used in Digital Betacam is a closed system, optimized for recording on tape. The DV format is more general-purpose, and can be interchanged between units in the native format – this avoids unnecessary decompression and recompression stages that would degrade the signal. The IMX format uses MPEG-2 compression.

Table 4.6 Digital Tape Formats

	Format	Tape width	Max. playing time (minutes)	Composition	Compression	Sampling
Digital composite	D-2	3/4 in	22	Metal	uncompressed	4 fsc
	D-3	1/2 in			uncompressed	4 fsc
Digital component	D-1	3/4 in	76		uncompressed	4:2:2
	D-5	1/2 in			uncompressed	4:2:2
	Digital Betacam	1/2 in	124	Metal	DCT 2.3:1	4:2:2
	Betacam IMX	1/2 in			MPEG-2 4:2:2P@ML	4:2:2
	Digital-S (D-9)	1/2 in	104	Metal Particle	DCT 3.3:1	4:2:2
	Digital 8			Metal Evaporated or Particle	M-JPEG variant	
	DV/DVC	1/4 in	Mini 60 standard 300	Metal Evaporated	DV 5:1	4:1:1/4:2:0
	DVCPRO	1/4 in	120	Metal Particle	DV 5:1	4:1:1/4:2:0
	DVCAM	1/4 in	180	Metal Evaporated	DV	4:1:1/4:2:0
	DVPRO-50	1/4 in	60 mins	Metal particle	DV 3.3:1	4:2:2

The compressed formats often can be copied between devices at higher than real-time, typically four times. This can be very useful for cutting down the capture time from tape to disk storage systems.

DV and MPEG I-frame

MPEG-2 at main profile/main level is ideal for program distribution, satellite DTH, and DVB transmissions. But the long group of pictures does not lend itself to editing. The ideal for editing is to be able to cut to the frame. DV does not use interframe Coding, so it meets the requirements for editing. The alternative for MPEG-2 is to adopt a profile that does not use interframe coding, or 'I-frame only.' It does not use the B or P frames (bidirectional and predictive). The drawback of the avoidance of interframe coding is that for a given video quality the data rate is much higher than regular MPEG-2. ENG users have adopted 24 or 25 Mbit/s; 50 Mbit/s is for studio use. Compare this with the maximum rate used by MP@ML of 15 Mbit/s. So DV and MPEG-2, I-frame only, deliver a similar level of video quality for a given bit rate, yet allow freedom to edit at random frames.

What format of VTR deck should I purchase?

If you are setting up an encoding station from scratch, the question of which format to use always comes up. There is no straight answer to this. A video dubbing facility may well have at least one of each format, but that is their core business. Of course the choice may be restricted – suppose you have decided to use a DV-based desktop editing system. It would make sense to opt for a DV format. Alternatively you may have a large archive of Betacam tapes. In that case one of the Sony 1/2-inch decks would be a better choice. The later models can play both analog and digital tapes. It is always useful to have a deck that can play VHS and S-VHS – a huge amount of corporate material is available in these old formats.

You could standardize on one format and outsource interformat dubbing to a video facilities house, but remember that this will add to turnaround time, which could cause problems with rush jobs.

Time code

Computers usually count time in *x* millisecond increments from a certain date. Television uses a system more suited to reading by humans. Since program tapes rarely exceed three hours in length, the time code needs to resolve only up to 1 day or 24 hours. The resolution needs to be to one frame. The SMPTE

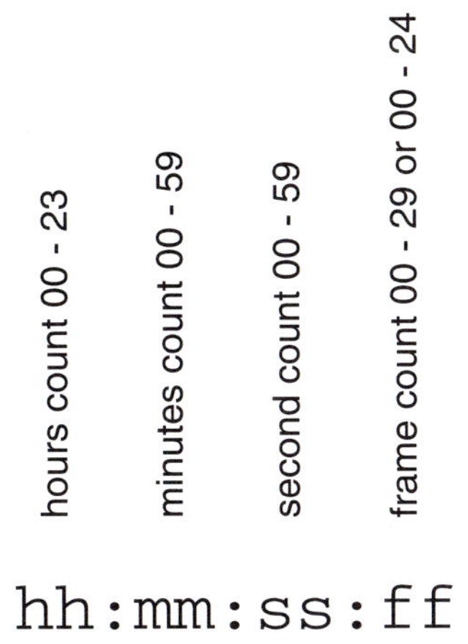

hours count 00 - 23

minutes count 00 - 59

second count 00 - 59

frame count 00 - 29 or 00 - 24

```
hh:mm:ss:ff
```

Figure 4.9 Time code format.

have a standard used throughout the television industry that counts each frame in frames, seconds, minutes, and hours.

Drop-frame time code

The NTSC standard further complicates the problem, with relation to program durations. The line and frame frequencies are derived from color subcarriers rather than from the arbitrary line and field rate values of PAL. The new line scanning frequency was defined as 2/455 times the subcarrier (3.579545 MHz), or 15,734.26 Hz, and the frame rate was defined as 1/525 times the line frequency, or 29.97 Hz.

With this frame rate of 29.97 Hz (rather than exactly 30 Hz), 30 frames last 1.001 seconds rather than precisely 1 second. This means the time code registering the frame count is not the same as the studio clock (probably locked to GPS). If the duration of a clip is calculated from the time codes, over a period of time this error will accumulate. This can be ignored for short clips like commercial spots, but for a two-hour movie the error amounts to a seven-second overrun. This may not sound like much, but with the tight scheduling of television commercials, seven seconds is potential revenue. To get around this, the SMPTE standard specifies an algorithm for dropping certain time code values. This drops the first two frames (00 and 01) of every minute, except every tenth minute. This amounts to dropping 108 frames per hour. This is 3.6 seconds, which effectively corrects the error.

Most editing equipment has configuration settings for time code, to select drop-frame (29.97 Hz) or non-drop-frame (30 Hz). Note that this setting is not required for PAL (625/50) because the frame rate is exactly 25 Hz.

Interconnection standards

Television companies have always preferred simple, robust interfaces that use coaxial cable and connectors. This is different from the computer industry, which has migrated toward the use of twisted pairs. Broadcasters prefer a single circuit, whereas computer interconnects frequently use multiple pairs. Any standard that departs from the single coaxial cable tends to be used for short interconnects; for example, a few meters. This policy is due partly to cost – coax can be terminated very easily and quickly – and partly due to a vast legacy of coaxial cable around the television plant.

- Analog composite
- S-Video or Y/C
- SDI (BT601)
- IEEE 1394

Analog composite

Analog composite uses the familiar 75 Ω coaxial format, with BNC connectors. Some consumer equipment uses RCA connectors. Analog composite is the de-facto standard interconnect; even today many low-cost video monitors feature only composite inputs.

S-Video, Y/C

S-Video is a spin-off from the S-VHS format. The chroma component, modulated on the subcarrier, is carried on a separate circuit from the luminance. This is to avoid the artifacts that result from the frequency interleaving of composite video. It uses a small four-pin connector.

BT601

BT601 uses 75Ω coaxial cable, but the high frequency (data rate 270 Mbit/s) demands better quality cable than analog composite. Belden makes cable designed especially for 601.

IEEE 1394

Originally developed by Apple as FireWire, it was adopted by IEEE as a standard and now is used by many other manufacturers. Sony uses the tradename i.LINK. There are two versions of the connector, a six-pin and a four-pin. The cable uses two pairs for data and one for power. The system can be daisy-

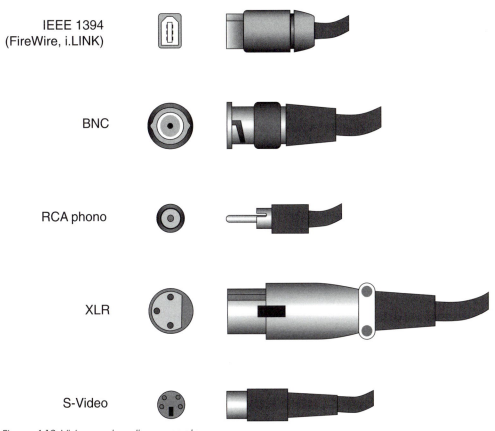

IEEE 1394
(FireWire, i.LINK)

BNC

RCA phono

XLR

S-Video

Figure 4.10 Video and audio connectors.

chained to a maximum of 17 devices. Each device regenerates the signal. If any device in a chain is turned off, the internal IEEE 1394 buffer is powered from the cable. The four-pin does not carry power and is used on self-powered cameras.

It can be hot-plugged, and likened to a high-speed USB connection in its simplicity of use. The data rates that are supported are 100, 200, and 400 Mbit/s for the original standard, and 800 Mbit/s for IEEE 1394b.

The interface carries not only audio/video data, but also remote control. So the capture card can stop, start, and cue the VTR over the IEEE 1394 cable. This makes for a very simple interconnection between the recorder and the encoding workstation.

Note that IEEE 1394 is not DV, although often called such, but it can carry DV compressed signals from a DV format camcorder.

Which interface to use

The priority for streaming interconnects should be as follows:

1. BT601
2. Analog S-video
3. Analog composite

If the source were using DV compression, then IEEE 1394 would be the first choice for a file interchange or streaming.

High definition

Everything in this chapter so far relates to standard-definition (SD) television. Although standard definition is great for small and medium-sized displays, once the screen diagonal gets above 750 mm the lines become very visible. Projection receivers and home theater systems demand higher resolution to equal the experience of watching 35-mm film.

The Advanced Television Systems Committee (ATSC) set about defining a new standard for high-definition television. The end result was a family of possible resolutions, leaving the broadcaster to make the choice. Both progressive and interlaced scanning are supported with 720 and 1080 being the line standards.

At the same time, studios were using digital processing for visual effects sequences in movies. Often using 2,048 × 1,556 or 4,096 × 3,112 pixels per frame (called 2k and 4k, respectively), such sequences can be composited seamlessly with the film stock. There had long been a demand to shoot productions on videotape rather than using film – that is, electronic cinematography. Rather than shoot at 30 frames per second, the same rate as film is used, which is 24 frames per second.

What has all this to do with streaming? Not much. An ATSC transmission uses a data rate of 18 Mbit/s, a long way from the requirements of a streaming file for less than 1 Mbit/s. If you are given HD source material you will have to convert the material to SD for encoding, a process called *down-rezzing* – lowering the resolution.

Maybe one day we will be able to view HD streaming, but that will have to wait for fiber-to-the-home and improved compression techniques.

Summary

Video formats have evolved from the standard definition color format developed by the NTSC in the late 1940s. This standard established the interlaced scan and the composite color encoding. Later, videotape recorders were developed. The pace of new formats has quickened, but the DV family has stood the test of time and has proved very popular for streaming video production. Future camcorders will use optical disk or memory cards as alternatives to tape, while retaining DV or MPEG compression.

Analog television is being replaced by digital formats, although analog composite is still the most used delivery format for the terrestrial receiver. The defining standard is BT601; this set the rules for the sampling structure that we see in MPEG compression.

Digital capture has a great advantage for streaming: there is less noise than analog systems. This makes for a better picture quality at a given bit rate. The compression codec and noise do not mix.

Domestic television formats are moving to higher definition standards, up to 1080 lines, and electronic cinematography is adopting a frame rate of 24 to be compatible with film, so there is ever-increasing diversity in standards and in tape formats. For the streaming video producer, this means cross-format conversion is likely to be part of the production workflow.

5 Video compression

Introduction

Compression reduces the number of bits used to represent each pixel in the image. The algorithms used to compress the images introduce, to a lesser or greater extent, visible artifacts. In general, the more complex algorithms introduce fewer of these artifacts. The processing power available to us increases with time, so more sophisticated algorithms always are being introduced into the codec products. This has to be done in a way that uses realizable computation, and has a short processing delay. The processing should not distort the image so that visible artifacts are generated.

As the level of artifacts decrease, so does our acceptance of the distortions. Once we were happy to watch monochrome television; now it must be color. Families were thrilled with the flickering home movies shot on 8 mm film; now a DV camcorder produces almost broadcast-quality results. Even so, the acceptable level of artifacts will depend on the application. If you paid to go to a movie theater to see the 70 mm print with Dolby Digital and they showed you a projection from a VHS tape, you would consider the picture unacceptable.

Compression systems exploit the mechanisms of human visual perception to remove redundant information, but still produce a compelling viewing experience. A typical example of the process is the persistence of vision, where an instantaneous view of a scene (for example, through a shutter) fades over about one-tenth of a second. This allows us to portray the continuum of time by a series of discrete pictures or frames. As an example, viewing a motion picture shot at 24 frames per second (fps) gives a good approximation of motion in the original scene.

Now there are artifacts – a classic is aliasing; for example, the wagon wheels of the stagecoach appearing to turn backward. Another potential artifact is flicker, where the brain is conscious of the discrete frames. If the refresh rate of the display drops below a certain threshold, the viewer will observe flicker.

Below 60 fps this becomes noticeable. To avoid flicker in the movie theater each film frame is shown twice, giving a display rate of 48 fps. The perception of flicker is reduced at low luminance levels. At the low levels of light used for projection in the theater, flicker is not a problem, even though it is lower than the optimal rate.

At the higher luminance levels used with television and VDU displays, refresh rates of at least 60 Hz must be used to avoid flicker. Television uses a similar system to film, but rather than repeating each frame twice it splits each picture into two – one half of the odd lines and the other of the even lines – in a process called interlaced scanning. These half-pictures are called fields; two fields make a picture of frame. Because European television systems use a 50-Hz field rate, under certain viewing conditions the flicker can be apparent.

Compression is always a trade-off between the level of artifacts and the bandwidth. Note that the shooting or encoding rate (chosen for realistic motion portrayal) can be different from the final display rate. We watch a film shot at 24 fps on a television receiver at either 25- or 30-Hz frame rates (50- or 60-Hz field rates).

Compression basics

A video clip is a sequence of pictures or frames. Each picture can be processed in isolation, much like a still image. A typical example is the JPEG standard.

Still images – JPEG

The JPEG format is widely used to compress continuous-tone grayscale and color images. JPEG compresses the file size by selectively discarding picture data. This is called lossy compression. The final picture is a representation of the original, but the original can never be restored from the JPEG file. The standard also supports a lossless compression with about a 3:1 reduction in data, but it is more commonly used in the lossy mode with ratios of 20:1 or greater. JPEG compression is based on a technique called the discrete cosine transform.

A lower compression ratio results in less data being discarded, but the JPEG compression algorithm will degrade any fine detail in an image. As the compression is increased, more artifacts become apparent. Wave-like patterns and blocky areas become visible, and there is ringing on sharp edges. The levels of artifacts that are considered acceptable depend upon the application. A picture reproduced in a magazine should have no visible artifacts, whereas minor distortions are to be expected with a thumbnail on a web page. It is more important to have a small file size with a short download time.

Intraframe compression

The compression of a single image in the spatial domain is called intraframe – within the frame. Video editing systems have used an extension to JPEG called motion JPEG, where the video sequence is compressed as a sequence of individual frames. When you are editing you need random access to each frame, and the ability to reorder the frame sequence.

Once the material has been edited into the final clip and is ready for dissemination, we no longer need the ability to freely cut a sequence on any frame. A streamed clip is delivered in a fixed order of frames. We now can take advantage of the redundant information in scene content that repeats from frame to frame.

Video and interframe compression

A sequence of video images has little change from one picture to the next, except at scene changes. This redundancy can be exploited by transmitting only the difference between successive pictures; by this means, a large reduction in the data rate can be achieved. This temporal or interframe compression allows the data rate for video sequences to be reduced much more than a sequence of unrelated still images. It typically allows a further 3:1 reduction over any initial spatial (intraframe) compression.

Visual perception

The human retina and visual cortex together process the visual scene in a way that detects edges and lines. This allows objects (like potential prey or predators) to be rapidly separated from the background. A consequence of this is that codecs that destroy or create edges will be viewed as creating perceptible distortions. Another feature is that fine detail near the edges of objects is not perceived with great acuity. So there are opportunities for perceptual redundancies and potential pitfalls where distortions are easily noticed. A good compression architecture has to exploit the mechanisms of visual perception.

Compression algorithms

Compression algorithms aim at lowering the total number of parameters required to represent the signal, while delivering a reasonable quality picture to the player. These parameters are then coded into data packets for streaming.

There are four main redundancies present in the video signal:

- Spatial
- Temporal

- Perceptual
- Statistical

Compression can be lossless or lossy. If all the original information is preserved, the codec is called lossless. A typical example for basic file compression would be ZIP. To achieve the high levels of compression demanded by streaming codecs, the luxury of lossless codecs is not possible – the data reduction is insufficient.

Spatial redundancy occurs where neighboring pixels in a frame of a video signal are related; it could be an object of a single color. If consecutive pictures also are related there is temporal redundancy. The human visual system has psychovisual redundancy; not all the visual information is treated with the same relevance. An example is lower acuity to color detail than luminance.

Finally, not all parameters occur with the same probability in an image. This statistical redundancy can be used in the coding of the image parameters. For example, frequently occurring parameters can be coded with fewer bits (Huffman coding).

The goal with compression is to avoid artifacts that are perceived as unnatural. The fine detail in an image can be degraded gently without losing understanding of the objects in a scene. As an example we can watch a 70-mm print of a movie or a VHS transfer and in both cases still enjoy the experience. If too much compression is applied, and the artifacts interfere with the image perception, the compression has become unnaturally lossy.

Table 5.1 lists some of the more popular technologies that have been used for encoding streaming files.

The techniques may be combined within codecs. For example, MPEG-2 divides the picture into blocks. Each block is encoded using a spatial transform, and the data is then run-length encoded. Blocks that repeat from frame to frame have temporal redundancy. Motion from frame to frame is approximated by the motion of a repeated block, which is encoded as the block with a motion vector.

Table 5.1 Compression Techniques

Spatial compression	*Other techniques*
Vector quantization	Frame differencing
Block Discrete Cosine Transform (DCT)	Motion estimation/compensation
Discrete Wavelet Transform (DWT)	Run-length encoding (RLE)
Fractal image compression	
Contour-based image coding	

Intraframe coding or spatial compression

To compress, the data required to recover each pixel must be reduced below the bit-depth of each pixel. Each pixel can be quantized separately – spatial quantization – but this would lead to posterization artifacts with any continuous-tone images. An alternative is vector quantization, where a group of pixels are quantized together. This theoretically offers the most efficient compression, but in practice it is computationally intensive and has a long processing delay. The alternative is transform coding, where a block of pixels is transformed to the frequency domain, and then quantized. Entropy coding can then be used to further reduce the data rate. The result can be as efficient as vector quantization, but without the processing overheads.

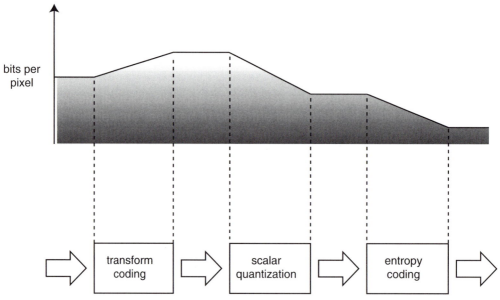

Figure 5.1 Compressing the bits.

Transform coding

Transform coding converts the spatial array of pixel blocks, a bit map, to the frequency domain. Although several different transforms have been proposed, the discrete cosine transform has been the most widely adopted for video codecs. Some other transforms investigated include Discrete Fourier (DFT), Karhunen Lo'eve (KLT), and Walsh–Hadamard (WHT).

The DFT was ruled out because it suffers discontinuities at the block boundaries. For typical real-world images, the DCT outperforms the WHT and DFT in the energy compaction. The KLT has the optimal decomposition but requires a very large number of operations, so it has the longest processing time. The DCT generally has been adopted because it approaches the performance of the KLT, but with a lower processing overhead. Any encoder that is to be used for video-conferencing or other live applications must have a short processing delay. So the DCT was chosen as the best compromise.

Wavelet compression

Although the DCT has been very successful, there has long been a demand for other compression schemes that do not suffer from the blocking artifacts that often are visible in DCT compression. Wavelet compression often has been cited as an alternative. It provides a time-frequency representation of the image and can achieve the same image quality as DCT at much higher compression ratios. It has been employed with some success in desktop video-editing systems as an alternative to motion JPEG. It is now becoming a more mainstream technology since it has been adopted as the core technology of the JPEG2000 standard for still image coding. Video applications include the QuVIS product line for the distribution of digital cinema files.

Model-based compression

This is an alternative to waveform coding. The codec attempts to model the scene and then transmit descriptors, rather than a representation, of the spatial image.

Fractal

The fractal compression technique relies on the fact that, in certain images, parts of the image resemble other parts of the same image. Similar sections of an image are located, and then the fractal algorithm is applied. Patents have restricted its use, and since wavelet compression offers better efficiency it has been the focus of more intense development effort.

Object-based coding

Object-based coding has been adopted as the basis for MPEG-4 coding. A scene – which can be in two or three dimensions – is represented by a number of video objects. Each object is described by its shape, texture, and motion. Conventional algorithms like the DCT and wavelet can be used to compress the objects.

Entropy coding

Entropy coding can yield a much shorter image representation with average content by using short code words for more likely bit sequences, and longer code words for less likely sequences. One of the first examples of entropy coding was Morse code.

Discrete cosine transform

This has formed the basis of all the popular video compression codecs. The picture is divided into regular blocks, and then the transform is applied block by block. The original coding schemes chose a basic block of 8 × 8, that is, 64 pixels. MPEG-4 introduced variable block sizes.

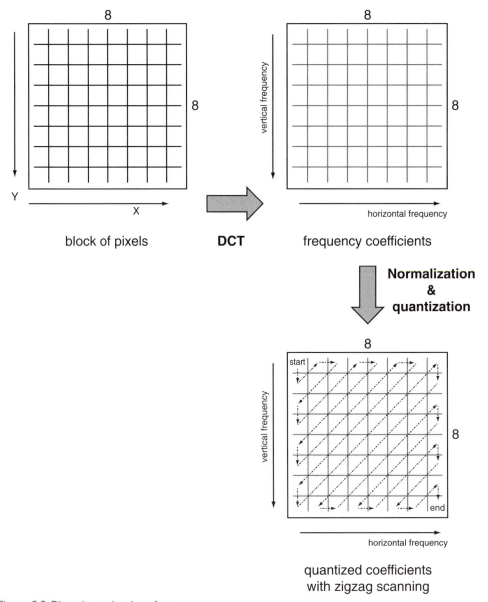

Figure 5.2 Discrete cosine transform.

Each 8 × 8 block of pixels is transformed to another 8 × 8 block of transform coefficients. Vertical edges in the picture transform as a horizontal frequency, and horizontal edges as vertical frequency coefficients. At this stage there has been no compression of the data. The goal is to gain a representation of the video signal in a form where perceptual and statistical redundancies can be used to reduce the data rate.

The coefficients are normalized and quantized. The quantization process allows the high-energy, low-frequency coefficients to be coded with a greater number of bits, while using fewer for the high-frequency coefficients. So as we go from top left to bottom right, the coefficients tend toward zero.

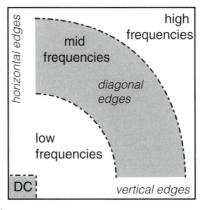

Figure 5.3 Spatial frequencies.

Variable-length coding (VLC)

By scanning the coefficients in a zigzag the result is long runs of zeros. The coefficients then are converted to a series of run-amplitude pairs. Each pair indicates the number of zero-value coefficients and the amplitude of the nonzero coefficient. These run-amplitude coefficients are then coded with a variable-length code. This uses shorter codes for commonly occurring pairs and longer codes for less common pairs – a form of entropy coding. These can be run-length encoded to reduce to the overall data rate.

Temporal or interframe compression

Video is a sequence of similar images, with step changes at scene boundaries. In many sequences there is virtually no change from one frame to the next. In scenes with subject motion, or where the camera is moving, there will be differences from one frame to the next, but there are many areas of the picture that do not change. This redundancy of information from one frame to the next can be exploited to lower the data rate. The basis of the compression is to transmit only the difference between frames – *frame differencing*. The player stores the entire picture in a frame store, and then reconstructs the picture from the previous frame and the difference information.

Since most of the difference between frames is from moving objects, there is further potential to reduce the data. The player already has the information to reconstruct the object; it is just in the wrong position. If a motion vector could be sent to say this block has moved from position A to position B then the block would not have to be retransmitted.

Of course it is not that simple. We are looking for a coding gain, where the total data rate is reduced with no apparent change to the picture quality. Motion vectors are additional data that have to be transmitted to the player. As an example, a scene with considerable subject movement coded to MPEG-2 at a rate of 6 Mbit/s can comprise 2 Mbit/s of motion vectors. That represents one-third of the total data.

Another problem is the reveal. As an object moves, what is revealed in its previous location?

Motion estimation

To generate motion vectors the encoder has to estimate the movement of picture elements. There are many ways to do this, some more complex than others. Since codecs like MPEG define the decoder rather than the encoder, the method used for vector generation is left to the encoder designer.

In a typical encoder, the motion prediction compares a previous frame with the current frame, and then estimates how blocks of the picture have moved. A local decoder generates the previous frames rather than using the original frames before intraframe compression. This is so that the predictor is using the same information that the player's decoder has available for computation.

The motion predictor makes trial moves of a block of pixels to establish the best match for the position of any moving elements. This match is then used to create a motion vector. Block matching is not the only technique for motion estimation, but it is one of the simplest to implement.

One consequence of the use of motion vectors is that the aggregate data rate will vary with the amount of motion in a scene. For a given image quality, a stationary scene may need 4 Mbit/s, and a scene with rapid movement may need 6 Mbit/s. A constant quality requires a variable bit-rate. This may conflict with the distribution medium; channels like telco circuits and satellite transponders have a fixed bandwidth.

Compression codecs

Compression codecs fall into three families:

- International standards
- Proprietary formats
- Open standards

International standards often use patented technology. A licensing authority controls the collection of the appropriate fees on behalf of the patent holders. Proprietary codecs collect revenues through a variety of methods. Open standards are usually under the umbrella of the open source community, and free for all to use.

Evolution of international standards

The video codecs we use today come from two backgrounds: the first is the telecommunications industry and the second is multimedia. These are some of the most used codecs.

H.261 – videoconferencing

This was the original video codec, and was the starting point for the MPEG-1 standard. H.261 was formulated under the auspices of the ITU for videophones and videoconferencing over ISDN lines. The videophone is now becoming a viable product, but videoconferencing has long been a key communication medium for business. One of the demands of both applications was real-time operation, so the codecs had to have a short processing delay.

The standard defines screen sizes of the Common Intermediate Format (CIF), 352×288, and Quarter CIF (QCIF) of 176×144 pixels. It uses progressive scan and 4:2:0 sampling. Data rates from 64 kbit/s up to 2 Mbit/s are supported by the standard. The compression is DCT-based with variable-length coding. As an option, intermediate predicted (P) frames could be used with integer-pixel motion-compensated prediction.

MPEG-1

This was the first successful standard developed by the multimedia community for audio-visual coding. The standard has long been used for video presentations on CD-ROMs. The normal resolution is source or Standard Input Format (SIF). Unlike the common interface format of H.261, the spatial resolution differs for PAL and NTSC systems (352×288 at 25 fps for PAL, and 352×240 at 30 fps for NTSC). It uses progressive scanning. The video compression, like H.261, uses the discrete cosine transform with variable-length coding. The motion prediction was improved over H.261 with subpixel motion vectors and the introduction of bidirectional predicted (B) frames.

It was designed for storage-based applications like the CD-ROM, at data rates up to 1.5 Mbit/s, and does not support streaming.

H.263

H.263 is a development of H.261 aimed at low bit rate applications. It dates from 1992. H.261 did not have a data rate low enough for operation at 28 kbit/s, so could not be used for videophone applications on analog phone circuits. For lower data rates a thumbnail size picture can be coded; the H.263 standard supports SQCIF, QCIF, CIF, 4CIF and 16CIF resolutions.

H.263 is now the baseline standard for MPEG-4 natural video coding.

MPEG-2

A higher resolution, high-quality system for broadcast television, MPEG-2 is intended to replace analog composite systems (NTSC, PAL) for digital transmission systems. It is also used for DVD encoding. Its primary applications use channel bandwidths greater than 4 Mbit/s. The main profile at main level (MP@ML) is a standard definition television frame rate and resolution with data rates up to 15 Mbit/s. The standard was extended to support high-definition television bit rates (up to 80 Mbit/s) and an I-frame-only studio profile (50 Mbit/s). MPEG-3 was to be a separate high-definition standard but was dropped in favor of extensions to MPEG-2 and MPEG-4.

MPEG-4

MPEG-1 and MPEG-2 were developed for specific applications. MPEG-1 is for multimedia CD-ROM presentations and MPEG-2 is for broadcast television. The spawning of so many potential multimedia applications, from hand-held wireless devices to high-definition home theaters, led to demands for a much more flexible coding platform. The support of the very low bit rates used for some streaming is one example of the new demands.

AVC (Advanced Video Codec, H.264)

H.263 is over ten years old, and, in many applications, no longer delivers the performance expected of a video codec. The MPEG and ITU realized that to separately develop new codecs was a waste of resources, so a joint video team (JVT) was set up to develop the advanced video codec or AVC. The fruition of this work was a new high-performance codec to rival the best proprietary codecs. It is designated H.264 by the ITU, and MPEG-4 Part 10 by the MPEG organization.

Much like MPEG-1 and MPEG-2, the standard defines the syntax of an encoded video bitstream with a reference decoder. The design of the encoder is left to each manufacturer. The advantage of this approach is that consumer devices can incorporate a compliant decoder that will play the output of any encoder. The manufacturers are free to differentiate their products by price and performance.

Table 5.2 Summary of Compression Formats

Compression format	ISO/IEC number Issue date	Target bandwidth bit/s	Typical resolution pixels	Application
H.261	1988–1990	384 k–2 M	176 × 144 or 352 × 288	Video conferencing, low delay
H.263	1992	28.8 k–768 k	128 × 96 to 720 × 480	Video conferencing
MPEG-1	11172 1993	400 k–1.5 M	352 × 288	CD-ROM
MPEG-2, MP@ML	13818 1994	1.5 M–15 M	720 × 480	Broadcast television, DVD
MPEG-4	14496 1998	28.8 k–500 k	176 × 144 or 352 × 288	Fixed and mobile web
AVC, H.264	14496–10 2002			General purpose

MPEG compression

MPEG compression divides a video sequence into groups of pictures. Each picture in the group then is divided into slices of macroblocks. A macroblock comprises four luminance blocks and one U and V color block each. The block is the basic unit for the spatial compression.

The concept of the slice first was introduced in the MPEG-1 standard. It divides the picture, so that if a fatal data error occurs within one slice, the rest of the frame still can be decoded.

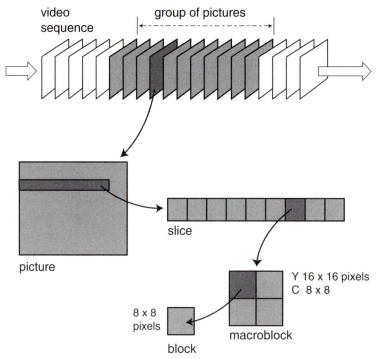

Figure 5.4 MPEG picture hierarchy.

Motion prediction

The temporal compression is arranged in short sequence of frames called a group of pictures (GOP). MPEG defines three types of frame within the group:

Intraframe or I-frame These are coded spatially, solely from information contained within the frame.

Predicted frame or P-frame These are coded from previous I- or P-frame pictures. The decoder uses motion vectors to predict the content from the previous frames.

Bidirectional frame or B-frame These pictures use past and future I and P pictures as a reference, effectively interpolating an intermediate picture.

I-frames provide reference points for random access to a stream. The number of pictures between I-frames is set by the encoder, and can be varied to suit subject material. The data in a typical P-frame are one-third of that in an I-frame, and B-frames are half that of a P-frame.

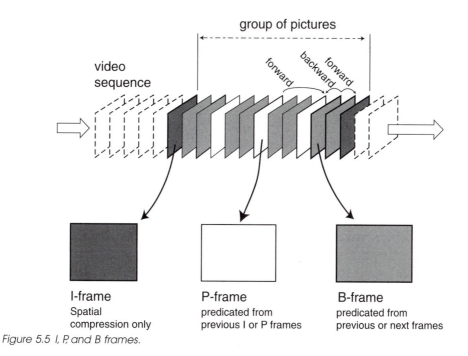

Figure 5.5 I, P, and B frames.

So that the decoder can make backward prediction from a future frame, the natural frame order is resequenced. The B-frames are transmitted after the next and previous pictures that each references.

MPEG-4 natural video encoding

MPEG-4 is the first MPEG system that supports streaming as part of the standard. The ability to stream is not related to the method of compression, but instead to the way that the video sequence is time-referenced, so that the media server can control the delivery rate to the player.

The requirements for the standard were for a flexible multimedia encoding format designed to support a very wide range of bit rates, from 5 Kbit/s up to 50 Mbit/s. This is sufficiently flexible to cover low bit rate wireless data through to HDTV applications. Version 1 MPEG-4 supports the following formats and bit rates:

Bit rates Typically between 5 kbit/s and 10 Mbit/s

Scan formats Interlaced as well as progressive video

Resolutions Typically from sub-QCIF to beyond HDTV

MPEG-4 broke from the rectangular and two-dimensional bit map of previous coding, and adopted object coding.

Video objects

Consider the cartoon as an analogy – cartoons are produced by cel animation. For example, consider a downhill skier. The animators deconstruct the story-board image into components: the background and the characters.

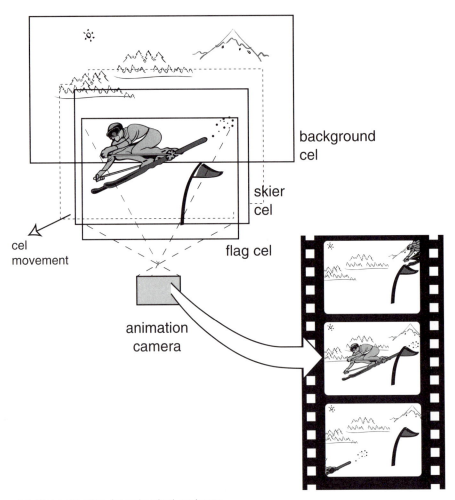

Figure 5.6 Cel animation for animated cartoons.

Each scene consists of a single background drawing, with a number of characters and foreground objects. Each is drawn separately on a clear sheet of acetate called a cel. Then each frame of a scene is photographed, with the cels stacked in the appropriate order. The skier cel can be moved for each exposure, or more likely a sequence of cels will represent the movement of the skier. So a great deal of drawing effort has been saved. Only one background has been drawn, and only one flag for the foreground. The savings by drawing each frame in its entirety is immense.

This deconstruction of a video sequence into different components or objects is the basis of MPEG-4 video coding, which is the big difference between MPEG-4 and earlier standards. Rather than the restrictions of coding a single two-dimensional rectangular video image, MPEG-4 allows both two-dimensional and three-dimensional objects to be mixed in a synchronized presentation. MPEG-4 breaks away from the cinematic representation and moves toward the virtual reality world of video games. This paradigm shift leads MPEG-4 to be a natural vehicle for rich media presentations. Immersive and interactive presentations can combine synthetic three-dimensional objects with two-dimensional stills and conventional video images.

An object has shape, texture, and motion. The object texture is equivalent to the information that was intraframe encoded in blocks by the earlier MPEG standards by the discrete cosine transform.

Consider a downhill racer again. The skier is moving, but the background (called a sprite) is essentially a still image. If the skier could be separated from the background, the background could be sent once, and the skier alone could be transmitted as a moving image. This potentially would save a large amount of data.

A sprite is defined as a large video object, possibly panoramic, and it is persistent over time. The media player can crop and spatially transform (warp) the sprite; for example, as a camera pans around the foreground objects. Rendering a number of video objects together in the player is relatively easy. Separating video objects from a two-dimensional scene within the encoder is nontrivial. This process is called video segmentation and is a subject of ongoing research.

The concept is a natural process for the human brain; we look at a scene and immediately decompose it into a number of objects. So, although the idea of object coding may seem foreign to a video engineer, to the neural physiologist it must seem like the obvious way to encode visual images. The scanned raster with which we are familiar is an engineering convenience.

In practice, object coding is not used for rectangular video scenes. Objects are used to combine video audio and graphics objects in interactive content, much like the DVD. A rectangular video image is encoded in much the

original scene

scene decomposed to objects

scene rendered in media player

Figure 5.7 MPEG-4 video objects.

Figure 5.8 MPEG-4 interactive objects.

same way as the earlier H.263 and MPEG-1 and -2 encoders. There are simpler ways of extracting objects that are suited to rich media presentations. The speaker could be shot on a blue-scene set, then extracted as an object. Figure 5.8 shows a typical application of objects for interactive content. The navigation elements and live video are combined over a background layer. Each object can be used as a hot-spot or link to other objects, giving the interactivity we are familiar with from the web page or DVD.

The arrangement of the objects within a scene is described by the scene descriptor, the Binary Format for Scenes (BIFS). Both natural video (pixel-based) and synthetic two- and three-dimensional objects can be encoded. The player stacks the object layers together to render a two-dimensional representation of the scene.

Shape coding A video object can be coded as an arbitrary shape. In the example the foreground flag could be coded as a separate video object. The shape of the object is defined by an alpha channel. To reproduce a complex edge structure the shape can be coded as a grayscale, giving an 8-bit resolution. A simple shape can be represented as a binary object (present or absent).

Texture coding The texture of a video object is conventionally coded by the DCT. The codec is similar to H.263, MPEG-1, and MPEG-2. The texture of static objects can be coded using the wavelet transform.

Motion coding The motion coding adds a global motion prediction. If an object is moving as a whole (like a camera pan), rather than code the motion vectors for each macroblock, the motion parameters of the entire object are transmitted. This can be very compact data.

Video encoder
Just like MPEG-1 and MPEG-2, the standard for MPEG-4 defines a standard player or *terminal*. The details of the encoder are left to the vendor, as long as the encoded bit stream can be played back on an MPEG-4 terminal.

A typical MPEG-4 encoder is shown in Figure 5.9. The texture and shape coding are new components. The basic encoder architecture is similar to MPEG-1 and MPEG-2 encoders. The enhancements to the coding do offer a small increase in efficiency over MPEG-2, typically 10–15 percent for typical material with the advanced simple profile. The AVC gives much better efficiencies, up to twice MPEG-2, albeit with a much higher complexity for the encoder and decoder.

MPEG-4 has a number of different profiles for natural video content. The most popular are:

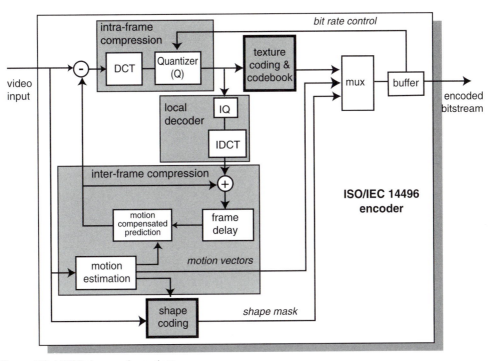

Figure 5.9 MPEG-4 encoder system.

Simple For low-bandwidth wireless and low-latency applications like video-conferencing and telephony.

Advanced Simple For interactive rich media applications, with bandwidth from 56 kbit/s up to high-definition at rates as high as 8 Mbit/s.

These two are joined by a third option of the advanced video codec, AVC. This offers much improved efficiency, but needs considerably more processing resources to encode and decode. As processors get faster and lower cost, AVC becomes the favored option for most fixed applications (rather than mobile).

AVC was created for conventional rectangular video, rather than the object-based coding of the MPEG-4, part 2, visual codec. It was formalized in 2003, with implementation in software and hardware becoming available in 2004. It achieves the same quality as MPEG-2 at around half the data rate.

These improvements are gained largely through improved prediction. AVC can use multiple reference frames within a GOP, rather than the bidirectional prediction of MPEG-2. The variable block size cuts down the mosquito effects, a common artifact of DCT block compression. AVC has three profiles: main (for broadcast TV), baseline (for mobile/wireless), and extended for high-definition reproduction. Developments (fidelity range extensions (FREX)) are planned for the standard to handle 4:4:4 sampling up to 12 bits per color. The initial standard is 4:2:0, 8 bit.

Other MPEG standards

MPEG-7
This is a standardized system for describing audio-visual content. This enables fast and efficient searching. You can compare this with the facilities provided with a search engine to locate textual content. Images and sound could be described in many abstract ways: textures, text descriptions of content, color. Much of this is open to interpretation. Consider somebody searching for a clip of a happy person. Happiness is an emotion that is not obvious from a description of the shape, color, and texture of the images. Content description is not a trivial task, but essential to the efficient utilization of audio-visual archives.

MPEG-21
MPEG-21 is a framework for integrating multimedia resources across a wide range of platforms and services. Streaming media is an important part of this framework. One focus of MPEG-21 is in value exchange, typically the sale of content. Key to this is the management of intellectual property rights.

MP3 misnomers
MP3 is the file extension for MPEG-1 and MPEG-2, layer 3 audio files, not MPEG-3. The latter was a proposed standard for HDTV that was dropped in favor of MPEG-2 high level.

Proprietary architectures

The proprietary architectures have been the most popular platforms for streaming. Windows Media has a very strong following, with other architectures moving toward compatibility with MPEG-4. There is the usual issue of proprietary versus international standard. Most vendors will claim that a proprietary solution brings higher quality encoding to the market quicker than the standards-based approach. Video codecs are a fast-moving product area. The list that follows gives the status as of 2004. It pays to use the latest versions of the encoders, since the quality is improving all the time, and often features like digital rights management are supported only in the latest versions.

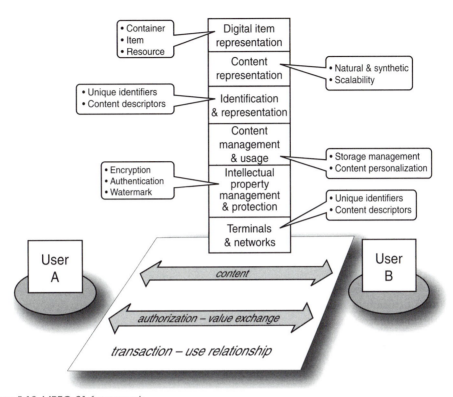

Figure 5.10 MPEG-21 framework.

Apple QuickTime

QuickTime supports a large number of video formats, including uncompressed, but came late to streaming. Most of the codecs are for authoring CD-ROMs. As a general-purpose multimedia production tool in an editing environment, Quick-Time can be used to wrap DV content and motion JPEG. Apple does not offer their own streaming codecs, but now supports the MPEG-4 codecs.

RealNetworks

The RealVideo 10 codec replaces earlier Real codecs with improved compression efficiency and support for high-definition video at 720 and 1080 lines. RealVideo 10 files are backward-compatible with RealVideo 9 decoder.

SureStream allows the content files to include video and audio encoded at different bit rates. The streaming server can optimize the delivery rate to suit the network conditions. Variable bit rate encoding can be used to maintain a constant video quality level. Two-pass encoding can be used for prerecorded video files (not live encoding) to give the optimum processing. This provides improved encoding quality with both constant and variable bit rates, but of course does lengthen the encoding time. RealVideo 10 now supports interlaced video as well as progressive scan.

As well as support for personal computers on the Windows, Linux, and Mac platforms, RealNetworks support mobile platforms like Symbian running on the ARM processor.

Windows Media 9 Series

Part of Microsoft's Windows Media 9 Series is the Windows Media Video codec. It is similar in principle to the MPEG-4 part 2 visual codec, but has been optimized to give better compression efficiencies. Microsoft played an active part in the development of the MPEG-4 standards, but in the interests of improved quality, has adopted the proprietary route. Microsoft has also forwarded the core codec for standardization by the Society of Motion Picture and Television Engineers (SMPTE) as video codec 9 (VC-9). This would open the way for third-party developers to adopt the VC-9 compression codec. Windows Media is Microsoft's implementation of the VC-9.

There are two video codecs, the basic codec and the Windows Media Video 9 Professional. The latter is for high-definition services, delivered by DVD or wide-band circuits, and supports line rates up to 1,080. The basic codec is more suited to regular streaming applications at bandwidths below 1 Mbit/s. The advanced profile will support 2,048 × 1,536 for digital film applications.

Windows Media 9 supports constant and variable bit rate encoding (see Table 5.3).

The video streams can be encoded at multiple bit rates for intelligent streaming over congested networks.

Table 5.3 Windows Media 9 Encoding Options

Bit rate	Encoding method	Notes
constant (CBR)		Stream data rate is constant
	one-pass	For live encoding
	two-pass	Improved quality over one-pass
variable (VBR)		Consistent video quality
	quality-based	Bit rate varies to give constant quality
	bit-rate based	Two-pass process, encodes for a set average bit-rate
	peak bit rate	Maximum rate constrained to fit streaming data channel, a two-pass process

Summary

Which codec offers the best compression? This is a moveable feast – codecs are improving all the time. Choosing a codec depends upon many factors. First there is the audience for your streams. What players do they have installed and what speed of connection do they use? You can make tests to see what codec gives the best quality at the required bit rate.

There are commercial concerns: What is the cost of an end-to-end solution? Then the producer may have a view. Does the architecture support all the rich media content that he or she may want to use? Only you can answer these questions. To recommend a codec for a specific task depends upon many factors.

Codecs are often compared to existing video formats – for example, VHS quality. It is difficult to sensibly compare an analog tape format with DCT compression. We quite happily watch the poor quality of VHS (compared to broadcast television) because of the constant level of artifacts like noise. The brain ignores continuing distortions. DCT-based coding produces changing levels of artifacts. This means that stationary pictures with low levels of fine detail look better than fast-moving fine detail. So the picture quality changes as the picture content changes. This is visually disturbing as the blockiness comes and goes. So it is meaningless to compare DCT coding with VHS. To achieve a constant video quality you have to resort to variable bit rate encoding, as adopted with the DVD format. That way the fast-action sequences get a higher bit rate than the stationary scenes. This is now an option with some streaming codecs.

Compression will always be a trade-off between bit rate and artifacts, but the use of perceptual coding now allows for compelling viewing over broadband circuits, DSL, and cable modems, using a fraction of the bandwidth of conventional television.

6 Audio compression

Introduction

For many consumers, Internet radio was their first exposure to streaming media. The other driver for interest in compressed audio has been the universal acceptance of the MP3 format for low data rate audio files. Although not a streaming format (it is for download and play), many popular streaming architectures can be used to wrap MP3 files for streaming. Although MP3 gradually is being replaced with the more efficient AAC codecs, it still retains a very wide user base. There are several audio-only architectures that come from the Internet radio arena: Nullsoft's Shoutcast and Winamp, and Audion for the Mac platform. The primary multimedia architectures – MPEG-4, Windows Media, QuickTime, and Real – all support audio-only streaming as well as video/audio content.

To stream audio you have to go through three processes:

- Digitization
- Encoding (compression)
- Packetization

The professional digital audio format, AES-3, is often the basis for digitization. The AES standard has a data rate of over 3 Mbit/s for stereo audio sampled at 48 kHz. To transmit this over a 28-kbit/s dial-up circuit, the data would have to be reduced by a factor of 100:1, and that excludes the overheads of packetization and error resilience.

The compression schemes split between the speech (voice) coding developed by the telcos and the military, and the general audio or waveform encoders developed for multimedia applications. The speech coding algorithms generally use a model of the vocal tract and transmit voicing parameters for reconstruction by the decoder into intelligible speech. Much of the Internet radio encodes music that can be distributed over a 28- or 56-kbit/s voice circuit.

There is a big difference in fidelity between conventional voice telephony and an acceptable system that can be used for the enjoyment of music, which has led to the development of a number of sophisticated compression schemes for general audio that can utilize such narrow-band channels. They are based upon the concepts of *psychoacoustics*, that is, the study of the mechanisms used by the human ear for the perception of sound. The problems for the developers of codecs stem from the very different waveforms generated by, for example, the piccolo or the castanets.

The quest to squeeze maximum fidelity from a channel started in the analog era before digital processing.

Analog compression

The compression schemes of analog audio originally were developed to counter the limited dynamic range of magnetic tape recorders. A typical recorder could have a range between peak level and the noise floor of 70 dB. High-quality recording demanded at least 90 dB.

Dolby A

Dolby A was the first commercially successful noise reduction product used by professional recording studios, dating back to 1965. It established the principal of splitting audio into sub-bands for processing, a system still used by MPEG codecs and by audio preprocessors. Multichannel recording added to the demands from recording studios for noise reduction. In a final mix-down, 40 or so tape tracks could be combined into a stereo signal. The noise from each channel adds, and without Dolby, the result would have been unusable. To get around the noise problem, the dynamic range of the input audio was compressed before recording on tape, then expanded back on replay, a process commonly referred to as *companding*.

To make the process inaudible was not trivial, especially using analog computing elements. Earlier proposals for noise reduction systems had suffered from noise modulation and poor transient response. The Dolby system made use of psychoacoustics to mask the effects of compression. With the low-cost digital processing available now, much more complex algorithms can be used.

Dolby B and C

This was a low-cost noise reduction system aimed at consumer products like the compact cassette. At the low tape speeds used, the frequency-dependent noise (tape hiss) was a big problem. It could be reduced to acceptable levels with Dolby noise reduction, and used a single sliding band of frequencies for companding.

Digital audio

Natural sounds are captured as an analog signal by a microphone. To convert the signal to a streaming format it passes through several processing stages.

- Pre-emphasis (optional)
- Sampling
- Analog-to-digital conversion
- Compression
- Packetization and wrapping

The first digital audio systems used uncompressed linear coding, and employed the first three processes, pre-emphasis, sampling, and analog-to-digital conversion. The most widely used was pulse-code modulation.

PCM

The basis of digital audio is pulse-code modulation or PCM. The microphone generates a voltage proportional to the air pressure (or velocity). This is sampled at regular intervals. The sample value is turned into a digital code word. The key parameters of the coding are the sampling rate and the resolution or bit depth. Pre-emphasis is a simple scheme to counteract hiss, or high-frequency noise, in electronic circuits. By boosting the amplitude of high-frequency content, the signal-to-noise ratio can be improved. It has been used in FM broadcasting, and is an option in some digital coding. It relies on there being less energy at high frequencies for typical content. It does trade dynamic range for lower noise, so is not essential to the process of conversion and coding.

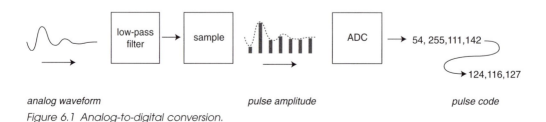

analog waveform   pulse amplitude   pulse code

Figure 6.1 Analog-to-digital conversion.

Sampling

The sampling rate is set by the desired frequency response. Sampling theory dictates that the sampling frequency should be greater than twice the highest frequency that is to be captured (the Nyquist criteria). The sampling rate is a compromise: the higher the rate, the more sample data is generated. Human hearing extends from 20 to 20,000 Hz, but speech uses a limited range in the center from 500 to 3,000 Hz. For high-fidelity applications, the sampling must be higher than 40 kHz, but a speech channel could use a rate as low as 6 kHz.

Resolution

The digital coding converts the analog waveform, with essentially a continuum of values, to a number of discrete levels – a process of quantization. The number of levels used determines the resolution.

Table 6.1 Main Audio Sampling Rates

Sampling rates	Frequency response	Application
8 kHz	200 Hz–3.3 kHz	Telephony
16 kHz	100 Hz–7 kHz	Wideband speech
32 kHz	50 Hz–15 kHz	Broadcast distribution
44.1 kHz	20 Hz–20 kHz	Consumer (CD)
48 kHz	20 Hz–20 kHz	Professional and broadcast
Max. 192 kHz	Up to 96 kHz	DVD-A
2.8224 MHz	DC to 100 kHz	SACD (uses bitstream coding)

The minimum step value sets the noise floor of the converted signal. In most conversions, each step has the same value, called linear PCM. Less demanding applications typically use 16-bit sampling. Professional users will demand a higher resolution of 20 or 24 bits. Table 6.2 indicates the potential dynamic range. In practice this will not be reached, as some noise will be present in the analog-to-digital conversion and in preceding stages between the microphone transducer and the converter.

The introduction of digital storage and transmission allowed the dynamic range to be increased when compared with analog systems. Even a 16-bit bit-depth digital system potentially offers a better dynamic range than an analog tape recorder.

The conversion stage is prone to distortions: the conversion process may be nonlinear, there may be circuit noise, and the sampling clock may have jitter.

Table 6.2 Dynamic Range versus Bit Depth

Code word length (bits)	No. of levels	Minimum step vs. full-scale* (dB)
8	256 (2^8)	−48.16
16	65,536 (2^{16})	−96.33
20	1,048,576 (2^{20})	−120.41
24	16,777,216 (2^{24})	−144.49

*Note. The ratio of the minimum step to the full scale in decibels = $-20 \log_{10}$ (No. of levels).

All these will impair the conversion process. A basic sound capture card may exhibit all these problems to a lesser or greater extent. Any distortions introduced will impair the later compression codecs and lower the quality of the audio delivered to the consumer's player.

In practice you would allow headroom between the maximum positive and negative excursions and the peak values. If the excursion reaches the peak values the waveform will be clipped. This produces unpleasant distortion, usually heard as a cracking sound.

Although the sampled waveform is bipolar (representing positive and negative sound pressure variations) the analog-to-digital converter ADC is usually a unipolar system. The pulse code often will use signed notation to represent the

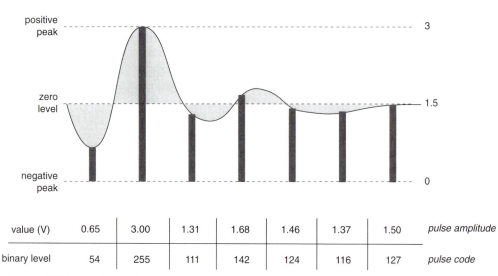

| value (V) | 0.65 | 3.00 | 1.31 | 1.68 | 1.46 | 1.37 | 1.50 | *pulse amplitude* |
| binary level | 54 | 255 | 111 | 142 | 124 | 116 | 127 | *pulse code* |

Figure 6.2 Pulse-code modulation.

bipolar waveform. It is possible for a DC offset to occur between the analog waveform and the digital code. This means that silence does not have a value of zero. Some codecs exploit periods of silence to lower the data rate. It is important to remove DC offset before compression.

Nonuniform coding

Linear PCM uses a fixed step value for the quantization levels. It is possible to use nonuniform steps – for example, a logarithmic scale.

G.711

G.711 is the international-standard encoding format for telephony set by the ITU. Two versions exist: μ-law (used in the Bell area) and A-law (used for international circuits).

The audio is sampled at 8 kHz (realizing a bandwidth up to a frequency of 3.3 kHz) with a linear 16-bit conversion. The 16-bit sample is coded to 8 bits using a logarithmic table. A 13-bit dynamic range is achieved, with three least-significant bits dropped. Both of the encoding schemes approximate to a logarithmic transfer function. This ensures that low-amplitude signals are sampled at a higher resolution, while maintaining enough dynamic range to encode high amplitudes. The output data rate is 64 kbit/s, the standard for a voice channel.

G.711 sets a baseline standard for speech encoding. It provides a reference fidelity that the listening public can use to assess the acceptability of a codec.

The actual encoding doesn't use logarithmic functions. The input range is broken into segments, each segment using a different interval between decision values. Most segments contain 16 intervals, and the interval size doubles from segment to segment. Figure 6.3 shows three segments with four intervals in each.

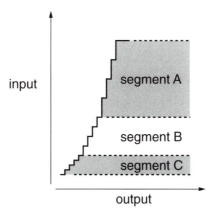

Figure 6.3 G.711 segments.

Both versions are symmetrical around zero. μ-law uses eight segments of 16 intervals each in each of the positive and negative directions, starting with an interval size of 2 in segment 1, and increasing to an interval size of 256 in segment 8. A-law uses seven segments. The smallest segment, using an interval of 2, is twice the size of the others (32 intervals). The remaining six segments are normal, with 16 intervals each, increasing to an interval size of 128 in segment 7. Thus, A-law is skewed toward representing smaller signals with greater fidelity.

As the levels are compressed and then expanded, this technique often is referred to as *companding* PCM (as opposed to linear PCM).

Floating-point coding
Some older computers were more efficient at floating-point arithmetic, rather than integers. Audio sampling schemes for these machines reflect this, using 32- or 64-bit floating-point sample values. Integers are used with AIFF and WAV formats (Audio Interchange File Format and Windows audio format).

Sampling rates

The sampling rate chosen determines the frequency range that can be reproduced. Telephony has an upper limit of 3.2 kHz; a sampling frequency of 8 kHz is used. Broadcast audio usually is limited to 15 kHz; this requires a sampling rate of 32 kHz. High-fidelity reproduction extends to at least 20 kHz, requiring sampling rates of 44 kHz or greater.

AES-3

This is the international standard digital audio interface. Its full title is Serial Transmission Format for Two-channel Linearly Represented Digital Audio Data. In simple terms that means it is stereo and uncompressed.

AES-3 was a joint development by the Audio Engineering Society (AES) and the European Broadcasting Union. The standard is based on balanced, shielded twisted pair cable, and is for transmission distances up to 100 meters. Three sample rates are supported.

Table 6.3 AES Sampling Rates

Sample rates (kHz)	Audio channels	Aggregate data rate (bit/s)
48	2	3,072,000
44.1	2	2,822,400
32	2	2,048,000

Table 6.4 Computer Audio Sampling Rates

Sample rates	Description
8 kHz	The G.711 telephony standard (μ-law and A-law encoding).
16 kHz	Used by the G.722 compression standard. Also specified for MPEG-2.
18.9 kHz	CD-ROM standard.
22.05 kHz	Half the CD sampling rate.
24 kHz	One-half 48 kHz rate.
32 kHz	Used in digital radio, and for TV audio distribution by the EBU.
44.1 kHz	The CD sampling rate.
48 kHz	The standard professional audio rate, AES-3. Used for DVD and DAT (Digital Audio Tape).

The AES rates are those most generally used for the capture of streaming media; 48 kHz is the popular professional recording rate.

Table 6.4 gives some other popular sampling rates that are in general use.

Mono, stereo, and multichannel

Audio can be transmitted as a single channel (monophonic) or can carry spatial information in a multichannel format. Stereo is very popular; most PC audio systems use two loudspeakers for reproduction. Although streaming codecs support multichannel audio, for many applications it pays to stick to mono. It saves valuable streaming bandwidth, and the luxury of stereo is lost on PDAs and laptop computers.

A halfway house is to remove stereophonic irrelevance – in other words, redundant information in both left and right channels. Human hearing does not perceive a stereo effect below around 2 kHz, so the lower registers can be transmitted as mono with no detriment to directional information at higher frequencies.

Cinema and home theater have introduced the public to surround sound, usually in the 5.1 format. The 5.1 refers to five channels plus a low-frequency effects channel. The effects channel can be reproduced through the main speakers or through a separate subwoofer. Most streaming audio formats now support surround sound, a consequence of the wider adoption of broadband and the higher bit rates that can now be distributed.

As the PC has evolved to be a home multimedia terminal and the television set-top box gains more functionality, the listener can take full advantage of surround sound.

The ear and psychoacoustics

Many of the characteristics of human hearing are exploited as part of perceptual encoding. The study of hearing is called *psychoacoustics*. The factors that are exploited by audio codecs include the following:

1. Threshold of hearing
2. Critical bands
3. Frequency or simultaneous masking
4. Temporal masking
5. Stereophonic irrelevance

Threshold of hearing

The human ear is relatively insensitive to low- and high-frequency sounds when listening at low sound pressure levels. The loudness button on consumer stereo equipment provides a partial compensation for this effect by boosting the high and low frequencies. Fletcher and Munson published typical sensitivity curves some 60 years ago. Note that the dynamic range at mid-frequencies is 120 dB.

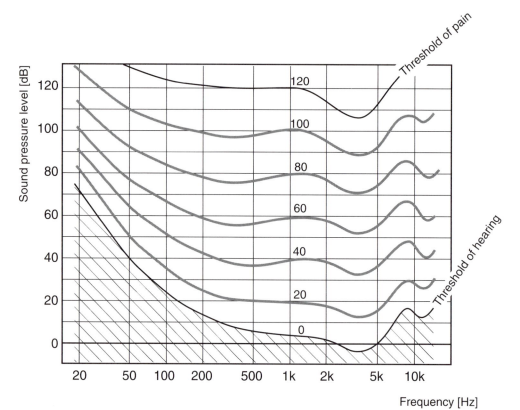

Figure 6.4 Fletcher-Munson curves.

Note also that the dynamic range falls off at lower frequencies, and to a lesser degree, at high frequencies. This means that less resolution is required from a codec to faithfully reproduce the bass registers.

Sub-bands

Studies of the mechanisms of hearing within the cochlea arrived at a model based upon a number of critical bands of frequencies. There are typically 24 critical bands from 20 Hz to 15 kHz. A unit, the bark, is used for this perceptual pitch scale, 1 bark representing the width of one critical band.

Masking

A characteristic of hearing is that, within one of these critical bands, a loud tone will mask low-level tones. The amount of masking is dependent upon the frequency and level of the tone. The greatest masking occurs closest to the masking signal. The second harmonic of high-level mid-frequency tones also has a masking effect (this indicates a nonlinearity within the ear).

Figure 6.5 shows a loud tone of 500 Hz. The threshold of hearing is modified at frequencies near the tone. Sounds within the gray area are masked by the

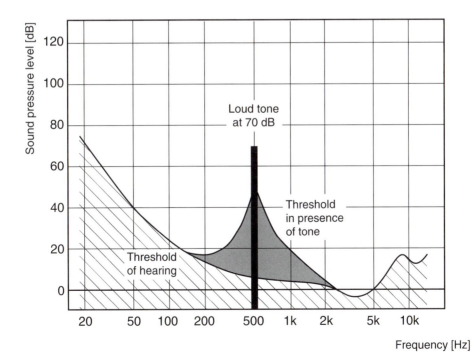

Figure 6.5 Noise masked by a loud tone.

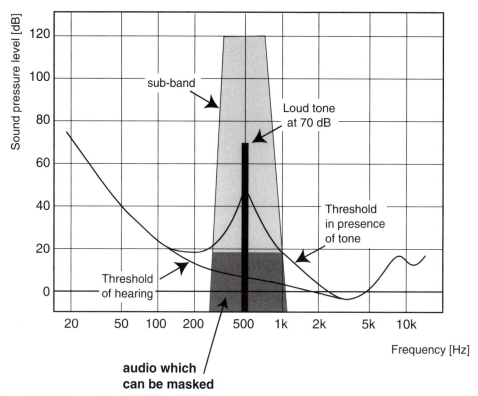

Figure 6.6 Noise masking threshold.

tone. This effect is called *noise masking* and is exploited by most general audio codecs to remove the masked audio information.

There is another, similar, phenomenon called temporal, or nonsimultaneous, masking. After a masking tone is removed, the masking effects gradually decay for about one-fifth of a second. There is a short premasking, less than 50 ms before the masking tone.

The human voice

Psychoacoustics apply only to hearing so are equally applicable to speech or general audio coding.

The other human characteristics that are used in compression are vocal tract models, which were established by research undertaken in the 1950s. If speech was broken into short frames (about 20 ms long), it could be considered as

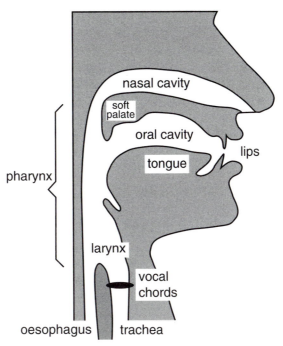

Figure 6.7 The human vocal tract.

steady-state sound. This sound could then be modeled by a combination of a 'buzz' generator for voiced sounds and a white noise generator for unvoiced sounds. A filter bank then reproduced the effects of the resonant cavities of the mouth, nose, and throat.

The vocal chords produce a buzzing noise. The fundamental is about 100 Hz for adult men and 200 Hz for women. The tone is rich in harmonics (overtones). The vocal tract then acts as a filter on this tone, producing vowel sounds (consonants or 'plosives' are formed by controlled interruptions of exhaled air). The vocal tract has three cavities: the pharynx, or back of the throat; the nasal cavity; and the oral cavity (mouth). The resonant frequencies, or formants, are changed by muscle actions in the jaw, tongue, lips, and soft palate. This gives voicing to the basic tones from the vocal chords. The nasal cavity acts as a parallel filter.

This is called the source-filter model of speech. These proposals were used to develop voice coders, or vocoders, that could be used to synthesize speech. The vocoders use the model to analyze speech and create a parameter set that can mimic the original speech.

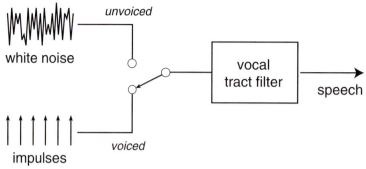

Figure 6.8 The source-filter speech model.

Lossy compression

Data compression can be lossless or lossy. A lossless codec allows the original samples to be reconstructed with no loss of information, but they offer limited opportunity to radically lower the data rates. Most media players include a lossless codec, but this is for the local archiving of music CDs rather than streaming applications.

To achieve the rates demanded for streaming, the developers have adopted lossy codecs. A lossy codec throws away data that can never be recovered. There are two ways this can be achieved. The first takes advantage of statistical redundancy in the data; the second exploits our knowledge of psychoacoustics to remove information that is perceived as irrelevant to the hearing process. Of course there are levels of judgment involved in this. What is considered irrelevant to a narrow band speech circuit is not going to be redundant for a broadband codec delivering music.

The fidelities delivered by speech codecs are classified by the application:

Broadcast This would be used for radio and television broadcast contribution circuits. The channel would have an audio bandwidth extending to 15 kHz with a minimum sampling rate of 32 kHz. The dynamic range would exceed 90 dB. Data rates exceed 64 kbit/s.

Toll Toll, or network quality, is equivalent to the speech quality for a regular analog telephone. The frequency range is 200–3,200 Hz; the data rate is over 16 kbit/s.

Communications Typified by cellular phones, this is a degraded version of toll quality where a lower data rate is demanded by the channel. Communications speech still sounds natural but has more audible distortions.

Synthetic A good example is LPC-10; although intelligible, the voice sounds unnatural. Used for low data rates below 4 kbit/s.

Music coders all fall into the broadcast category, and generally use higher bit rates than speech to support an increased sampling rate and larger sample word size.

Statistical redundancy

Lossy compression can use statistical redundancy in the audio waveform, with no regard to psychoacoustics. The best examples are DPM and ADPCM.

Differential PCM (G.726)

In Adaptive Differential PCM (ADPCM), 4 bits are used to quantize the prediction error sample, giving a bit rate of 32 kbit/s. This is found in ITU-T Recommendation G.726.

Perceptual compression

This uses knowledge derived from the study of the psychoacoustics of human hearing. Redundant information that can be called perceptually irrelevant is removed from the sample data.

Compression schemes are split between those developed specifically for speech using very low bit rates (sometimes referred to as vocoders), and the more general-purpose or waveform codecs that can be used for any material, especially music. The success of a speech codec is measured by how natural and intelligible it sounds.

General audio codecs

Compressing general audio is far more complex than speech. A speech codec is encoding a single voice, and can use the human voice-tract model to represent that voice. A general audio codec has to reproduce a wide gamut of sounds. Consider musical instruments; these range from the almost sinusoidal tones of the flute to the complex spectrum produced by percussive instruments. This could be a harpsichord, castanets, or bells. Then there are the many non-musical sounds: explosions, audience applause, the wind. Some have harmonic relationships, others are completely atonal. A general codec should perform reasonably with any such source.

The input to codecs is a time-varying voltage, represented by a regular series of discrete samples. Perceptual codecs generally sample a finite-length frame of samples, and then perform a time/frequency analysis of that frame. Frames are typically a few milliseconds long. A coarse time frame is optimum for long pure notes; a fine resolution is more efficient for percussive transients.

Sub-band coding

Designers of waveform codecs do not have the luxury of the model for speech generation used in the vocoder. Instead, they look to the perceptual irrelevancies identified by the study of psychoacoustics. The core for general audio coding is the masking effect – a consequence of the critical bands of human hearing.

Sub-band coding is the basis of most general audio codecs. The audio spectrum is split into a number of sub-bands that approximate to the critical bands. Within each sub-band, information that is masked by louder components can be discarded. Although this is a lossy compression, if suitable algorithms are used, the final listener will be unaware of the missing information.

The filter banks have to meet a number of criteria, not the least being a fast processing algorithm. Desirable characteristics are perfect reconstruction (in the decoder), good stop-band attenuation, and constant group delay.

The filter banks convert the frequency spectrum of input waveform into time indexed coefficients representing the frequency-localized power within each of the sub-bands.

The Pseudo-Quadrature Mirror Filter (PQMF) was adopted for the MPEG-1 algorithms. Later codec designs have used the Modified Discrete Cosine Transform (MDCT) to decompose the frequency components into the sub-bands.

Avoiding pre-echo

One problem that can arise with transform codecs is pre-echo distortion. If a transient occurs near the end of a sample frame, a pre-echo can be heard. MPEG-1 used four different windows (short and long), switched as appropriate to the signal content.

Rating codecs

Some key parameters are used to select a suitable codec:

1. Compression ratio achieved
2. Processing power required by encoder (MIPS)
3. Coding delay
4. Audio fidelity

In general, the more compression offered, the more processing power is required. The codec's cost is related to the processing power, so there is a direct cost/benefit relationship.

Codecs

Codecs fall into three groups: those defined by internationally agreed standards, proprietary systems, and open source. Each has their proponents and supporters. If you are trying to decide which route to take, many factors have to be considered beyond the obvious one of audio quality. Different codecs will have different licensing costs; there is interoperability to think about, and then the level of support offered by the vendor.

The key technical parameters are the number of bits per sample (a measure of compression), the encoding delay, and the processing power required for encoding (MIPS). The encoding delay is very relevant for any two-way working. A natural conversation becomes more difficult as the delay increases – we have all seen television anchors interviewing a contributor over a satellite feed.

Table 6.5 Summary of Codec Algorithms

Organization/family	Algorithm	Codec
MPEG		MPEG-1, layer 1, 2, 3 MPEG-2, layer 2 & AAC MPEG-4, AAC
ITU-T	PCM ADPCM	G.711 PCM (μ-law, A-law) G.726 ADPCM at 16, 24,32 & 40 Kbit/s (replaces G.721 at 32 Kbit/s and G.723 for 24 and 40 Kbit/s)
Interactive Multimedia Association	ADPCM	IMA/DVI
US DOD Federal Standard	Linear predictive CELP	LPC-10E (1015) (1016)
ETSI	Linear predictive	GSM 06.10 (global systéme mobile)
3GPP	ACELP	AMR (adaptive multirate)
Proprietary	ACELP ACELP ATRACS	Voiceage Sipro Sony ATRAC3

The processing resources required primarily impact mobile and telephony applications. Mobile applications have limited power resources and telephony demands low-unit-cost encoders. For the general encoding station for streaming, cost is only a small factor.

Codec standards

Military vocoders

The US DOD has developed low-bit-rate speech coders for use with secure telephone units (scrambled phones). The same coding principles, called (Code Excited Linear Prediction (CELP), have been adopted by MPEG-4.)

LPC-10E

LPC-10E stands for Linear Prediction Coder (Enhanced) with 10 predictive coefficients. It is a US DOD Federal Standard (No. 1015). The bit rate is 2,400.

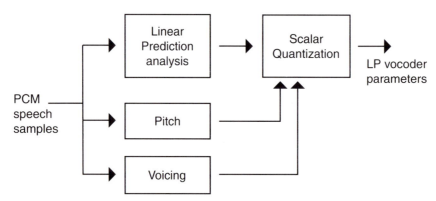

Figure 6.9 LPC vocoder.

Linear Prediction uses a simple model of the vocal tract. The speech is fitted to this model. The result can be understood, but sounds somewhat robotic. The main disadvantages of LPC are the buzzy sound from the parameter updates and the poor modeling of nasal sounds – but in practice the results are satisfactory. It is not suited to mobile applications, because it does not work well with high ambient noise levels.

CELP

The US DOD Federal Standard 1016 defines Code Excited Linear Prediction (CELP). Sometimes LPC and CELP are taken to mean the same thing, but the

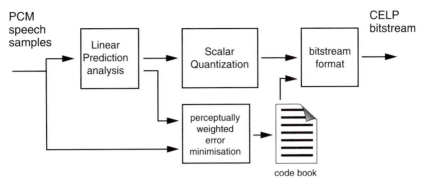

Figure 6.10 CELP vocoder (simplified).

CELP standard is much more sophisticated. It does the same simple speech analysis as LPC, but compares the result with the original speech, and transmits a compressed form of the errors. This uses a code book for compression, hence the term, code excited. The result is a much higher quality of speech. It has a data rate of 4,800 bit/s, but the intelligibility has been compared to an ADPCM codec at 32 Kbit/s (G.721).

Mobile telecommunications

The mobile phone industry has another set of codecs used for streaming multimedia to third generation (3G) wireless terminals. 3G services use adaptive-multirate (AMR) coding for speech, with MPEG-4 H.263 coding for video. AMR uses ACELP coding and can be used with bit rates from 12 to 4.75 kbit/s. The CDMA2000 variant of the 3G infrastructure (3GPP2) also supports Qualcomm's CELP codec (QCELP) at similar data rates.

MPEG general

MPEG (from the Moving Picture Experts Group) is the international standard for multimedia. It incorporates both audio and video encoding at a range of data rates. MPEG audio and video are the standard formats used for digital television (along with Dolby audio).

MPEG-1

The work undertaken to develop the MPEG-1 audio compression standards forms the foundation stone for the technology of streaming audio. The ubiquitous MP3 standard set the benchmark for good quality music encoding at low bit rates. Figure 6.11 shows the basic MPEG-1 encoder.

There are three types of MPEG-1 audio encoding – layer 1, layer 2, and layer 3 – in order of improving sound quality and increased encoding time. This is to

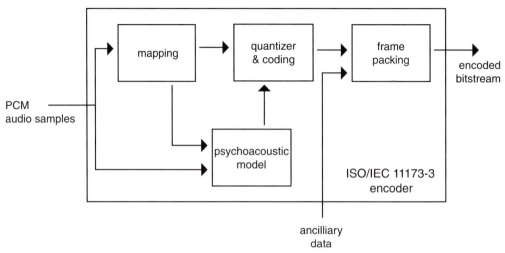

Figure 6.11 MPEG-1 encoder.

cover a wide range of different applications. MPEG codecs are asymmetric, which means that the decoder is simpler than the encoder. This is ideal for consumer products, where the player is the most used application.

Layer 1 evolved from the PASC compression used in Digital Compact Cassettes, and layer 2 is based on the MUSICAM compression format. The lowest data rate supported for MPEG-1 mono audio is 32 kbit/s. Sample rates of 32, 44.1 (audio CD), and 48 kHz (Digital Audio Tape) are supported. Consumer equipment that supports recording requires a basic encoder that can be at a low cost for compact, battery-powered products. The lowest layer, layer 1, is used for such applications; a typical example is the Digital Compact Cassette (DCC).

Layer 2 uses a more complex encoding algorithm based on the MUSICAM system. The data rates from a typical layer 2 encoder are around 192 kbit/s.

Table 6.6 Summary of MPEG Audio

	Bit rate range (kbit/s)	Target bit rate (kbit/s)	Typical compression ratio
Layer 1	32 to 448	192 (mono)	1:4
Layer 2	32 to 384	128 (mono)	1:6 to 1:8
Layer 3 (MP3)	32 to 320	64 (mono)	1:10 to 1:12
		128 (stereo)	
AAC	32 to 128	96 (stereo)	1:16
HE AAC	32 to 128	64 (stereo)	1:24
HQ Parametric		24 (stereo)	1:64

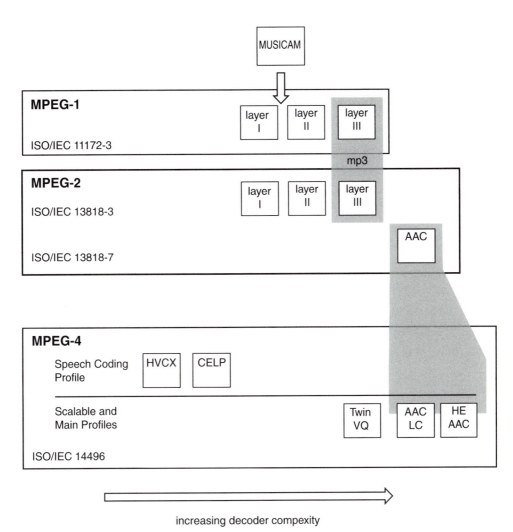

increasing decoder compexity

Figure 6.12 The evolution of MPEG audio formats.

Layer 3 (usually called MP3) is very popular for Internet Radio due to its combination of high quality and efficient compression.

MPEG-1 decomposes the input into 32 bands, an approximation to the 24 critical bands of the human ear. The filter bank is a pseudo-QMF, and a Fast Fourier Transform is used for the psychoacoustic analysis. Layer 2 has several enhancements to lower the data rate.

MPEG-1 layer 3 (MP3) uses a more sophisticated hybrid filter bank with a modified DCT following each polyphase filter. This gives better high-frequency resolution and improved pre-echo control. Huffman coding is used to remove redundancy in the data stream.

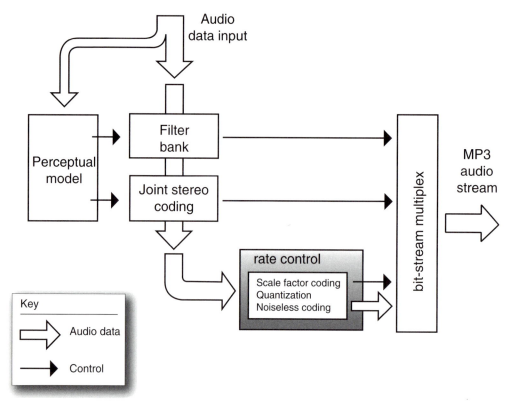

Figure 6.13 MP3 audio coder.

MPEG-2

MPEG-2 provides broadcast quality audio and video at higher data delivery rates. MPEG-2 standard added to the original work on MPEG-1 to provide a high-quality audio format for digital television. In some applications, Dolby AC-3 has been used as an alternative to accompany an MPEG-2 video stream. The original MPEG-2 standard (ISO/IEC 13838–3) supports a Low Sampling Frequencies extension (LSF, 16, 22, and 24 kHz) and multichannel audio (MPEG-1 is mono or stereo). The original standards were backward-compatible with MPEG-1. To take advantage of newer coding algorithms, backward-compatibility was abandoned. This led to the definition of the Advanced Audio Coding scheme (AAC), ISO/IEC 13838–7.

Advanced Audio Coding (AAC)

The original goal was to produce a coder that could compress CD format audio (44.1 kHz sampling, 16-bit sample, more than 2 Mbit/s) to less than 384 Kbit/s, yet be indistinguishable from the original. This represents about 3 bits per sample.

AAC was based on layers 1, 2, and 3, and introduced several new tools:

Filter bank window shape adaptation The MDCT filter bank can switch between two alternative window shapes depending on the spectral character-istics of the input. This maximizes the coding gain. The filter banks approximate more closely to the critical bands than the original MPEG-1 filter banks.

Spectral coefficient prediction For redundancy elimination with steady-state signals.

Bandwidth and bit rate scaling The rate-control feedback loops are more complex. These control the quantization process through the exploitation of psychoacoustic irrelevancy.

Noiseless coding The entropy coding of the quantized coefficients has been improved with the use of 12 Huffman codebooks. Much like video coding, the grouping maximizes runs of zero-value data.

MPEG-4 scalable audio profile

The MPEG-4 standard departs from the simple structure of the MPEG-1 and MPEG-2 audio coding. The MPEG team wanted to give a much wider flexibil-ity. MPEG-4 was designed for use in a much wider range of applications than the focused remits of MPEG-1 and MPEG-2. Rather than adopting a number of levels, each more complex than the layer below, MPEG-4 offers a number of profiles.

The first departure is that two groups of codecs are used, one for general audio coding, or waveform audio, and the other for speech. The speech coding is based on the vocoders developed for secure voice communication by the military. The general audio is based primarily on the previous work of the MPEG-2 team. MPEG-4 uses the following algorithms for encoding at different bit rates:

1. HVCX
2. CELP
3. Twin VQ
4. AAC

Speech coders

Harmonic Vector eXcitation Coding (HVXC)

The HVCX is a parametric vocoder operating at 2 and 4 kbit/s, and offers a good speech quality for the low data rate.

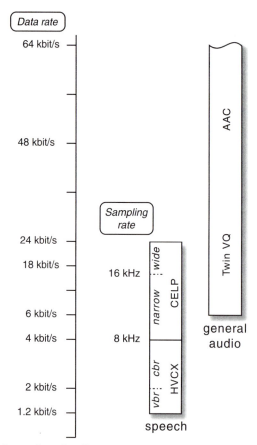

Figure 6.14 MPEG-4 audio coding algorithms.

Code Excited Linear Prediction (CELP)

The CELP speech coding tools offer encoding from 6 kbit/s (for a narrow audio bandwidth of 3.5 kHz) up to 18 kbit/s at a higher sampling frequency for wideband speech.

The MPEG-4 speech coding tools differ from legacy standards such as ITU-T G.723 in that they offer three new functionalities: multiple bit rate coding, bit rate scalable coding, and bandwidth scalable coding (the latter for CELP only). This variable rate is important for support of streaming applications to cope with network congestion, and for the wide variety of playback devices.

General audio coders

Advanced Audio Coder (AAC)

This is based on the MPEG-2 AAC low complexity audio coding algorithm. It includes an additional tool called PNS (Perceptual Noise Substitution) to lower the data rate. MPEG-4 AAC has been designed with full backward-compatibility with the low complexity profile of MPEG-2 AAC (where prediction is not used). You can use an additional object type with long-term prediction.

AAC coding is close to the maximum data compression that can be achieved using perceptual masking. To lower data rates further other techniques are required. One such technique is spectral band replication or SBR. One way to decrease data rates is to lower the original sampling rate, but this also restricts the reproduced frequency range according to the Nyquist criterion. SBR exploits the correlation between low- and high-frequency components of the waveform. In simple terms, the upper frequency band is not coded, but replicated by the decoder from the lower frequency band using some control data. SBR is now an extension to AAC, and called high efficiency AAC (HE AAC). It offers efficiency gains of up to 40 percent when compared with standard AAC. A stereo signal can be coded at quality near to the CD at a data rate of 48 kbit/s.

The MPEG developers are now looking at parametric coding to achieve lower data rates. The new tool is High Quality Parametric Audio Coding. The target data rate for this codec is around 24 kbit/s. Applications for codec include high-quality speech coding where pitch and tempo scaling need to be conveyed. Distance learning of languages or spoken books are possible uses for this extension to MPEG-4 audio.

Twin Vector Quantization (Twin VQ)
Twin VQ is a general audio coder that is optimized for encoding music at ultra-low bit rates, typically 8 kbit/s. It uses an interleaved vector quantization of the same scaling factors and spectral data that are used in the AAC processing. It has a higher coding efficiency than AAC, but the drawback is that it always suffers a minimum loss in the audio quality. The break point in audio quality (with AAC) is about 16 kbit/s.

The general audio coder has many similarities with original MPEG-1 architecture. The psychoacoustic model is used to generate control parameters for the spectral processing tools. The output of the spectral processing is then quantized.

MPEG-4 tools

Long-term predictor (LTP)
The long-term predictor tool reduces the redundancy between audio frames for stationary harmonic signals with AAC and Twin VQ. It is a new feature for AAC and is introduced with MPEG-4.

Perceptual noise substitution (PNS)
Since one noise sounds like another, it is not necessary to transmit the fine grain structure of noise. The coder substitutes the actual spectral components of a noise signal with data that represents a noise-like signal. The tricky part is determining which part of the input signal is noise.

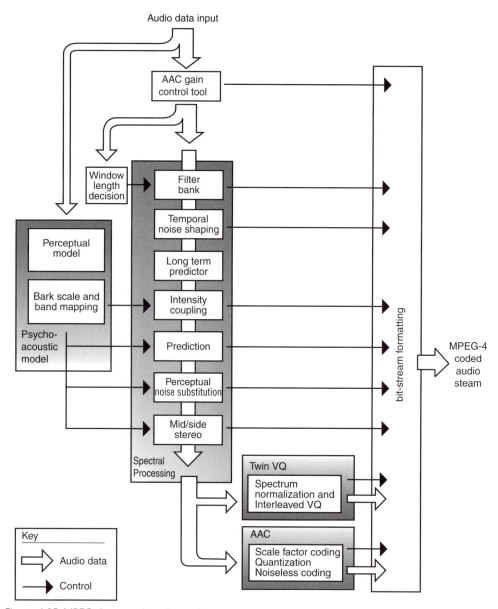

Figure 6.15 MPEG-4 general audio coder.

Joint stereo coding

Rather than transmitting a stereo audio signal as two separate channels, left and right, the two signals can be matrixed into mid and side signals, much as FM radio uses a mono signal (for compatibility) and a difference signal (modulated on a subcarrier). Since there is a great similarity between left and right for typical audio material, the side or difference signal carries much less information than the mid signal. By this method of processing, the redundancy in information between left and right is eliminated.

MPEG-4 levels

The following four levels are defined for MPEG-4 audio:

1. Maximum sampling rate of 24 kHz, one mono object.
2. Maximum sampling rate of 24 kHz, one stereo object or two mono objects.
3. Maximum sampling rate of 48 kHz, one stereo object or two mono objects.
4. Maximum sampling rate of 48 kHz, one 5.1 channel object or multiple objects with at maximum one integer factor sampling rate conversion for a maximum of two channels.

Note that a stream can consist of several audio objects. For example, this could be a speech object giving commentary and a music object. Different objects could carry different languages.

Proprietary codecs

There are three popular multimedia compression architectures: Apple Quick-Time, RealNetworks, and Windows Media. Each supports a choice of different codecs for speech and music. There are also a number of audio-only systems for Internet radio, notably the MP3-based Shoutcast from Nullsoft.

Microsoft Windows Media

The Microsoft Windows Media Player control acts as a universal player for rendering most standard multimedia formats. The player can decode live and interactive streams or play back local content that may have been downloaded at some earlier time.

Version 9 of Windows Media includes four codecs:

- Windows Media Audio 9 Professional for surround sound at data rates from 128 to 768 kbit/s
- Windows Media Audio 9 Lossless (to archive CDs rather than streaming)
- Windows Media Audio 9, with improved performance over version 8; backward-compatible with earlier players
- Windows Media Audio 9 Voice for bit rates below 20 kbit/s; can be used for music as well as speech

RealNetworks

The RealAudio streaming audio players used CELP compression for the original version 2.0 audio codec for 28 kbit/s delivery. They have since developed a proprietary codec, RealAudio.

The RealAudio format started as Progressive Networks Audio (PNA). It was the first compression format to support live audio over the Internet and thus gained considerable support. It requires proprietary streaming server software in order to provide the real-time playback facility. The server also supports repositioning during real-time playback. Version 2.0 offered two encoding algorithms; the original 8 kbit/s data rate and a higher data rate to give higher audio quality for music using higher sampling rates (11, 22, and 44 kHz).

RealAudio10

RealAudio 10 has two main codecs, the RealAudio for bit rates below 128 kbit/s, and MPEG-4 AAC for higher bit rates. RealAudio is compatible with RealPlayer 8 and later. They also have introduced two new codecs, a lossless codec for archiving music, and RealAudio Multi-channel for 5.1 surround sound applications.

Note that the version 10 RealOne Player is designated version 2. The Real codecs are also supported by the Helix community.

Apple QuickTime

Apple QuickTime supports a large number of codecs, although only a few are streamable formats. The following are the main choices:

- AAC MPEG-4 is the high-quality standard for general compression and is particularly good for music encoding.
- QDesign Music 2 codec is a high-quality music codec, which claims to offer better performance to MP3 at lower rates. Typical stereo audio bit rate is 24 kbit/s.
- Qualcomm PureVoice for speech encoding at low bit rates, typically 6.8 kbit/s; it is based on CELP coding.
- AMR Narrowband is an adaptive multirate codec that is variable rate for wireless applications at bit rates between 5 and 12 kbit/s.

Open-source codecs

The alternative to the licensed formats like MPEG, and proprietary formats like Windows Media and RealAudio, is to use an open-source standard like the Ogg

Vorbis codec. This has been developed by a team with roots in the academic community at MIT, under the general umbrella Xiphophorous. Vorbis is a waveform coder for general audio applications, and uses MDCT coding. The bit stream is in Ogg format. Data rates supported range from 16 to 128 kbit/s, with sampling at 44.1 or 48 kHz. It claims to offer a better audio quality than MPEG-1, layer 3 coding, and comparable with MPEG-2 (AAC). The format can be streamed in real-time using the Icecast server. This is another Xiphophorous project and is an open-source streaming server for the Vorbis audio codec. I suggest you look at their web sites for further details, and for downloads of the source code if you are interested.

Summary

There is no one-size-fits-all outfit for audio encoding. At the very least when you stream you will want to choose between speech and music. Speech can use one of the super-efficient vocoders, whereas music will use a general audio or waveform coder. The MPEG-4 standard recognizes this reality, and offers a number of different technologies to cover data rates from 1 to 64 Kbit/s and higher.

Streamed audio has been able to exploit speech-processing algorithms developed for secure military communications and for cellular radio. These codecs feature the low coding latencies required for a two-way conversation and the efficient processing demanded by compact, battery-powered hardware.

General audio coding has undergone similar developments. The consumer audio industry needs high compression ratios to give reasonable download times for Internet music sales. Again, the limited battery power places constraints on the available storage.

The latest audio codecs utilize the full resources of our understanding of psychoacoustics to remove perceptual irrelevancies in the audio waveform. Redundancy in the data signal then allows further reductions in bit rates.

A wide range of codecs are available – some vocoders, some for general audio. Bit rates vary from a few kbit/s for speech up to a few hundred kilobits per second for multichannel audio. The compressionist can choose the optimum codec to match the quality requirements and the bandwidth available.

Section 2

Streaming

7 Introduction to streaming media

Introduction

Less than 10 years after its initial development, streaming joined the mainstream of communication media. The ubiquity of the Internet led many multimedia content owners to search for a way to deliver video content over an IP network. Video and audio are a more natural way to communicate than the text and images used for the first decade of the Internet. We only have to look at the overwhelming success of television. Combine live delivery over IP with video and audio and you have streaming.

The first multimedia applications used the Internet just for file transfer to the PC. Once the entire file had been downloaded, it could be played back locally, much like a CD-ROM. This is called download-and-play. True streaming is media content that is delivered to the viewer's media player in real-time. That means that it is transferred at the same rate as it is displayed. So a 10-minute clip will take 10 minutes to download over the network. There is no intermediate storage of the content between its origin and the player. The data is processed as it arrives at the player, and then discarded.

Three developments introduced this seed change in media delivery: the streaming server, advances in compression algorithms, and the improvements to the 'last mile.' Progressive Networks developed a way to control the delivery rate of a file, so that it could be transmitted in real-time. The ongoing developments in audio compression led to codecs that could deliver a reasonable quality music stream at 28 kbit/s. Alongside this evolution of the streaming architectures, the telcos and cable service providers were rolling out broadband Internet to the home. The cable modem and ADSL now could offer download speeds higher than 1 Mbit/s. The delivery of video over IP became a reality.

There have been many startups with innovative codecs but, from a plethora of technologies, the MPEG-4 standards are beginning to dominate. RealNetworks showed it was possible, and have developed a comprehensive range of products for producing, serving, and playing rich media content. Microsoft developed their Video for Windows multimedia platform into Windows Media –

focused now on the streaming of video and audio. It has strong support for integrated presentation graphics for the world of corporate communications. Apple came from the QuickTime multimedia world. A favorite for CD-ROM production, it was later extended to support streaming. It now offers support for a wide variety of media formats, from 3D to audio and video. Both Apple and Real-Networks now support the MPEG-4 standard.

All these products have developed from a background of the traditional rectangular picture that we know from film and television. The focus has been delivery to the PC, but that is not the only possible display.

The world of multimedia is expanding into new platforms, and finding new ways to use old platforms. The production community has requested international standards for the delivery of multimedia content unrestrained by the platform. MPEG-4 has been the outcome of this work. Interactive content can be authored for a whole range of platforms: hand-held wireless devices, games consoles, interactive television. The PC is just one of many means to view content.

MPEG-4 has broken away from the traditional methods of audio/video coding as a two-dimensional rectangular raster used by MPEG-1, MPEG-2, and the H.261 video-conferencing standard. MPEG-4 supports new types of media objects in addition to regular audio and video: three-dimensional (from virtual reality technology) and synthetic video and audio. It supports interactivity at the client and server-side. It is highly scalable and covers resolutions from a thumbnail size image suited to mobile wireless applications, to high definition for digital cinema.

Audio- and video-conferencing

Video-conferencing has much in common with streaming. Much of the streaming codec development started with the H.261 and H.263 video-conferencing standards. The latest, H.264, is called the advanced video codec (AVC). The real-time protocols also are shared by conferencing and webcasting. But there are also major differences. Video-conferencing demands very low latency so that natural conversations can be held; for webcasting the propagation delays and processing latencies are not important – if it takes 3 or 4 seconds for a live webcast to arrive it is of little concern. Another difference is the connection. Video-conferencing is peer-to-peer between at least two participants; in contrast, webcast streaming is server–client.

What are the applications of streaming?

Streaming media potentially can be employed wherever the CD-ROM or video-tape previously has been used for content distribution. The initial applications very much followed the functions of the CD-ROM: training, corporate communications, marketing, and entertainment.

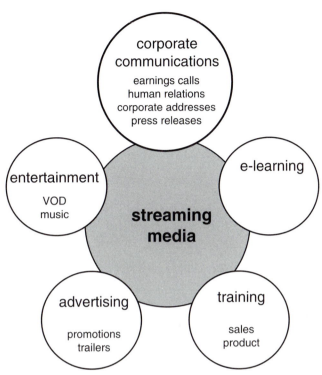

Figure 7.1 Streaming media applications.

Legacy formats

Before streaming media was developed, if you wanted to distribute a live broadcast to a multiple-site corporation, the main option was to rent a satellite transponder for the duration of the presentation. The cost for the distribution is not inconsiderable; in addition to satellite time, there is the rental of the uplink truck. The next problem is that most businesses do not have many television receivers. How many times have you taken a VHS tape home because it was the easiest way to view it?

The alternative for prerecorded content is the videotape cassette or CD-ROM. The tape is fine for linear programming (except for the just-mentioned lack of televisions), but is totally unsuited to random access. This was the strength of the CD-ROM. First, it can be played back on a PC, ubiquitous in the office. Second, the viewer could use interactive navigation, essential for applications like training.

The drawbacks with tape and CD are the duplication and distribution costs. There is also the delay while material is shipped out, so it always lacks the immediacy of a live broadcast.

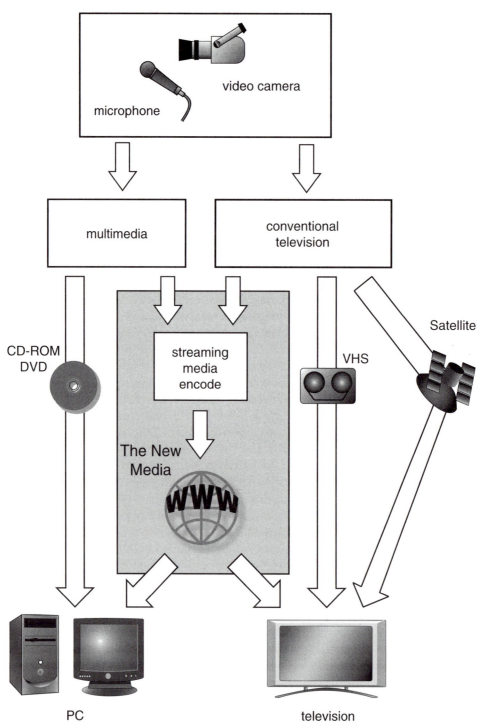

Figure 7.2 Streaming media as an alternative to videotape, satellite, and the CD-ROM.

The other form of distribution was on-demand. If you want a training presentation, you look up a suitable tape in a catalog and order a VHS tape for overnight delivery. When it arrives the next day, you preview the tape and find it is not what you want. Three days could elapse before you have the correct tape in your hand. With streaming media you can browse the online catalog, preview a clip, then once satisfied, download the stream. The whole procedure may have taken 15 minutes.

Which is the most productive? Which has the highest distribution costs? Streaming can replace the videotape cassette and courier, just as the PDF file has replaced the wait for a catalog in the mail.

If you were to adopt streaming, it is quite possible that the corporate wide area network can be used. If it does not have the capacity, the Internet infrastructure also can be used. One of the big advantages is that most of the audience can watch from their desktop PC. Home-workers or the field sales force can even dial up a company extranet server to watch on a laptop.

Corporate communications

Streaming opens up a whole new way to communicate. Until the advent of streaming, if a company executive wanted to communicate to the organization, the options were limited. A group e-mail could be sent out but it lacked impact, and would be buried in all the other messages. The alternative was to hire a conference facility in a suitable venue and make a stand-up presentation. Although effective, the cost of the latter option is considerable, both in time and money.

Using streaming media a webcast can be made from the CEO's office direct to all the staff, over the corporate WAN/LAN. The VP of Sales can address customers using the company extranet – the opportunities are endless.

The more natural feel of video and audio can be used as an adjunct to press releases, to give a more direct communication of important news. Investor relations can benefit greatly from streaming. It is becoming *de rigueur* to stream the quarterly earnings call.

Distance learning

Distance learning, often called e-learning, takes a big step forward when you can add video and audio content. One problem that distance learning has always suffered from is a high drop-out rate. In the past it has been limited to communication via e-mail and the telephone. Streaming now presents the opportunity to add video to help to convey facts and information in a far more compelling way. Video can help the student relate to the tutors, giving a boost to the success rates of the courses.

Product and sales training

This is rather different from distance learning, in that it is more likely to be aimed at a group of staff or customers, as opposed to the one-to-one interaction of e-learning. For product training, streaming can replace the traditional slide presentation with a rich media show – slides, video audio, and text – plus the opportunity for interactivity with web meetings. Of course it could also be a one-to-one training session – the boundary between e-learning and e-training is blurred.

Advertising

Many surveys have shown that streaming media users spend more online, so they are suitable targets for Internet-delivered advertising. Streaming ads are one step further than the banner ads of the web page. The technology has to be applied with care. Viewers will not be pleased if the result of a stalling download is a commercial for a loan they do not want.

One of the first major applications for advertising was the movie trailer. Streaming is an obvious vehicle, offering on-demand video teasers for upcoming films. The music business has also adopted streaming as part of interactive rich media promotions for new albums.

Entertainment

In some circles streamed entertainment has gained notoriety after the blatant abuses of intellectual property rights practiced by peer-to-peer content distribution systems like Napster. The widespread distribution of entertainment calls for an industrial-strength rights management solution to protect the potential revenues. Entertainment did get off to a slow start. Who wants to pay to watch a jerky, fuzzy video over a dial-up modem? The advent of broadband to the home changes all that. With high-performance content delivery networks and ADSL or a cable modem, the viewer can now watch at a quality that is comparable to VHS. Pay-per-view becomes a viable proposition.

The streaming architecture

There are four components to a streaming architecture:

- Capture and encoding
- Serving
- Distribution and delivery
- Media player

Capture and encoding take the raw audio and video from the microphone and camera and process them into a compressed computer file. These files are then stored on a content server, which has special software that can control the real-time delivery of the stream.

The distribution channel connects the server to the player. This may involve many interconnected networks and cache servers. The network may be anything from a local area network to the Internet. Distribution can use digital rights management (DRM) to protect intellectual property.

The media player, usually a plug-in to a web browser, receives the stream and decompresses back to regular audio and video, where it can be displayed on the PC.

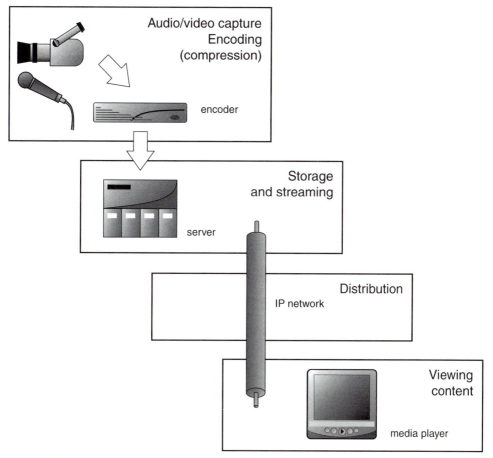

Figure 7.3 The four stages of streaming.

Capture and encode

The capture and encode processing takes regular audio and video signals in a television format and converts them to a streaming file. There are a number of stages to this:

- Capture to computer file format
- Compress the media data
- Packetize data with hints or index

A straight video signal cannot be handled by software until it is in a compatible format, typically AVI. A video capture card installed in the capture workstation converts analog or digital video and audio into the AVI format. The card most likely also scales down the picture size to one-quarter of the original resolution. This gives a data rate that can be handled easily by the processor and ease the storage requirements for the final file.

The compression algorithm is embedded in a software application called a compressor-decompressor, or *codec* for short. The compressed takes the raw audio/video file and reduces the data rate to match the bandwidth available for streaming. The decompressor is found in the media player, and renders the data stream back to audio and video. The encoder also wraps the data with special hint or index metadata that the server uses to control the real-time delivery. Note that the compression and stream wrapping do not necessarily have to be from the same software vendor. As an example, QuickTime can wrap many different codecs, with Sorenson being one.

Serving

The encoded file is uploaded to a server for delivery out to the network. The server is a software application, like a web server, rather than the physical server hardware. A streaming server is more than just a fancy file server, it controls in real-time the stream delivery – this is what sets it apart from similar products like the web server.

Streaming versus download

Downloading was the normal way to receive files over the Internet. We are used to requesting a web page, then waiting an indeterminate period while all the files for the page are downloaded to the web browser for rendering. The recall of a page places no special requirements for the network bandwidth. A high bandwidth network will allow rapid delivery; conversely, a large file will be delivered slowly over a narrow band network (28 kbit/s). The process is

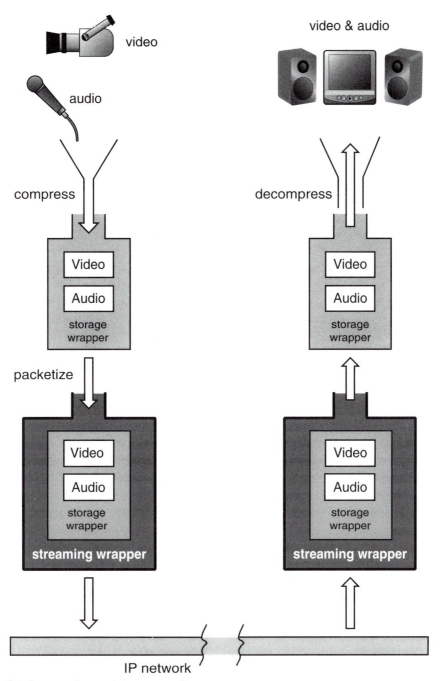

Figure 7.4 Compression and decompression.

asynchronous. The term bursting is used to describe the rapid download of low bit rate media files over broadband circuits.

Download-and-play, just like a web page download, will use best effort to download as fast as the IP channel allows. So a 30-second clip encoded at 56 kbit/s will take at least 1 minute over a 28 kbit/s dial-up modem, or it could be less than 2 seconds over a high-speed 1 Mbit/s link.

Animated vector graphics in the Flash format are often described as streaming media, but actually are delivered as a progressive download. A streaming file has to be encoded at a data rate that can be delivered by the circuit. If you want to stream to analog modems, then you have to encode at 40 kbit/s. Here lies a problem: It is rare to have control over the last mile to the viewer. They may have a high-specification ADSL link, or they might be using the 56k modem. The user who is paying the monthly rental on a broadband circuit wants to see a higher bit rate – that is why he or she is paying the extra cost.

The way around this, adopted by the early codec architectures, is to encode several copies of the clip at different bit rates. The server and media player negotiate to select the optimum file for the prevailing network conditions and available bandwidth. That does solve the problem, but at a price. Encoding has to be done several times over, and additional file space is needed on the content servers. Both add to the costs of serving content.

Progressive download

Progressive download is an intermediate step between download-and-play and true streaming. Rather than waiting for the complete file to be downloaded to the local disk before playback, the file can be opened while the remainder is still downloading.

The difference from streaming is two-fold. The first is that the server is not delivering the file in real-time, so the player can run out of material if the transfer is slower than the encoded rate. How many times have you watched the race with the progress bar on a progressive download? If the player catches up with the download, the screen goes black – there is nothing to do but wait for more of the file to download. The second difference is that the entire media file is stored locally to the player.

Live and on-demand

Streaming can be used in two ways. Media can be pushed to the viewer, much like a regular television channel. This is live streaming. The alternative is for the viewer to pull, or request, the media from a content server, just like using a library. This is called on-demand.

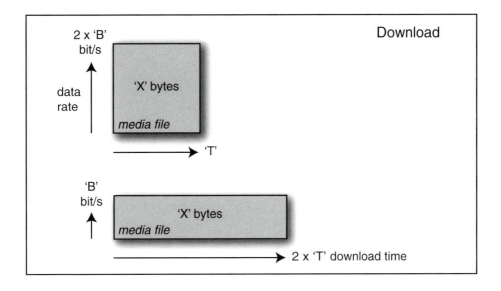

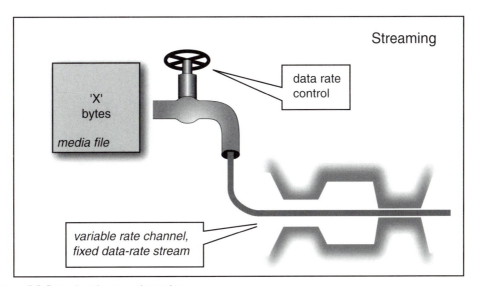

Figure 7.5 Download versus streaming.

A special case of live streaming is *simulated-live*, where the content is delivered by a server-side request. This can be mixed at will with a live presentation. So a speaker could be introduced with a promo, speak live to camera, and then show a prerecorded clip from the server.

Streaming requires a persistent client-to-server connection and continuous data flow. Contrast this with the burst transmissions of a web server connection.

On-demand and interactivity

One major delineator of streaming from regular television is the interactivity. The viewer can interact with on-demand content files. The player has VCR-like controls (PLAY, STOP, FF, REW) and random access to any part of the clip. Hotspots on the video screen can take the viewer to another part of the file, or to a different file, at the click of a mouse – hypervideo replaces hypertext.

To support this functionality a special streaming server is used rather than a regular web server. The streaming file is time indexed to enable the random access. This means that a long program can be split into 'chapters' with random access by the viewer to any chapter at will.

Live streaming

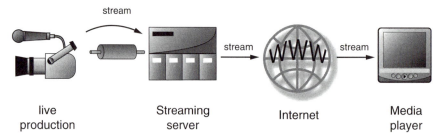

| live | Streaming | Internet | Media |
| production | server | | player |

On-demand streaming

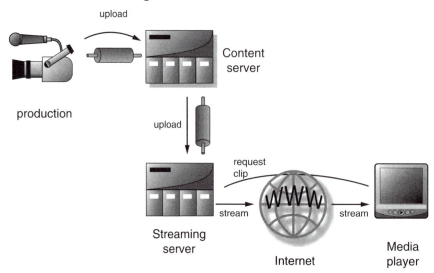

Figure 7.6 Live and on-demand.

Distribution

In principle, the distribution is simple. As long as there is IP connectivity between the server and the player/client, the requested packets arrive at the player. In practice, it is not that easy. No doubt you have seen a stalled media file; the video is distorted and blocky, the audio has silent passages. The problem is that the Internet was not originally designed to support continuous streams over persistent connections. It is basically a packet-switched system for asynchronous data.

Several different developments are aiding improvements to the delivery quality. First is increased bandwidth for the last mile to the consumer. Through either the cable modem or DSL, downloads of 1 Mbit/s or higher can be achieved. The next development is the content delivery network (CDN). These use a smart overlay on the Internet to provide content-aware routing. The final development is the quality of the Internet. More and more fiber is installed, and QoS protocols help differentiate priority traffic.

The catch is that as quality improves, more companies will use streaming. This creates more traffic and potential congestion – the race that never ends.

Player

A regular web browser can render text and images only in JPEG, PNG, and GIF formats. A special media player is required to render streaming files. Players are usually supplied as free downloads, or are pre-installed with the operating system. Some vendors also have a fully featured player available for a small charge.

Plug-in, player, or portal

The player can be used as a plug-in to a web browser. The alternative is to use a stand-alone player. These players have been developed into media portals, with navigation to popular material, and often offering unique content specific to a given architecture.

Download versus streaming

Download-and-play is what it says: The file is downloaded to the local hard drive, and once the entire file has been delivered, the viewer can play the file locally. In contrast, streaming is processed chunk by chunk as it arrives, and is rendered directly to the display; then the data is discarded. So there is no waiting; if you do not like what you see you can quit the stream immediately, rather than downloading the entire file before you decide. Note that there is no local copy of the file stored on the hard drive. This greatly aids in the protection of content from illegal copying, although it is not foolproof against the determined hacker.

Download-and-play

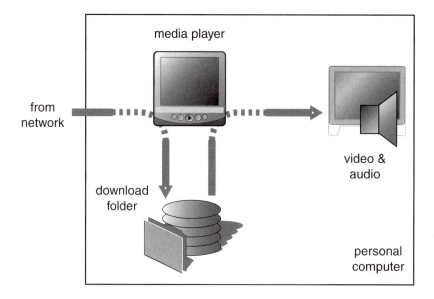

Streaming

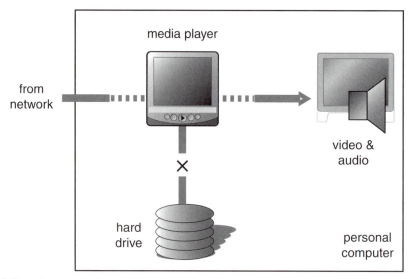

Figure 7.7 Download-and-play and the streaming player.

Bandwidth, bits, and bytes

The units bit and byte occur throughout this book. Although you know that a byte is 8 bits, it is very easy to get the two mixed up. Most of this stems from the abbreviations:

B = byte
b = bit

To avoid confusion it is always best to spell out the abbreviations in full. Have you ever purchased eight times more disk storage than you needed because b and B were swapped around? Alternatively, midway through a live webcast the disk archive is completely filled. In general, bits refer to streams and bytes to memory and storage. So a 10-second clip at 80 Kbit/s (that is, 10 Kbyte/s) needs 100 Kbytes of storage. The other point is that although the standard multiplier of kilo-means 1,000, in the computer industry it represents 1,024 (or 210). The two are abbreviated to k and K, respectively. If they are mixed up the error is going to be only 2 percent.

1 byte = 8 bits
1 kbit = 1,000 bits
1 Kbit = 1,024 bits

Bandwidths and file sizes

Streaming is very different from other media in the sheer range of bandwidths that can possibly be encoded. Whereas television is essentially a fixed bandwidth (although the bit rate can vary within close limits), streaming may be delivered down anything from an analog phone line to a high-speed local area network, or 28 kbit/s to 2 Mbit/s or higher.

The starting point for uncompressed audio is a bit rate of nearly 3 Mbit/s from a CD. For video the studio interconnection standard is 270 Mbit/s. The compression used with DV camcorders has a video data rate of 25 Mbit/s (although it can be transferred at different rates over the IEEE 1394 interface).

The streaming media has to be compressed to match the capacity of the user's connection. These vary widely; an analog modem will have a maximum rate of 56 kbit/s, although many users still use 28 k or 14 k modems (although the latter are not adequate for video streaming).

Most connections quote a maximum rate, but usually this is not achieved, except for ISDN and T-1, where the data rate is guaranteed. The dial-up modem will be limited by propagation conditions on the line, factors like noise pickup. The cable modem uses a shared fiber back to the head-end from your

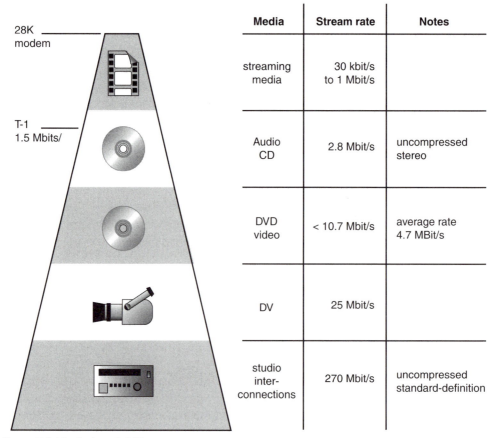

Media	Stream rate	Notes
streaming media	30 kbit/s to 1 Mbit/s	
Audio CD	2.8 Mbit/s	uncompressed stereo
DVD video	< 10.7 Mbit/s	average rate 4.7 MBit/s
DV	25 Mbit/s	
studio inter-connections	270 Mbit/s	uncompressed standard-definition

Figure 7.8 Media bandwidths.

Table 7.1 Typical Carriers for Delivery of Streaming

	Maximum	Actual	Notes
Dial-up modem	56 kbit/s	35 kbit/s	
Dual ISDN	128 kbit/s	128 kbit/s	
Cable modem/DSL	1–8 Mbit/s	300 kbit/s–2 Mbit/s	Rate varies with supplier
T-1	1.5 Mbit/s	1.5 Mbit/s	
10 base-T LAN	10 Mbit/s	3 Mbit/s	Typical

local node. If everyone on the block tries to watch high-bandwidth streams simultaneously the contention for the available bandwidth will cause degradation of the streams. DSL, much like the analog modem, will be limited by line conditions.

The rule is always to encode at a lower rate than the maximum the circuit is specified to carry. If you are using standard encoding tools these will have headroom already built into the encoding templates.

Proprietary codec architectures

There are three popular codec architectures: Apple QuickTime, Microsoft's Windows Media, and RealNetworks. Each product supports a number of different compression codecs, although there is more choice of audio versus video codecs.

Apple QuickTime

QuickTime is Apple's multi-platform, multimedia software architecture. It originally was used by content creators to author and publish CD-ROMs. It also offers virtual reality with 3-D views of objects and panoramas. The initial support for IP delivery was by progressive download. It was extended to support true streaming in version 4, utilizing the RTSP framework. QuickTime 6 expands support for international standards, MPEG-4, and for third-generation wireless applications 3GPP and 3GPP2. Because QuickTime has an established position in multimedia authoring there is a large community of users.

Some of QuickTime's features include the following:

- Multiple delivery channels: WWW, CD-ROM, DVD, wireless broadband, kiosk, presentations
- Players for Mac and Windows
- Powerful interactive capabilities
- Synchronized graphics, sound, video, text, music, VR, and 3-D for rich media production

QuickTime is the dominant architecture for CD-ROM video. It enjoys an impressive market share due to its cross-platform support, a wide range of features, and free licensing. For these reasons QuickTime is used on the vast majority of CD-ROM titles.

The MPEG-4 team adopted the QuickTime stream serving methodology (with the use of a hint track and RTSP/RTP) as the basis of MPEG-4 streaming.

Scalability

QuickTime offers multiple bit rate delivery through its alternate movies feature. At the beginning of playback, the QuickTime Plug-In requests an alternate version according to the settings the viewer has configured in their QuickTime Settings control panel. Content creators may create as many alternates as they need when they are encoding the movie, and specify complex criteria for when particular versions will be displayed. This allows for delivery of content based on bandwidth of the user's connection, playback platform (Mac or Windows), Quick-Time version and language (to select different audio tracks), or the CPU speed.

QuickTime can be served from the Mac OS X server or the open-source Darwin server. The QuickTime Pro can be used for authoring, with the Quick-Time Broadcaster product adding facilities for live streaming.

RealNetworks

RealNetworks pioneered streaming as a usable communication medium under the name Progressive Networks. Before the Real player, audio-visual content was delivered as a download, to be played later from the local drive.

The Real 10 platform, incorporating RealAudio and RealVideo, is a network-oriented, streaming media architecture developed by RealNetworks. Real 10 provides further improvements in quality, supported media types, and features over earlier versions.

Real 10 is a streaming architecture, offering both server-based true streaming and serverless HTTP streaming (also known as progressive download). There are performance and scalability advantages with the server, but you can get started without one. High volume sites, however, definitely need a server for improved delivery performance.

Real 10 is most appropriate for network delivery of audio, video, and other media types, such as text and Flash animations.

Users can view Real 10 movies with the RealPlayer 10 (Real One), a free client application available from RealNetworks. The enhanced RealOne Super-Pass provides additional features, and must be purchased from RealNetworks.

Real 10 supports Synchronized Multimedia Integration Language (SMIL, pronounced *smile*). This language enables the content creator to synchronize media and actions within a web page to the video and audio tracks. For example, SMIL can control the loading of multiple movies at given times, URL page flips, transitions, text tracks, and advertisement insertion.

Scalability

Real 10 offers dynamic stream switching called SureStream. During playback, the RealPlayer and RealServer continually communicate and can repeatedly switch between versions to deliver the highest-quality stream that the viewer's connection can support at any given time. This real-time switching effectively handles changing network conditions, such as congestion. Switching of audio and video is handled independently, and you can indicate whether the video or audio should be given preference as the viewer's throughput drops.

In addition to the SureStream feature, the RealPlayer can also drop frames and/or degrade the image quality to maintain real-time playback over slower connections. If the available bandwidth drops very low, the RealPlayer can omit the video track entirely and simply play the audio track.

See Real and RealNetworks web sites for comprehensive background information.

Windows Media

Windows Media 9 Series is Microsoft's complete solution for delivery of Internet multimedia. The architecture includes a number of products for encoding, serving and distribution, and an integrated and fully featured rights management system. An SDK allows integration into wider systems. Although the main product line is available only on the Windows operating system, Microsoft has a player for Mac OS X, and embedded players for consumer devices from DVDs to portable music players. Windows Media 9 has applications beyond streaming to PCs, and also can be used for the delivery and distribution of high definition television with high-quality surround sound. DVD players and set-top boxes are beginning to offer support for these new facilities.

The Windows Media tools include the Windows Media 9 encoder and Windows Media Services for control and configuration of the media server. This supports both live and on-demand video, and forms part of the Windows Server 2003 product. This potentially can offer a low-cost media and web server solution.

The Windows Media rights management allows content creators to set up a full e-commerce system to sell or rent streamed content. It also can be used for delivery of confidential media clips. The initial releases of rights management supported pre-encoded content. With version 9, Microsoft introduced DRM support for live content.

Scalability

Windows Media Server offers scaling of the transmitted data rate through the use of multiple video tracks, called *intelligent streaming*. At the beginning of playback, the Media Player and the Windows Media Server negotiate to select the video track that best matches the viewer's connection. If the network's performance degenerates, the server automatically sends a lower rate video stream. If the amount of available bandwidth decreases more, the server degrades video quality further, until only the audio is left. This ensures that the clip can be followed even during excessive congestion.

Version 9 added several enhancements to the servers including a fast-start, thus avoiding the usual long buffering before a stream starts to play. The latest free downloads, as well as more information, are available at Microsoft's Windows Media web site and through the Microsoft Developers Network.

Summary

The development of the streaming file format and the associated streaming server were the original drivers for the technology. Sophisticated compression algorithms have enabled transmission of video and audio over very modest bandwidths. The Internet is the ubiquitous glue that connects the far corners of the world, so that we can send the video and audio long distances without resorting to the expensive medium of television, affordable only for mass market programming.

One of the drawbacks often cited for HTML is the need to design pages that render effectively with different browsers. Although the experienced web designer will get to know all the tricks, there are many pitfalls for the novice. The end result is the many unpredictable page views that we encounter by chance across the Internet.

Unfortunately, streaming media has perpetuated this rather chaotic position, with the coexistence of a number of proprietary architectures. Although there are ways around this that involve authoring in a number of formats, the problem is exacerbated if you want to use interactive rich media. The three proprietary architectures do not have exactly complementary feature-sets, although there is a gradual move toward the MPEG-4 standards.

Audio and video communications have developed throughout the twentieth century. From film to television to IP streaming, system developers have striven to deliver the optimum quality that the channel will support at a reasonable cost to the consumer. The twenty-first century promises to offer new business opportunities for content owners to exploit not only the Web, but wireless and broadband delivery channels.

The MPEG-4 team has embraced these new channels. From use of the Web, CD-ROMs, and DVDs, consumers expect interactivity. Other sectors, especially games developers, have shown how virtual reality can contribute to entertainment. MPEG-4 embraces this concept, along with graphics and synthetic audio, to offer a new platform for the authoring of creative and compelling content. Although the early applications of MPEG-4 have been as a conveyor of a rectangular natural video picture with associated audio, its object-based approach has great potential for the creative content developer.

You must never forget that content is for the users, not the creators. It is vital that the complex technology application is transparent to the potential consumer. The early viewers of streaming media may have overcome any technical obstacles, but the bulk of the public will not tolerate quirks or unpredictable behavior if streaming is to be a mainstream media. It must be as easy as watching television or a DVD.

With careful HTML design, you can make smart decisions about which file format to direct a browser to by detecting the plug-ins installed in the browser.

Standardization often is put forward as the answer to some of these issues. If there was one player that could render any media format, perhaps using proprietary plug-ins, all would be simple. After all, we can receive a television broadcast from any station without needing a special receiver. The flip side to this is that it is extremely unlikely that streaming could have developed from inception to be a mainstream communication medium in the period of only five years. The proprietary architectures can continuously improve without the constraints of standards, and are spurred on by intense competition.

Whether this situation continues as streaming moves out of the PC environment into general consumer devices remains to be seen. There is far more pressure to standardize when streaming is deployed to set-top boxes or wireless devices. The life of a television receiver or set-top box can be 10 times that of a software release, so there will be a drive to standardize.

8 Video encoding

Introduction

Encoding is the conversion of a video signal into a streaming media file. The video signal first must be compressed, then packetized, and finally encapsulated within a streaming wrapper. This chapter covers the encoding stage from a video signal to the point where the streaming file is transferred to the streaming server.

The encoding takes place in several stages. The first stage is to capture a conventional video or television signal and convert it to a file format that can be processed by computer software. The second stage is data rate reduction by scaling and compression to a bit rate that can be delivered over dial-up or broadband circuits. The third stage is to wrap the compressed video in a packetized format that can be streamed over an IP network.

The majority of developments that have led to the rapid adoption of streaming media lie at the second stage, compression.

There is no standard way of encoding; there are many different ways to get from video to a streaming format. The route that you choose will depend upon the hardware platform that you have selected, the required throughput of encoded material, and the final viewing quality that you require. This chapter describes some typical architectures, but is not intended to be prescriptive.

To find the optimum solution for your application, you may want to undertake comparative trials between some different solutions. It is quite possible to assemble your own system from PCs, video capture cards, and suitable choice of software. Alternately a shrink-wrap solution can be purchased. Do you require the best quality at very low bit rates? Do you encode a few hours a week, or do you have a large archive to put online? All these factors have to be considered before deciding upon an encoding solution. Broadly speaking the price will rise with performance and with the convenience of operation. Some high-end applications allow automated batch encoding. If the encoder will be used in a integrated workflow with other systems, how easy is it to interface with the encoding process?

Distribution channels

A broadcast teleproduction usually is created in a single format. If other formats are needed for distribution, then standards conversion will be used, but as a separate downstream process. In contrast, when encoding media for streaming it is common to produce multiple output formats. You may be called upon to encode up to 20 different versions of a video clip. These are files at different stream rates, each rate repeated for a number of different streaming codecs.

Television has an allocated bandwidth, and the MPEG-2 compression is configured to fit. It may be variable bit rate, but within narrow limits; for standard definition it could be 2 to 6 Mbit/s. The channels used to deliver streams vary from 3G wireless, dial-up modems, to E-1/T-1 lines.

Table 8.1 Typical Distribution Channels

	Channel data rate	Guaranteed bandwidth	Notes
601	270 Mbit/s	Yes	Uncompressed, standard definition video
Digital television	4–6 Mbit/s	Yes	Variable bit rate
T-1 (E-1)	1.5 Mbit/s (2 Mbit/s)	Yes	
DSL	144 kbit/s–8 Mbit/s	No	
Cable modem	128 kbit/s–1 Mbit/s	No	
Dual ISDN	128 kbit/s	Yes	
ISDN	64 kbit/s	Yes	
Dial-up modem	56 kbit/s	No	Typical capacity 35 Kbit/s

In Table 8.1, the digital television example is the standard definition television that is broadcast to the DVB standard, and uses MPEG-2 MP@ML coding. It is very similar in quality to DVD video.

Some channels offer a guaranteed bandwidth; others are dependent upon the capacity of the local loop, plus the contention ratios within distribution nodes. Typically the local ends offered to the consumer do not have a guaranteed quality of service (albeit they are at a much reduced cost compared to the traditional telecoms circuits).

To encode video for all these different applications, the video is delivered with a range of basic parameters. Table 8.2 shows some typical data rates for the video alone, excluding audio and control data.

Table 8.2 Channel Data Parameters

	Uncompressed SD video source	SD broadcast television	ADSL or cable modem	Analog modem
Frame size	720 × 480	720 × 480	192 × 144	160 × 120
Frame rate	30	30	15	5
Color sampling	4:2:2	4:2:0	YUV12	YUV12
Video source rate	166 Mbit/s			
Uncompressed data rate after scaling		124 Mbit/s	5 Mbit/s	1.15 Mbit/s
Target data rate		4 Mbit/s	500 kbit/s	35 kbit/s
Total data reduction to meet target rate		40:1	330:1	4700:1
Scaled data rate		1:1.33	1:33	1:144
Compression from scaled rate to target rate		30:1	10:1	30:1

Note: SD is standard definition.

The table shows how scaling down before encoding reduces the uncompressed data rate. A thumbnail video for a dial-up modem requires that the data rate is reduced to nearly 1/5000 of the original. This is accomplished by scaling down by a factor of 144:1, and then compressing by a further 30:1.

Figure 8.1 shows the relative file sizes for encoded media.

Data compression

The raw data rate from a standard definition television camera is 166 Mbit/s. This has to be reduced to rates as low as 30 kbit/s for delivery to dial-up modems. How is a reduction in video data of almost 5000:1 achieved, while retaining a viewable picture?

This reduction takes place in several steps. The scaling usually takes place on the video capture card. The compression is performed by the codec, a software application running on the main processors.

The usual way to encode is first to capture the video with a dedicated PCI card installed in the encoding workstation. The card converts the video signal into an intermediate format that can be handled as a computer file, usually one of the Audio-Video Interleaved (AVI) formats. AVI has become the

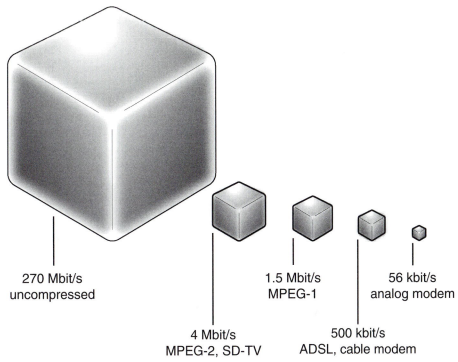

270 Mbit/s
uncompressed

1.5 Mbit/s
MPEG-1

56 kbit/s
analog modem

4 Mbit/s
MPEG-2, SD-TV

500 kbit/s
ADSL, cable modem

Figure 8.1 Relative file sizes.

de-facto standard for computer audio and video files. From this point on, regular desktop computer technology now can be used for downstream processing.

The AVI files themselves cannot be delivered over the Internet for two reasons: one, AVI files are usually very large, each second of video can be more than 1 Mbyte of data; two, AVI files can't be streamed in real-time over the Internet. You must download the entire file to a local drive before you can play it. Hence the need for compression and packetization.

Once captured, the AVI file is routed to the encoding software. The encoder uses a software codec to convert it to a streaming format (typically MPEG-4, Windows Media, Real, or Apple QuickTime). Finally, the streaming file is uploaded to a server for delivery over the Internet.

If you are making a live webcast, this process has to take place in real-time. The computer will need a minimum level of processing power; this varies from codec to codec.

Codec

Codec is short for **co**mpression/**dec**ompression. Codecs are software programs that employ a mathematical algorithm to squeeze the media files into a more

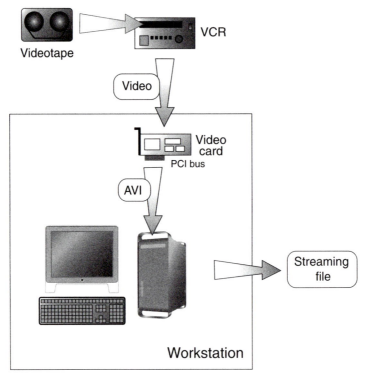

Figure 8.2 Encoder system.

compact streaming format. Decompression then takes place in a compatible decoder, or media player, installed in the end-user's computer. The process can be likened to zipping and unzipping a file on a PC.

Codecs can be symmetrical or asymmetrical. A symmetric codec usually requires less processing and is more efficient. Streaming media codecs are usually asymmetrical; this means the encoding process requires much more processing than the decoder. Since only one encoder is required, but all the viewers need a decoder, it makes sense to put the complexity in the encoding end.

The players usually are downloaded over the Internet, so the executables must be kept to a reasonable size – very large downloads are not popular with the public.

Ingest station

The video capture can be carried out on a separate ingest station ahead of the compression process and the intermediate AVI file stored on a server. These files can be very large so you will need a generous-sized array of disk drives. Also beware of the 2 GByte limit for the file size for the original AVI format.

Most video content is edited into a finished program before conversion to a streaming format. The final cut can be dubbed onto videotape to transfer into the streaming encoder, but it is often simpler to transfer the program as a file directly from the editing system to the streaming media processor over a LAN.

Video capture

Most streaming media content is created in a conventional television format, either direct from a camera or as an edited program on videotape. Live streaming is a special case of encoding and places more exacting demands on the processing hardware.

The first step is to convert the television signal as a computer file format, often Audio-Video Interleaved (AVI). In the case of a live event the capture will take place at the venue. With videotape the capture usually will be at the encoding center. It is also possible to ingest files directly from nonlinear editing systems.

The first problem you will encounter with video is that there is a large number of different formats that you might want to encode: analog or digital, component or composite.

Videotape also comes in many formats, as shown in Table 8.3. This list is by no means exhaustive; there are older analog composite formats (1-inch) and a number of other digital formats (D-1, D-3, D-5, D-9). The source material may even be supplied in a high-definition format like HD-CAM.

I haven't mentioned audio-only sources. Again, these can be analog or digital, and delivered on tape, cassette, and mini-disc, or burnt onto a CD-ROM.

Table 8.3 Tape Formats

Tape width	Name		Color encoding	Notes
3/4 inch	U-matic	Analog	Y/C	Archive material
1/2 inch	VHS	Analog	Y/C	Consumer format
	S-VHS	Analog	Y/C	
	Betacam (SP)	Analog	Y/C	
	Digital Betacam	Digital	YUV	
	Beta SX	Digital	YUV	
8 mm	DV	Digital	YUV	
	DVC-PRO	Digital	YUV	
	DVCAM	Digital	YUV	

live encoding

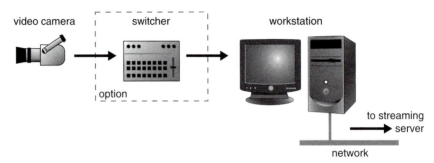

option

to streaming
server

network

encoding from tape

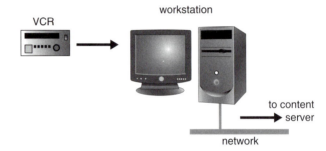

to content
server

network

file transfer from editing system

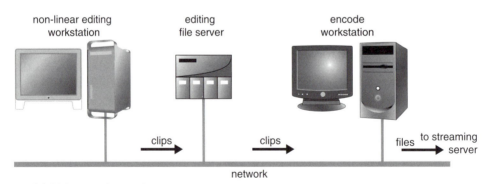

clips

clips

files to streaming
server

network

Figure 8.3 Video capture systems.

There are different interconnection formats for video to add to all these formats:

- Analog composite (NTSC, PAL)
- Y/C or S-video (analog)
- Digital component (601, 4:2:2) – 270 Mbit/s (SDI)
- DV (FireWire, IEEE-1394) – 25 Mbit/s, 5:1 compression

As you can see, encoding is partly video format conversion.

Interconnections

Interconnection formats include analog composite and component, and digital component. All require processing to arrive at the final AVI file format. To this end the video capture card has several components: a composite decoder, analog-to-digital conversion, DV decompression, and possibly hardware scaling.

If modern digital tape decks use component recording, why do most video cards have analog composite inputs? For historical reasons analog composite has become a standard for interconnections and is still in very common use.

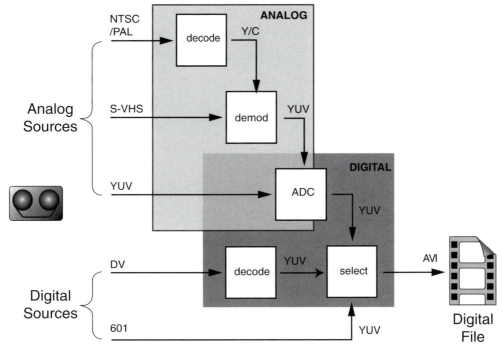

Figure 8.4 Capture card blocks.

It is possible to find video cards with digital inputs (DV and 601) and these do offer the potential for higher quality encoding. The video cards also include a preview output so that the encoded files can be viewed on a conventional television monitor. Many video cards are designed as platforms to support non-linear editors, so they will have many additional facilities that are not required for a straight encode.

In an ideal world the streaming format would be encoded directly from a 4:2:2 source (at 270 Mbit/s); in fact, this is the way that DVDs of motion pictures are encoded. In this way the studios can ensure the best possible picture quality for the DVD release.

To get the best possible encoding, a digital source should be used, with a clean picture and a low level of noise. If a 601 source is not available, DV can be used as an alternative. The mild DCT (discrete cosine transform) compression used by DV should not produce significant artifacts visible in the final stream.

The second best is an analog source; here Y/C is preferable to composite. Analog sources exhibit more noise, which potentially can use up bandwidth at the compression stage. Composite signals are first decoded, and there will be visible artifacts that will produce a slight impairment of the final encoded quality (called cross-color and cross-luminance).

There are different ways of compressing; the intermediate AVI may be at the same resolution as the original video, or it may be scaled to the target size. Each method has advantages and disadvantages. It is a trade-off between video quality and data rate. If many different output formats are required, an intermediate file may have to be stored for the duration of the encoding process. This file should be at least the size of the largest encoded picture, if not larger. So if you are encoding to 160 × 120 and 192 × 144, you may want the intermediate file at SIF resolution 352 × 240. The AVI file may even be archived. But the higher the quality, the higher the storage costs.

The other consideration is the processing time, as a high-resolution file will take longer to process. The processing time can be important for two reasons. First, it could impact the throughput of work in a busy encoding center. Second, with live feeds the encoding has to take place in real-time, so the lower the resolution, the less CPU power required for the codecs.

VTR control

It is much simpler to encode a tape if the video capture application has a remote control facility for the VTR. This means that you do not have to start the capture on the fly, plus it allows batch encoding to a prepared schedule. Most professional tape decks can be controlled via an RS-422 port (DV decks also can be controlled through the IEEE-1394 interface). The port allows full transport control – Play, Fast Forward, Rewind, and Stop – and gives status feedback plus a readout of the tape time code. Frame-accurate control allows the exact in and out points of the clip to be set in a record list. This avoids the need to trim the clip later in the encoding process.

Lowering the bit rate

A standard resolution television frame is 720×483 pixels (720×575 for 625/50), RGB sampled at 13.5 MHz, and has an 8-bit resolution per sample. At a rate of 30 frames per second this is a total data rate of 248 Mbit/s, and that is without any synchronization or control data.

To stream video to a 56 kbit/s modem the bit rate has to be reduced by a factor of over 4,000. How is this achieved while still producing a recognizable picture?

There are two methods used to achieve this. The first is to scale down the video data. This can achieve a reduction of over 130:1, clearly a long way off the target ratio of 4000:1. To reach this target a further reduction of 30:1 is required. This is achieved using sophisticated compression algorithms to remove redundant data, while retaining a viewable picture.

Scaling

The simplest way to lower data rate is to scale down the original video size. Three techniques are used to scale down the signal; the first and most apparent is to use a smaller video frame size than a television picture. Since video is often shown as a window in a web page, it is perfectly acceptable to reduce the picture to one-quarter size (320×240 pixels) or even smaller.

This is called *spatial scaling*. It produces an instant reduction of data rate to one that is more easily processed by desktop workstations.

The second scaling is *temporal*. Broadcast television uses 25 (PAL, SECAM) or 30 (NTSC) frames per second to give good portrayal of motion. Film uses 24 frames per second. Video material that originally was shot on film is converted to one of the two television rates during the telecine process.

The third method of scaling down is to decrease the color resolution.

Dedicated hardware processors in the video card can be used for the scaling, or it can be a straight software process using the main CPU. For live encoding it is best to use the video card and relieve the main processor load.

Spatial scaling

A smaller window can be used to display video; typical window sizes have resolutions of 320×240 or 176×144 pixels. This radically reduces the number of

Table 8.4 Common Image Formats

Image format	Resolution	Frame rate	YUV	Application
HDTV, 1080i	1920 × 1080	30 interlaced	4:2:2	Broadcast television
HDTV, 720p	1280 × 720	30 progressive	4:2:2	Broadcast television
CCIR-601 (NTSC)	720 × 486	30 interlaced	4:2:2	Broadcast television, DVD
CCIR-601 (PAL)	720 × 576	25 interlaced	4:2:2	
SIF (NTSC)	352 × 240	30 progressive	4:2:0	Streaming video, CD-ROM,
SIF (PAL)	352 × 288	25 progressive	4:2:0	MPEG-1
CIF	352 × 288	30 progressive	4:2:0	Video conferencing, streaming video
QCIF	176 × 144	30 progressive	4:2:0	Video phone, streaming video

Note: Standard Interface Format (SIF); Common Interface Format (CIF); Quarter Common Interface Format (QCIF).

samples to one-quarter or one-eighth of a full-size television resolution picture. Table 8.4 shows common streaming resolutions compared to television.

Figure 8.5 shows these frame sizes in relation to an SVGA monitor display for NTSC territories. Note that the BT.601 standard has been scaled to compensate for the nonsquare pixels.

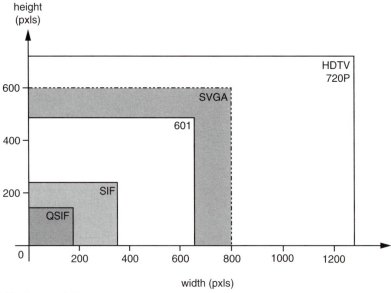

Figure 8.5 Display resolutions.

The QCIF frame is the ideal size to place a video window within a web page. There is still room left for the menus and textual content of interactive applications. The larger frame sizes are more useful where video is the primary content and will occupy most or all of the display.

Temporal scaling

This is the process of dropping frames below the normal video rate of 30 frames per second (fps). For certain subject material the frame rate can be reduced to one-half or even more without serious degradation in picture quality. The deciding factor is the amount of motion in the picture. A talking head can be viewed at rates as low as one-fifth of television rates – of course a fast-moving subject like a sportscast would not be satisfactory at these low speeds.

This sounds like a big problem for streaming video, but much of the demand for low bit rate content is for applications like distance learning. Here the typical program uses a talking head, just the kind of material that can stand the highest temporal compression.

RealVideo will encode at a variable frame rate. The user sets the maximum rate, and then the codec automatically adjusts the frame rate based on the clip size, the target delivery bit rate, and emphasis set for smoothness or visual clarity. One scene may be 7 fps, for example, while another is 10. A maximum set to 15 fps means the frame rate could vary anywhere between 15 and 0.25 fps.

Color resolution

The camera and display are both RGB devices. The usual coding is to take an 8-bit sample each of the red, green, and blue values at each sample point or pixel. This gives a total of 24 bits, but it is often padded for ease of processing to give a 32-bit word. A 24-bit pixel can display 16 million colors. To reduce the bit rate of the streaming video, the bit depth of a sample can be reduced, albeit at a reduction in the number of colors displayed.

Table 8.5 AVI Formats

AVI format	Bit depth			Padding	Bytes per pixel
	R	G	B		
RGB32	8	8	8	8	4
RGB24	8	8	8		3
RGB16	5	6	5		2
RGB15	5	5	5	1	2
RGB8		Indexed palette			1

It can be reduced to 16 bits (5:6:5, giving 65,536 colors), 15 bits (5:5:5 giving 32,786 colors), or to 8 bits (giving 256 colors). Note that the designation indicates the bit depths for R:G:B. Eight-bit coding uses a predefined palette of colors (indexed).

For very low bit rate channels, the reduction in color resolution can be acceptable, but continuous-tone objects will exhibit a posterization effect.

Subsampling

The alternative to reducing the bit depth is to use the perceptual redundancy of human visual perception. This allows the color resolution to be reduced relative to the luminance resolution, without apparent loss of picture resolution. This is achieved by *subsampling* the color information.

YUV format

The red, green, and blue signals from the camera are matrixed to give a luminance signal (Y) and two color-difference signals (Blue–Y) or U, and (Red–Y) or V. This is called YUV. It allows compatibility with legacy monochrome systems, and allows the color resolution to be reduced to save on channel bandwidth and reduce program storage requirements. YUV coding is the standard for interconnecting video equipment, whether as the 601 digital format, in IEEE-1394 compressed digital format, or encoded as a composite analog signal (NTSC and PAL). Raw RGB occasionally is found in graphics equipment, and is the standard for display drivers (VGA).

Early composite digital video systems chose to sample analog video at four times the NTSC color subcarrier. This rate of 13.5 MHz (4×3.375) was adopted for digital component sampling standards. Since the human visual system primarily uses the luminance information to resolve scene detail, the color information can be sampled at a lower rate with no apparent loss of detail. This is a form of perceptive compression. The luminance sampling rate is referred to as 4 after the multiplier used. The color sampling rate may be a half (2) or one quarter (1) depending on the performance required. So a YUV sample is referred to by the ratios of the sampling rates of the three different channels – 4:2:2 or 4:1:1.

YUV formats are divided into two groups: packed and planar. In the packed format, the Y, U, and V components are stored in a single array. The 601 standard uses a single array. With the AVI formats two pixels are stored as a single unsigned integer value in one macro-pixel. In the planar format, the Y, U, and V pixels are encoded as three separate arrays.

It should be noted that 4:2:2 sampling represents a two-thirds reduction in bit rate over RGB 24, and 4:1:1 is a reduction of one-half. The number of

Table 8.6 Sampling Formats

Format		Nomenclature	Sampling
601	Packed		4:2:2
AVI	Planar	IYUV/I420	4:2:0 or 4:1:1
		YV12	4:2:0 or 4:1:1
		YVU9	16:1:1
	Packed	YUY2	4:2:2
		UYVY	4:2:2
		YVYU	4:2:2

bits per pixel averages to 24 bits for 4:4:4, 16 for 4:2:2, and 12 for 4:1:1 and 4:2:0.

More detail on these formats can be found in Chapter 4.

Result of scaling

The typical scaled video data rate at a size and frame rate used with analog modems is 1.15 Mbit/s. Compression to a rate suitable for delivery below 56 kbit/s will require a further 30:1 reduction. To reduce the rate even further, some form of image compression has to be employed.

Compression

Compression removes information that is perceptually redundant; that is, information that does not add to the perception of a scene. Compression is a trade-off between the level of artifacts that it causes and the saving in bandwidth. These trade-offs sometimes can be seen on satellite television. If too many channels are squeezed into one transponder, fast-moving objects within a scene can become blocky and soft.

Like scaling, compression of video splits into spatial compression (called intraframe) and temporal or (interframe) compression.

Intraframe compression

Single frames can be compressed with spatial, or intraframe, compression. This can be a simple system like run-length encoding, or a lossy system where the original data cannot wholly be reconstructed. A typical example of a lossy system is JPEG, a popular codec for continuous-tone still images.

Interframe compression

The next method to compress video is to remove information that does not change from one frame to the next, and to transmit information only in the areas where the picture has changed. This is referred to as temporal or interframe compression. This technique is one of those used by the MPEG-1, MPEG-2, and MPEG-4 standards.

Compression classes

The different algorithms are classified into families:

1. Lossless
2. Lossy
   - Naturally lossy
   - Unnaturally lossy

If all the original information is preserved the codec is called lossless. A typical example for basic file compression is PKZIP. To achieve the high levels of compression demanded by streaming codecs, the luxury of the lossless codecs is not possible – the data reduction is insufficient.

The goal with compression is to avoid artifacts that are perceived as unnatural. The fine detail in an image can be degraded gently without losing understanding of the objects in a scene. As an example we can watch a 70-mm print of a movie or a VHS transfer, and in both cases still enjoy the experience, even though the latter is a pale representation of the former.

If too much compression is applied, and the artifacts interfere with perception of image, then the compression has become unnaturally lossy.

Packetization

This usually is implemented within the compression codec. There are two facets to the packetization. One, the compressed video file has to be formatted into IP packets to allow transmission over a standard IP circuit. The second is to wrap control data around the compressed video and audio data, so that the streaming server can control the real-time streaming of the media data.

Streaming wrapper

The packetization of the media is followed by a packet builder. This generates a Real-Time Protocol (RTP) hint track (metadata) that instructs the server how to stream the file. This is covered in more detail in Chapter 11. Note that there are proprietary streaming formats that do not use RTP.

Encoding hardware and software

Streaming media usually starts with a program recorded on videotape. (I will consider the special case of live streaming in a different chapter.)

The output of the VCR is connected to a video and audio capture board that is fitted to the encoding workstation. The board converts the video to a digital format, usually an Audio-Video Interleaved format (AVI). Apart from the video interfacing, the board has several functions that can ease the processing load on the workstation CPU.

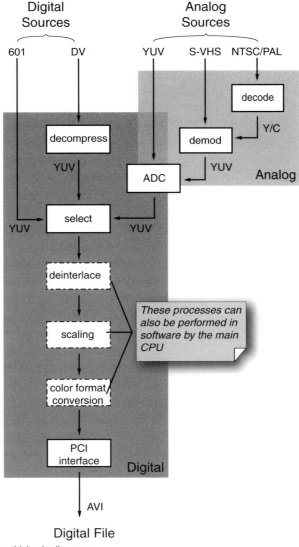

Figure 8.6 Video card block diagram.

The functions of the card include the following:

- Decoding composite analog NTSC and PAL into a YUV format
- Demodulating the color component of S-video to U/V
- Analog-to-digital conversion
- Decoding DV (IEEE-1394) to uncompressed YUV
- Color pixel format conversion to an AVI format
- Interfacing to the PCI bus

The cards usually have a number of other facilities; these vary with different models and their manufacturers:

- Spatial scaling
- De-interlace filter
- VCR control port
- Video preview output

The video preview facility may use Microsoft Direct Draw for DMA (direct memory access) to the workstation video driver. This saves loading the CPU, because a real-time preview at 30 fps would take considerable processor resources.

To achieve optimal system performance it may be necessary to use a computer with fast or multiple processors, especially for live events. The performance of the disk drives should not be forgotten. For archiving or file conversion, use a high-performance disk drive, for example a 10,000-rpm SCSI. This can help to offload performance requirements from the main CPU, freeing up more processing power for the encoder.

Encoding sessions

From the previous description of encoding and compression, it is clear that there are a huge number of possible parameter sets for encoding. It would not be productive to set up all these parameters from scratch for each encoding session. Instead, templates or profiles can be set up to suit typical content. Most codecs come with a number or profiles already prepared. For example, a template might be stored to encode a Beta SP tape to MPEG-4/AVC for delivery over a corporate network at 500 kbit/s.

Encoding enhancements

Multiple bit-rate encoding

Early deployments of streaming media often posted links to the media file at perhaps three different rates: 30, 100, and 300 kbit/s. So the onus was on the viewer to select the correct streaming file. First, this is an unnecessary complication for the viewer, and second it does not take into account network congestion.

The leading codec suppliers developed multiple bit rate codecs to allow several streams of different bit rates to be bundled into one file. The streaming server then negotiates with the end-user's media player to determine the optimum rate to use for the stream delivery. No user interaction is necessary.

A typical example is SureStream from RealNetworks. With SureStream technology, up to eight different bit rates can be encoded. The Helix Server automatically selects the best bit rate to serve for the network conditions. The Microsoft Windows Media Intelligent Streaming is a similar feature.

All the viewer sees during network congestion is a gradual lowering of quality, rather than freezes typical of a fixed rate system.

Variable bit rate (VBR)

Streaming codecs by default use constant bit-rate (CBR) encoding. DVDs and digital satellite television both use variable bit-rate encoding. The DVD has a maximum file size; so, to give the maximum playing time, a low bit rate is indicated.

The MPEG-2 compression used differs from an analog recording like VHS. The VHS tape has a fixed video quality, whereas at a fixed bit rate, the MPEG video will have a variable quality, dependent on the entropy of the original content. To avoid visible MPEG artifacts, the DVD encoding rate increases when there is rapid subject movement. During scenes with motion the bit rate increases from a typical value of 3 Mbit/s up to a maximum of 8 Mbit/s. The end result is a constant video quality for the viewer. The bit rate is a trade-off between artifacts and the file size. To achieve the optimum encode within the limit of the maximum file size of the DVD, two passes are used. The first analyzes the material, the second encodes using the parameters from the first. The process can be automatic, or for the best quality transfers the compressionist will adjust the encode rates manually on a scene-by-scene basis.

Similar variable bit rates can be used for multiplexed digital satellite television channels. The technique of statistical multiplexing allows channels to aggregate bit rates up to the total that a transponder can carry. If one channel needs more bits, it can borrow from the other channels. This technique is more successful the more channels there are in a multiplex. Statistical multiplexing can be used to add additional channels to a transponder, or to give better quality output when compared with an equal number of fixed bit rate channels.

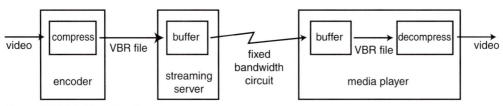

Figure 8.7 Variable bit buffering.

These techniques have been utilized by some proprietary streaming codecs, again to improve video quality within the constraints of the average channel bandwidth. The codecs use the server and player buffers to average the data, so that a continuous bandwidth is transmitted across the IP connection.

Figure 8.8 shows two streams, one constant and one variable, used across the same fixed bandwidth channel. Note that, during the action scenes, the VBR channel has an increased bit rate. The CBR channel will have a lower quality during these scenes.

Again, like DVD encoding, two-pass encodes give better results with VBR. The first pass analyzes the entire video file to find the best encode rates. The second pass is the true encode and uses the data gathered from the first pass.

Obviously this technique can be used only when encoding a video file, rather than a live stream.

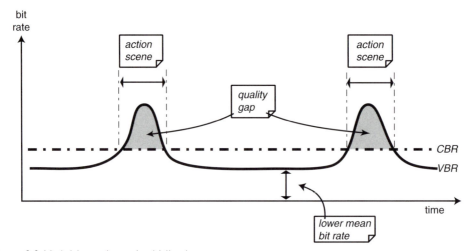

Figure 8.8 Variable and constant bit rates.

Batch encoding

Anybody who wants to encode more than two or three files will benefit from batch encoding. Most of the proprietary codecs offer some form of automation to process a large number of files. The alternative is to use a product like Discreet Cleaner or Anystream, designed for high throughput encoding.

Live encoding

Live encoding often is used for live events. The output of a camera or video switcher can be streamed directly to the Web. The main issue to watch for here is that the processing has to be in real-time. The software codecs have to keep pace with the incoming video signal; this usually means using a dedicated workstation, possibly a multiprocessor. To improve performance the workstation should not be running any other applications that may consume CPU resources. One typical application is a video preview; buy a video capture card that offers preview facilities without drawing on the main processor resource.

Import from video editing systems

Rather than using videotape as the medium for the final edited version of the program, video can be ingested directly by file transfer from a desktop video editing system. This can be as a DV, AVI, or QuickTime file. A video capture card is not obligatory, but if the source file is in DV format it is decompressed to raw YUV before encoding. Hardware decompression on the card will increase the speed of the file encode as software decompression is processor intensive.

Encoding products

There are many products that you can buy for encoding. Both Microsoft and Real supply comprehensive encoding applications for their proprietary architectures. If you are going to be encoding into several different architectures and formats you may want to consider a third-party product. The first step is to decide what output formats you want. If you are coding for material for internal distribution on a company intranet, you may have the luxury of a single codec and a single data rate. If you are running the encoding shop of a web agency, you may have to produce streaming files in Real and Windows media, both at six different bit rates (with smaller resolution for the lower rates), an MPEG-4 file for wireless applications, and 1 Mbit/s MPEG-1 files for distribution as progressive download over corporate networks. You also may have to encode in different versions of a codec, as older browsers may not support the latest version of a codec.

You may well have to produce 20 versions of a video file. To keep down the cost of encoding it pays to use tools that can automate the encoding process. When you are choosing such a tool, you also need to consider what sort of pre-processing that you want. Even the most basic codecs offer simple clean-up facilities: cropping, normalization, and levels.

Another consideration is integration with the rest of your workflow. If the streaming media is to be integrated with a rich media presentation, what architectures do you want to use? Do you want to use SMIL to synchronize the multimedia files? What platforms do you want to use: Windows, Linux, Mac?

There are so many options that it may pay to get advice from a consultant. Alternatively, you could outsource the encoding.

RealProducer 10

RealNetworks provides two versions of RealProducer 10: the basic version for personal use and the Plus version with extra facilities for the professional. Real-Producer Plus is a full set of tools for encoding RealVideo 10 and RealAudio 10 files. Variable bit-rate encoding with two-pass processing gives the best encoding quality. The product includes de-interlacing and inverse telecine. For live encoding, redundant paths can be set up to the streaming servers. Both versions can run on Windows and Linux platforms.

Windows Media 9

Microsoft supplies a complete set of tools for encoding audio and video into the Windows Media format for streaming. Version 9 adds many new features including VTR control, multichannel audio encoding, rights management for live streaming, plus encoding for CD, DVD, and portable music players.

More sophisticated control of encoding can be done with the command line utility. This can be used for automation and batch encoding. Windows Media Encoder 9 replaces versions 7 and 8 in one product.

Apple QuickTime

Apple has two encoding products: the QuickTime Pro 6 for general authoring, and QuickTime Broadcaster for live encoding. QuickTime Pro 6 and Broad-caster take the standards route, with MPEG-4 encoding 3GPP and 3GPP2 file formats for wireless devices. Broadcaster can take live video direct from a camera via FireWire without the need for a video card. Like other Apple products they can both be automated with AppleScript.

Discreet Cleaner 6/XL

These products, originally from Terran, have become the most popular encoding tools: XL for Windows and 6 for the Mac. They are a complete suite of applications to capture, preprocess, encode, and publish rich media. They support the three main architectures: Apple QuickTime, Microsoft Windows Media, and RealNetworks RealVideo, as well as mobile formats like Kinoma.

The product has comprehensive processing options for video and audio content. A preview window lets you see the effects of filters. The audio optimization includes dynamic range compression, noise reduction, and high- and low-pass filters. Video processing includes de-interlace and inverse telecine.

Anystream

The Anystream Agility Workgroup XE provides the solution for the busy encoding station. It can capture a video signal, either live, from tape, or from a file, in a single pass. Files could be in AVI or Avid formats. This input signal then can be compressed to a number of different formats, each with a different set of parameters. Before encoding the signal can be preprocessed. The Anystream system includes cropping, de-interlace, reverse telecine, and color correction for the video. The audio processing includes dynamic range compression, noise reduction, and low-pass filtering. The big advantage of Anystream is that you can encode an MPEG-2 program stream for a DVD, a 320 × 240 QuickTime file, and 160 × 112 Real and Windows Media for streaming, all in the same session. The encoding parameters are programmed into profiles, so jobs can be set up very quickly.

The output formats range from broadcast MPEG-2 down to PacketVideo MPEG-4 for wireless applications.

Once material is encoded, the Agility can be programmed to e-mail content producers to alert them that the content is ready for streaming.

Limits on file sizes

The original AVI format files were limited by the size of disk partition. The 16-bit file allocation table (FAT) used by the original MS-DOS had a maximum partition size of 2 Gbyte. FAT32 extends the partition size to 4 Gbyte. Partitions using current file systems such as the Windows NT File Systems (NTFS) are not subject to the 2-Gbyte limit (the NTFS file system is available on Windows NT, 2000, and XP operating systems).

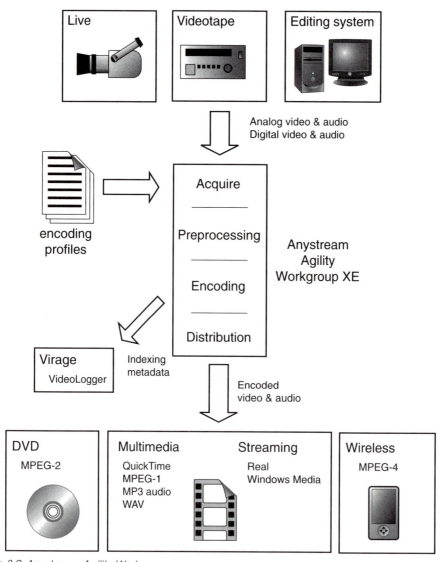

Figure 8.9 Anystream Agility Workgroup.

The current AVI format (called AVI 2.0, AVI Type II, or extended AVI) supports larger file sizes, but older capture software or hardware may support only the original format.

Table 8.7 gives files sizes for some typical streaming files. Note that a typical CIF resolution file reaches the 2-Gbyte limit in only nine minutes.

Table 8.7 Streaming File Sizes

Bit rate	Bytes per second	Gbytes per minute	Gbytes in 1 hour	Duration of 2-Gbyte file (hour:min)	Duration for 4-Gbyte file (hour:min)
30k	3,750	0.00	0.01	148:09	296:18
100k	12,500	0.00	0.05	44:27	88:53
500k	62,500	0.00	0.23	8:53	17:47
CIF, 352 × 240, YUV12, 30 fps	3,801,600	0.23	13.69	0:09	0:18
601 video (166 Mbit/s)	20,750,000	1.25	74.70	0:02	0:02

As an example of a current format using 64-bit addressing, the Windows Media file container supports files up to 17 PetaBytes (peta is 10^{15}). This is equivalent to 200 million hours of uncompressed 601 sampled video.

Summary

This chapter has described the processes of capture and compression. A straight encode can be a simple operation, but the need to encode in different formats and resolutions can complicate the processes. Much of this complexity can be hidden from you if you are using tools like Discreet Cleaner or Anystream Agility.

Choosing the parameters for an encoding session is a compromise between the acceptable level of artifacts and the data rate of the bit stream. The choice of codecs is determined by many factors: the architectures that you are using, the video quality required, the processing latency, the CPU resources required, and, of course, the cost.

Closely allied to encoding is the preprocessing of the video material. This cleans up the video signal before the compression, removing artifacts like noise. Noise is the enemy of compression as it eats up valuable data bandwidth. So an encoding session most likely is combined with the preprocessing stage.

Streaming media could never have happened without the compression codecs available today. Video codecs saw much development in the 1990s with video-conferencing, MPEG-1, and MPEG-2 all blazing the trail in techniques and algorithms. The result has been some very effective systems that can stand alongside legacy consumer distribution formats. MPEG-4 has continued with this development, with a range of encoding profiles suited to applications from low bit-rate mobile and wireless to high-definition video.

9 Audio encoding

Introduction

Audio encoding can look easy beside video. It takes only a few seconds to set up a PC to rip your favorite CDs to an MP3 file. The MP3 industry has spawned a large number of encoding applications, many that can be used to process streaming audio.

There are a few pitfalls to avoid, but a modest investment in equipment can produce very good results. The problems encoding audio are most likely to arise if you want to set up live webcasts on location. You lose the control that you had ripping CDs back in the workshop. Also, music CDs are carefully crafted, with excellent mixes, controlled dynamics, and superb sound quality. At the live event, you are recording direct from microphones via an audio console, and you may need several tweaks to the sound to realize the optimum audibility for your stream.

Your local AM and FM radio stations use several techniques to ensure maximum audibility and to increase the apparent loudness. If you want your webcast to sound as good, you will have to follow a similar path. It is easy to overlook or neglect audio sweetening for the Web. After spending hours editing the video until the pictures look great, the audio is processed with a simple preset template. But great pictures with unintelligible audio are not going to convey your message. Learn from the radio guys, they have been in business for a long time.

Much of the audio processing can be done with a PC workstation fitted with a sound card. The external equipment required depends on the job, but it could include an audio editing system, an audio mixing board, and a variety of play-back decks – CD or DAT. The audio source may well be a camcorder or VTR if it is an audio/video production.

This chapter has four sections: audio formats, capture, encoding, and the final section describing some of the more popular audio file formats. Audio encoding starts with a live audio stream from a microphone or mixing board.

The stream is captured as a computer file then processed before encoding as a compressed file using a streaming codec. The result is another stream, but now it is in streaming media format.

The captured file may need some basic adjustments before compression, or it may need a comprehensive clean-up (see Chapter 10 for further details). Audio encoding may be for an audio-only stream, maybe Internet radio, or synchronized to a video signal for a multimedia presentation.

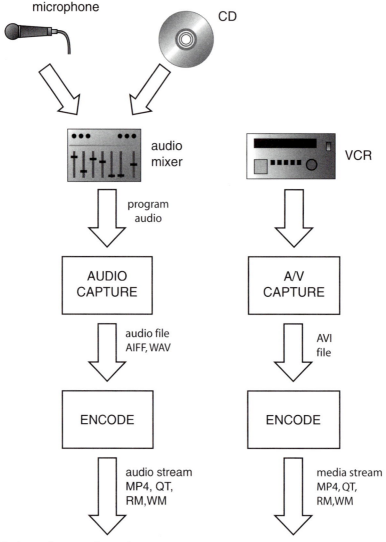

Figure 9.1 Basic audio encoding system.

Audio formats

Even in a digital world, there is a vast legacy of analog audio equipment. Analog interconnections often are used between digital equipment. The most familiar audio connector is the RCA phono connector, often used for audio and video interconnections of PCI cards. Although it can be used successfully for occasional use it is not suited to repeated mating and unmating. Many professional encoder cards have breakout boxes with professional connectors. The alternative to the PCI card is the outboard interface with a USB or FireWire connection to the workstation. The simplest interface converts the analog output from an audio board to digital audio. An example is the Edirol interface, with RCA phono connectors for audio, and a USB interface to the PC (see Figure 9.2).

The Mbox from Digidesign is a typical example of a professional audio interface for the PC (see Figure 9.3). It has control over levels, and includes microphone preamplifiers and S/PDIF input/output. The Mbox unit connects to the workstation with a USB connection.

If you want reliable equipment that will not let you down during an important webcast, do not stint on connectors and cables. The best connector for audio is the very rugged XLR. You can drive a truck over one without damage, bar some surface scratches. Local interconnects between equipment can use unbalanced connections, but for the best performance use balanced connectors. These avoid grounding problems that can introduce hum, and also reject noise pickup in the cable.

Some equipment has poor immunity against RF interference. You would not want the chirping of a cell phone breaking across an important corporate broadcast. The only way to establish the RF immunity is by tests, as manufacturers rarely give any information. Most professional equipment is very good in this respect, but beware if you use consumer equipment.

Figure 9.2 Edirol UA-1A analog audio capture. © Edirol Corporation.

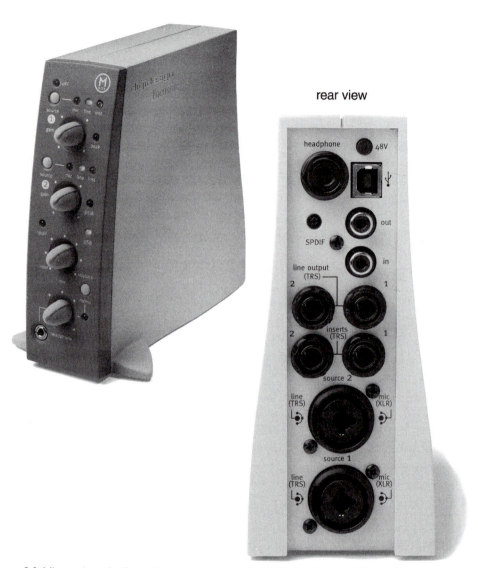

Figure 9.3 Mbox micro studio music production system. © Digidesign, a division of Avid.

AES-3

The full title for this international standard digital audio interface is Serial Transmission Format for Two-channel Linearly Represented Digital Audio Data. That means it is stereo and uncompressed. It was a joint development by the Audio Engineering Society (AES) and the European Broadcasting Union. The standard is based on balanced, shielded twisted pair cable, and for transmission

Table 9.1 AES Parameters

Parameter	
Channels	Two: left and right or A and B
Bit depth	16–24
Coding	Linear 2's complement
Sampling rate	48, 44.1, 32 kHz
Pre-emphasis	On or off
Time reference	Time-of-day time code, hours:minutes:seconds:frames

distances up to 100 meters. The usual connector is the three-pin XLR. The key parameters are shown in Table 9.1.

The AES standard supports three sample rates: 32, 44.1, and 48 kHz. The usual rate that you will encounter is 48 kHz, the standard rate for professional equipment. Unfortunately if you want to incorporate material from CDs, the different sample rate of 44.1 kHz is used. To mix the two, the sample rate of the CD signal must be converted to 48 kHz. This can be done in software or in real-time by hardware. If you use software beware of the processing overhead.

The 48 kHz rate is well above the Nyquist criteria for sampling audio with a frequency response extending to 20 kHz, but allows for variable speed operation without losing the upper register. Most professional audio equipment uses this standard for interconnections. The signal also can be transmitted using unbalanced coaxial cable and BNC connectors. This means that you can use regular 75 Ω video cable and analog video distribution equipment to interconnect your digital audio system. Note that the AES format represents a continuous real-time stream, and is not a file format.

Table 9.2 AES Data Rates

Sample rate (kHz)	Data rate (MHz)	Upper frequency limit (kHz)	
48	3.072	15	Professional
44.1	2.822	20	Consumer (CD)
32	2.048	20	Broadcast

S/PDIF

Some consumer equipment is fitted with the Sony/Philips Digital Interface (S/PDIF). There are many converters available to interface S/PDIF and AES connections.

Interconnecting equipment

Unlike analog audio, if you interconnect several pieces of digital audio equipment they must be synchronized to a common clock. This has always been the case with video equipment, where a master sync pulse generator (SPG) is used as a reference. To lock audio equipment together a word clock, AES signal, or video reference signal can be used.

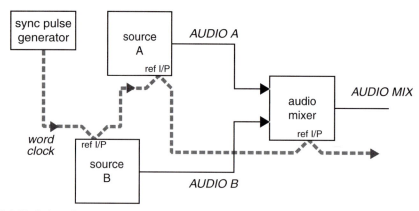

Figure 9.4 Digital audio synchronization.

Capture

Audio capture is the process of acquiring the live audio stream and converting it to a computer file format. This process is very simple. The files are composed of a number of chunks. The header chunk describes the file format and the number of samples. The data chunk contains the audio samples as frames, much like the AES standard. The file formatter adds a header chunk with all the necessary data to read the audio samples. To encode audio you really do not need to understand the file formats. Usually the configuration consists of just selecting the relevant format from a drop-down box on the user interface.

   There are two common file formats: AIFF and WAVE. The AIFF (Audio Interchange File Format) is used by Apple Mac and UNIX platforms. The other, WAVE (Waveform Audio), is a proprietary Microsoft format and is the common

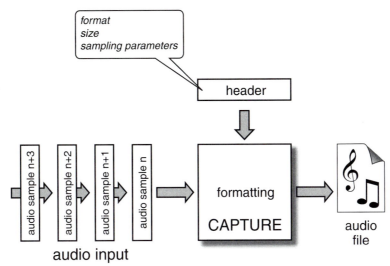

Figure 9.5 File formatting.

format for PC applications. So the decision as to which file format to use is simple.

DC offset

A silent audio input should produce a code value of zero. DC offsets in analog processing can give a zero offset. There are two reasons to avoid an offset. The first is to allow equal positive and negative excursions to maximize the dynamic range. The second is that some codecs do not encode periods of silence to lower the audio data rate. The offset can be nulled out using the audio codec.

Ripping

Ripping is the conversion of audio CDs (recorded to the Red Book standard) into an audio file, usually MP3.

There are many programs that can be used to rip audio from a CD, ranging from freeware to professional packages with full technical support. Most will read the CD at faster than real-time. This is a great bonus if you have a large number of CDs to encode.

Parameters to be adjusted when encoding are:

- DC offset
- Equalization

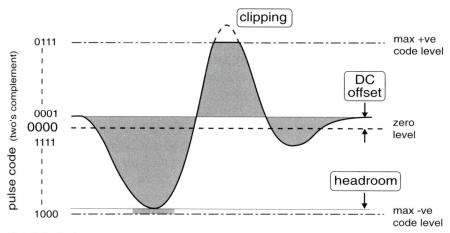

Figure 9.6 DC offset.

- Dynamic range compression and limiting
- Noise gates
- Normalization (gain)

Normalization

Once you have removed any offset, then set suitable compressor-limiter parameters, the signal should be normalized. This ensures the optimum code range is employed by the codecs, by ensuring that the correct gain is set between the input and the codec. This can be adjusted manually, but most encoders will normalize a file automatically.

The goal of normalization is to ensure that the signal level is at a maximum without clipping. A small amount of headroom is set between the maximum excursions of the waveform and the high and low code levels. Typically the headroom will be set to 0.5 dB.

Normalization is always the last step to take with a file, so you should not press the button until all the other adjustments have been made.

Encoding

Once you have decided which codecs to use, it is straightforward to actually encode the audio files. You can use either the tools provided by the main architectures – QuickTime, Real, and Windows Media – or by third-party products like Discreet Cleaner. The advantage of using the latter is that multiple format streams can be created in one encoding session.

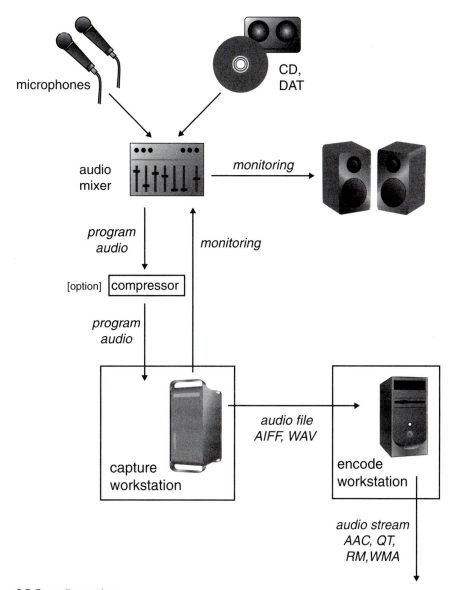

Figure 9.7 Encoding system.

Most encoding tools have similar operation. You start with the target bit rate for the stream, then choose speech or music coding:

- Target audience, 28 k modem, ISDN, DSL, or T-1
- Speech or music
- Mono, stereo, or surround

Typically, a codec template will exist for each combination of these choices. There may be further selections, for example to select codecs compatible with legacy players. You can also create new templates if the default settings are not to your liking. Once an encoding template is selected all that remains is to start the encode.

QuickTime

Apple QuickTime can be encoded with QuickTime Pro, an upgrade to the Quick-Time player, or if you want to do live encoding, QuickTime Broadcaster. The latter is a comprehensive application that supports MPEG-4 and runs on a Mac OS X server.

QuickTime supports a large number of different audio codecs, but only a few can be used for streaming. For speech the choice is between the Qualcomm PureVoice (QCELP) and AMR. The Qualcomm can encode intelligible speech at a data rate of around 7 kbit/s. There is a choice of two rates, full and half. The full rate gives about 9:1 compression ratio, the half rate is about 19:1. For low bit-rate streaming to wireless players that use the 3GPP and 3GPP2 standards, QuickTime supports the AMR narrowband codec.

To encode music you have a choice between the MPEG-4 AAC and QDesign's Music 2 codec. The AAC codec supports multichannel audio and can be encoded at variable bit rates. Typical data rates for stereo audio are 64 kbit/s. The QDesign can encode stereo at rates of around 24 kbit/s, compared to MP3 at around 64 kbit/s for a mono channel.

RealAudio

Real Networks audio encoding is part of the RealProducer 10. This uses the proprietary RealAudio 10 encoder for stereo coding at mid to low bit rates (below 64 kbit/s). At higher bit rates the MPEG-4 AAC codec is used, replacing the ATRAC3 codec that RealNetworks used in earlier versions of RealAudio. In use, the operator selects an encoding template for voice or music, and a target bit-rate. There is a choice of mono, stereo and surround sound. The RealAudio 10 streams can be played on the RealOne player and RealPlayer 10; earlier versions require an upgrade.

Windows Media

Microsoft provides the Windows Media Encoder 9 Series as a free download. It runs on Windows XP or 2000 with DirectDraw installed. The Media Encoder gives complete control of the encoding process, with easy to use templates like voice, FM, or CD quality, plus multichannel and set up for multiple bit rates.

Microsoft has its own set of Windows Media codecs for audio compression. Windows Media Audio 9 is a variable bit-rate codec for stereo music. The Professional version adds surround sound. Typical high-quality 5.1 audio can be encoded at rates from 128 kbit/s for streaming up to 768 kbit/s for download applications. For speech there is the Windows Media Audio 9 Voice codec. This can be used for speech and music at bit rates around 20 kbit/s, ideal for dial-up modems.

There is also a lossless codec in the set, but this is for local archiving of CDs rather than streaming.

File formats

There used to be a large number of audio file formats before the drive to standardization. Sun, SGI, IRCAM, Soundblaster, and Amiga all spawned different file formats. Most were developed to support computer-based music creation and editing systems, rather than for general audio sampling. The move now is to limit use to AIFF for Mac and WAV for PC. In professional circles an enhanced version of WAV is also found – the Broadcast WAVE Format or BWF.

Most of the formats carry the device parameters and encoding in the header – these are called self-describing. Some older, raw formats use fixed parameters that define a single encoding; these are headerless formats. An example of a headerless format is the G.711 (mu)-law encoding.

Table 9.3 is by no means an exhaustive list of the formats that each player can process.

Audio Interchange File Format (AIFF)

This format was developed in the late 1980s by musical developers. It conforms to the Electronic Arts Standard for Interchange Format Files, EA-IFF 85. The file has a number of chunks. Three are obligatory: the header, common, and sound data. A number of optional chunks can be added as required.

The format supports mono, stereo, three-channel, quad, four-channel, and six-channel (5.1). The bit depth can range from 1 to 32 bits per sample. Note that four and quad relate to different loudspeaker layouts.

Microsoft Waveform Audio (WAVE)

This Microsoft format is derived from the Microsoft/IBM Resource Interchange File Format (RIFF). There are three data chunks:

Table 9.3 Some Popular Audio File Formats

	Extension		WM player	Real player	QuickTime player
Audio streaming formats					
Moving Picture Experts Group standard 1, layers 1, 2, 3	.mpa		Y	Y	Y
	.mp2		Y		
	.mp3		Y	Y	
	mpg			Y	
QDesign					Y
RealAudio	.ra			Y	
Windows Media Audio	.wma		Y		
Non-Streaming (local playback) audio formats					
Audio Interchange File Format	.aif, .aiff	Apple, SGI	Y	Y	Y
Audio Interchange File Format, compressed	.aifc	Apple, SGI	Y	Y	Y
Sound File	.snd	NeXT	Y		Y
UNIX Audio	.au	Sun	Y	Y	Y
Waveform Audio	.wav	Microsoft	Y	Y	Y

Table 9.4 AIFF Chunks

Chunk name	Chunk ID	
Header	FORM	Form type 'AIFF'
Common	COMM	Number of audio channels Number of samples in sound data chunk Bit depth Sample rate
Sound data	SSND	Audio sample frames
Marker	MARK	Pointers to positions in a file Example: start and end
Instrument	INST	Musical instrument/sampler control
Comment	COMT	
Name	NAME	
Author	AUTH	
Copyright	(c)	
Annotation	ANNO	(Use comments instead – COMT)
Audio recording	AESD	Channel status data (per-emphasis flags)
MIDI	MIDI	MIDI data
Application specific	APPL	

- RIFF chunk (file format WAVE and file size)
- Format chunk (mono/stereo, sample rate, bits/sample: 8 or 16)
- Data chunk (audio samples)

The format originally supported 8- and 16-bit mono or stereo. It has been extended to support many more formats, as the audio industry demands multiple channels, greater bit depth, and higher sampling rates. These include MPEG-1, A-law, μ-law, and Dolby AC3. Encrypted content found in Windows Media digital rights management is specifically supported.

EBU Broadcast Wave Format (BWF)

The European Broadcasting Union has developed a file format to meet the special needs of broadcasters. Their requirement was for seamless interchange of files between equipment from different manufacturers, and for program exchange between broadcasters. It is based on the Microsoft WAVE format. It adds a broadcast audio extension with essential metadata, plus a unique material identifier (UMID) to reference the audio content. The broadcast extension is analogous to the text chunks in the AIFF; the extension carries information about the audio program originator plus a date/time reference. Linear PCM and MPEG-1 formats are supported.

Summary

To many people audio encoding is MP3. It has been a phenomenally successful codec for the distribution of audio files, although now it has been supplanted by the AAC codec, which offers more efficient compression with the same quality at a lower bit rate.

Audio encoding often is thought of as an adjunct to the video encode. We are blasé about digital audio; the CD has been here for a long time. Ripping CDs to MP3 files is widely used and abused. The audio encoding should not be dismissed as trivial. The bandwidths available to Internet radio for streaming are much lower than an MP3 encode.

The intelligibility of the soundtrack is a prime deciding factor in the acceptance of streaming media by the audience. It is important that live recordings are cleaned up before encoding to remove noise and compress the dynamic range. Music CDs should not require much preprocessing, since the recording will be very clean.

The main streaming architectures all offer alternative codecs to MP3 that offer higher compression while delivering a high quality. These codecs can even be used for audio-only streaming to 28 kbit/s modems. One easy way to almost halve the demands on the codec is to use mono encoding. Do you really need stereo for a talking-head presentation?

When you are encoding audio, the requirements can differ widely. If it is for an Internet radio station, or to accompany video on middle to lower bandwidth circuits, you may want to use one codec. To encode music at a high bit rate for download to portable music players a different codec may be chosen. A third codec could be selected for speech.

The audio codecs available today are suited to a wide range of applications, from low bit rate speech for wireless applications to high-quality surround sound with on-demand streaming movies for the broadband user.

10 Preprocessing

Introduction

The previous two chapters described video and audio encoding. The final quality of a media stream delivered over the network usually can be improved by judicious preprocessing. Plus, compression algorithms provide the best results with a very clean source.

To optimize the picture quality for a given stream bandwidth, a number of steps can be taken to clean up the audio and video signals before compression. Perhaps the greatest distortion that impacts upon compression codecs is noise. In general, digital sources are better than analog in this respect. A signal from a DV camera is much quieter than a VHS tape. Unfortunately you will not always have control over the source; you may have had to use archive material.

There are many other distortions that can impair codec performance; one example is the redundant fields present in material originated on film. To transfer film at 24 fps to video at 30 fps, the telecine machine repeats fields to compensate for the different frame rates.

So, if you want to get the optimum results for your streams, the audio and video signals will benefit from some preprocessing before the encoding stage.

Video processing

Spatial compression can exploit regions of flat texture to reduce the data rate. Any noise in the area of even texture will stop this potential redundancy being removed. Temporal compression removes information that is repeated across many frames. This typically includes the background and other static elements in a shot. Information that changes between frames, for example a moving object, is transmitted as new data each frame.

If the original video material is of poor quality, it may exhibit excessive noise and other distortions. The compression algorithm will interpret this as information that changes from frame to frame, so will encode as data. For a given bandwidth of streaming, a noisy picture will use up valuable data space that could be used for real picture information.

So to get the best quality encoding for your streaming media, it is important that you use a high-quality master free from visible noise. The lower the final bit rate, the more this holds true.

If the only available videotape of the program to be encoded carries visible artifacts and distortions, then the video signal should be preprocessed prior to compression. Several techniques can be used to clean up the video; these include noise reduction and color correction. Similarly the audio may require treatment; for example, compression of dynamic range to suit limited audio playback facilities.

Video levels

Eight-bit television coding does not use the full 256 values for the range from black to white. The analog television waveform has negative excursion below black, used for synchronization. The composite waveform of NTSC and PAL has modulated color information above white level. As it was possible to exceed the black and white bounds, headroom was built in to digital coding. The BT 601 standard defines 220 levels from black to white. Computer video is much simpler: black has the value 0 and white 255. To reproduce the full gamut of color values on the media player, the video range of 220 steps is rescaled to 255 steps.

To give the optimum range, the black level may have to be adjusted; this is called *lift* (analogous to the brightness on a monitor). The gain control then sets the peak white level to the correct value (contrast on a monitor).

Gamma

Gamma adjusts the mid-tones of the image relative to the black and white. There are two default target gammas: Apple Macs use a value of 1.8 and Windows PCs use 2.2. This means that a given encode will appear darker on a Windows PC than a Mac. If you don't know what display the viewer is using, you will have to compromise, with a value of 2.0. It also means that you should preview the resulting encoding on a browser on each operating system to check the settings.

De-interlacing

Television uses an interlaced scan, whereas the PC display uses a progressive scan. The streaming formats are all progressive, so the interlaced video source has to be converted to a progressive scan. An interlaced frame comprises two

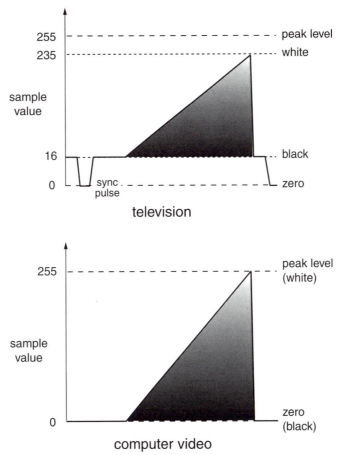

Figure 10.1 Video levels.

fields, one with the even numbered lines and one with the odd (in NTSC, fields are captured every 16 ms). To generate the progressive frame the two fields are combined. Unfortunately if there are any moving objects in the scene, the result will be a horizontal streaking or feathering effect.

A de-interlace filter smoothes the two fields to give an average position for the object. Most codecs offer a de-interlace filter to improve rendition of fast-moving objects. The filter is required only for interlaced video.

Cropping

One easy way to cut down the amount of data is to crop the picture. Surely you want to encode the entire frame? Well, the edges of the frame rarely contain useful picture information.

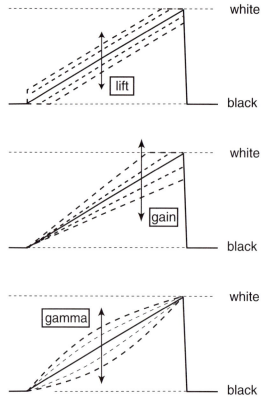

Figure 10.2 Lift, gain, and gamma.

The original tube television receivers had poor voltage regulation for the EHT supply to the CRT. This meant that the picture size was inversely proportional to the picture brightness. To mask this change in size, the picture was over-scanned; that is, the raster was larger than the CRT display area. This also covered up poor scan geometry and drifts with age. So the viewer saw only the center 90 percent of the picture. Aware of this, the cameraman would insure no important action took place at the edges of the picture. Any graphics also are designed to sit well within the actual display area. This is called the safe text area.

Media players display the entire picture, so the edge – usually lost on a television – is also displayed. This means that a picture can be cropped to the safe action area before encoding with no loss of useful picture information. If material is shot specifically for streaming, then the camera operator can crop in closer.

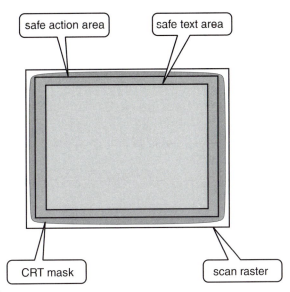

Figure 10.3 Safe text area.

Noise reduction

Noise comes in many different forms. It can be random, caused by electrical noise or film grain. Film-originated stock also has scratches and dirt. Tape is not without its problems – videotape suffers from tape dropouts. FM noise causes sparkles on satellite contribution links. If your material has already been compressed and then decompressed, there may be visible block errors. Although they are artifacts rather than noise, cross-color and cross-luminance from composite video sources also eat into your bandwidth budget.

All these forms of noise require different treatment, although some noise is difficult to remove satisfactorily without introducing a different set of artifacts. For example, very heavy filtering can produce motion artifacts; this will cause smearing of fast-moving objects. There are three popular types of filters for cleaning up video: the two spatial filters, median and the brick wall; and the temporal recursive filter.

Median filter

These are used for the suppression of impulse noise, such as tape dropouts or switching glitches. Impulse noise is usually black or white. A threshold detector separates the impulse noise from the picture information. A median filter then replaces the noise pixels with the median (not the mean) of a window of surrounding pixel values. It is also called a sliding window spatial filter. One of the advantages of the median filter is that it does not soften the edges of an object.

Brick-wall filter

A brick-wall filter allows both the horizontal and vertical spatial resolution to be filtered extremely sharply above a preset frequency point. This lets you reduce high-frequency detail out of band detail that cannot be resolved in scaled-down pictures at low bit rates. Typically film grain and electrical noise have a high frequency spectrum, so this filter will remove both. To avoid the softening of edges, the brick-wall filters can apply a boost just inside the pass-band. Note that a brick-wall filter will smear out impulse noise, so the median filter should be applied first.

Recursive filter

Recursive filters are used to remove the random noise from film grain or electrical noise. For typical video material the main change from one frame to the next is noise. A recursive filter averages one frame with the next, reducing the noise but leaving repeated picture information unchanged.

The only picture information that does not repeat should be moving objects within the scene. A motion detector can be used to separate real moving objects from noise. The recursive filtering can be made adaptive, and can be applied solely to the stationary areas of the picture. This avoids the smearing of moving objects if too much filtering is applied in an attempt to clean up a noisy picture.

Sharpening

Sometimes a picture needs sharpening. This is difficult without adding noise to the edges of objects. Once a picture has become soft, maybe through excessive dubbing, information has been lost forever. If you are careful a picture can be given a bit more snap, but beware of using too much sharpening.

Unsharp masking

Many video processors offer a technique called unsharp masking, or USM. This is a traditional technique to sharpen edges in an image that has been borrowed from film compositing. A thin, soft negative is sandwiched with the original positive. When a new exposure is made it sharpens the edges without increasing noise in flat areas. It produces a more pleasing effect than a straight sharpen.

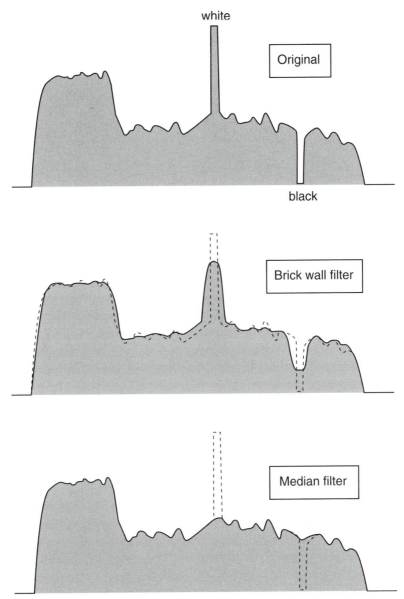

white

Original

black

Brick wall filter

Median filter

Figure 10.4 *Median versus brick-wall filter with impulse noise.*

Inverse telecine and 3:2 pull-down

When film is transferred to video (a process called telecine), to maintain the correct television timebase, the film shot at 24 frames per second has to be processed to 30 frames per second. Normally each frame is scanned twice,

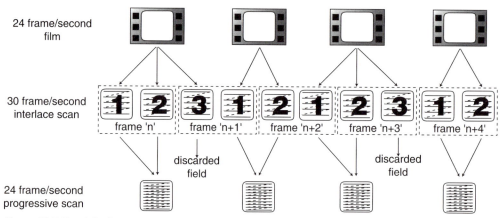

24 frame/second
film

30 frame/second
interlace scan

frame 'n'   frame 'n+1'   frame 'n+2'   frame 'n+3'   frame 'n+4'

discarded
field

discarded
field

24 frame/second
progressive scan

Figure 10.5 The telecine sequence.

giving two interlaced fields. In the case of film this would give a field rate of 48, rather than the 60 of video.

To correct the field rate, alternate frames are scanned three times; that is, the first and third fields are duplicated. This gives a 3:2:3:2 sequence to the scanning so that 24 frames become 60 fields, the normal rate for video.

Note that a video frame can be made from fields from two different film frames.

If this video signal is to be encoded efficiently, the duplication of one field every five is redundant information that could be removed. This task is not as simple as it appears – the repeated field carries no label to indicate the duplication. The duplicate field has to be detected in the presence of analog noise (from the telecine image sensor). This noise makes the duplicated fields slightly different.

The second problem is that if video transfer of the film is edited, the 3:2:3:2 sequence can be disrupted. So that means that once a duplicate field is detected, the next duplicate cannot be assumed simply by counting fields.

This process of removing the duplicate fields is called *inverse telecine*.

625/50 systems completely avoid this process. The film simply is run slightly fast, at 25 frames per second, and scanned directly to 50 fields in a normal interlace sequence. The 4 percent increase in speed is ignored.

Audio

Most audio content will need some preprocessing before the streaming codec. This will include equalization, dynamic range compression, peak limiting, and noise reduction.

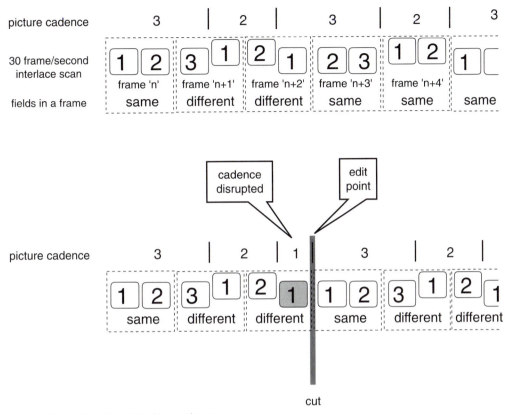

Figure 10.6 Editing the telecine cadence.

Equalization

Often called EQ, equalization is seen everywhere from car audio to the recording studio. Equalization allows you to adjust the frequency response of the audio chain. The simplest equalizers are bass and treble controls.

Equalizers can be used to compensate for deficiencies in the original recording, and to allow for limited audio replay facilities of the average PC.

Bandpass filters

These give comprehensive control over frequency response with a number of bandpass filters, often called graphic EQ from the graphic layout of the controls.

Parametric equalizers

The most flexible filters allow the bandwidth and center frequency of each filter to be adjusted. They are used more often in the recording studio, where there

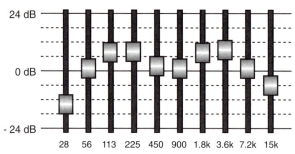

Figure 10.7 Graphic equalizer.

is the luxury of more time than you are likely to have for a webcast. Always apply equalization with care; too much will not enhance the final result. For streaming, typical adjustments could be as follows:

- Low-pass filter to remove high-frequency hiss
- High-pass filter to remove hum and air conditioning rumble
- Mid-frequency mild boost to give presence to speech

You may find problems with sibilance from some speakers. It can sometimes be reduced with a microphone shield; otherwise, a combination of EQ and multi-band compression can assist.

Dynamic range

Modern home audio systems can reproduce a very large dynamic range. DVD-A and SACD both offer 24-bit coding; home theater systems also offer a wide dynamic range. In contrast, streaming audio often is listened to with the limited facilities built into laptop PCs. A loudspeaker, maybe 1 inch in diameter, driven with a modest power amplifier, cannot hope to reproduce a wide dynamic range. So, much like AM radio, intelligibility is improved if the dynamic range is compressed. Two processes are employed: compression and peak limiting. The compression ensures that the average loudness of the signal is relatively constant. This requires more sophisticated processing than a simple automatic gain control.

The more complex dynamic processors split the audio into bands, typically five. This band splitting was developed for the original AM radio processors, to give the most natural sound with high levels of dynamic range compression. By using phase-linear filters for the band splitters, the final mix will be free of non-linear group delay.

If you are going to host corporate webcasts, usually the executives will address an audience from a podium. As the speaker moves about, the audio

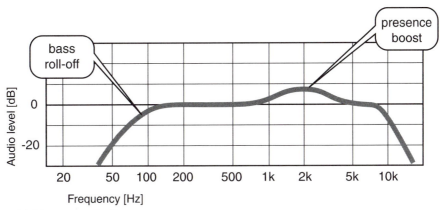

Figure 10.8 Voice equalization.

levels will change. During pauses in the presentation you do not want to amplify the background noise.

Peak limiting

Simple clipping generates unpleasant audible artifacts. For the best results you should use a look-ahead peak limiter. They reduce the gain fractionally before a peak, gracefully reducing peak levels without the apparent distortion that you get with straight waveform clipping. The amount of peak limiting you use depends upon the program content. If you want to retain musical transients to give punch to the audio the limiter should be used with caution.

Noise reduction

A noise gate reduces gain radically below a preset threshold. One application that can be very useful is to stop the dynamic range compressor from sucking up noise during pauses in a presentation. It should not be used if the background is contributing to the audio track; an example would be background music. If the noise gate were to cut the music in and out this would be irritating to the listener. The only way to set the threshold for the noise gate is to listen to the effect. The threshold can be increased gradually until the background noise cuts out. If there is unacceptable breathing of the background, it can be backed off until an acceptable result is achieved. The noise gate usually has temporal adjustments, so that there is a delay before it cuts in and out. If the gate is maladjusted, it can lead to clipping of the presenter's speech.

A noise gate offers a great advantage if your compression codec has silence detection. During periods of silence the compressor effectively shuts down. This

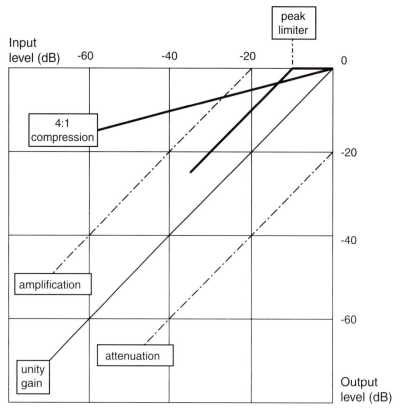

Figure 10.9 Compressor–limiter transfer characteristics.

means that the data rate can be reduced by a useful amount. Codecs that offer this feature include CELP and the Qualcomm PureVoice.

The compression ratio alters the slope of the input/output transfer characteristic. The compressor will also have a gain control, as a compressed signal will sound louder than the uncompressed. The limiter prevents the output level exceeding a preset threshold.

Attack and release times

The dynamic range controls do not change gain instantaneously; that would just modulate the sound with its own level. Instead there is a delay before the control parameter is changed – the attack time – and another delay as the applied parameter is restored – the release time. The attack time is customarily very short, just a few milliseconds. It is long enough for brief transients; the limiter takes care of them. The release time is much longer, up to several

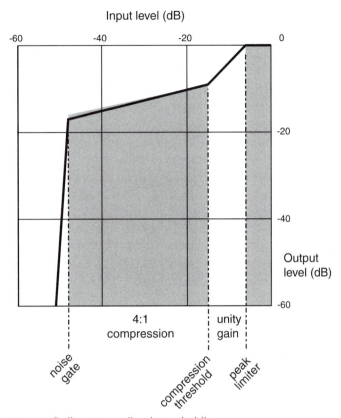

Figure 10.10 Compressor–limiter composite characteristics.

seconds. This prevents the modulation effects that you would get with a very short release time.

Usually all these controls are used together. The peak limiter is set to remove transients, then louder sounds are passed at unity gain. Below a set threshold, the quieter sounds are compressed to improve intelligibility. Everything below a lower threshold is treated as noise and gated out. This may seem like a lot of adjustment, but once you arrive at some good settings they can be stored for reuse with similar content.

Processing applications

Typical streaming media encoder applications include many facilities to pre-process audio. Some are implemented in software, some in hardware. The hardware products are best if you want real-time processing for live webcasts. A good example of a comprehensive encoding package is Discreet's Cleaner.

Discreet Cleaner

Cleaner is not just a clean-up tool. It has all the facilities to take raw content and publish to the streaming servers. It processes both the video and audio. Cleaner 6/XL can perform the basic de-interlace and reverse telecine on the video. The signal levels and color can be adjusted and the noise cleaned up. The adaptive noise reducer uses spatio-temporal processing to clean up flat areas of color without degrading the edges of objects.

Figure 10.11 Discreet Cleaner 6 audio controls. © Autodesk Inc.

Cleaner 6/XL also has powerful audio processing capabilities. The product has a wide range of filters, including high- and low-pass filters with adjustable turnover frequencies. It has control of dynamic range, and a noise removal filter to reduce unwanted background noise. A useful addition is the deep notch filter that can be set to remove power line hum, which is often a problem at live events. If you want to change the sampling rate of the audio, it can resample an input file. Cleaner can add reverberation to the audio to give a presentation the sound of a big auditorium. Once a file is processed it then can be encoded on the same platform.

Processing hardware

Preprocessing is not limited to software applications. Some manufacturers have hardware developed specifically to clean up video and audio. The dedicated hardware products process in real-time. Companies like Orban and Omnia have been making high-performance compressors for the radio business for many years, and now have products targeted at the webcasting market.

The Orban product line includes the Optimod-PC and the Opticodec-PC. The Optimod is a PCI card with on-board DSP that gives automatic gain control (AGC), equalization, multiband gain control, and peak-level control. The Opticodec is a complete solution for compression and encoding aimed at the Internet radio station. The preprocessing includes AGC, multiband dynamics compression, and look-ahead limiting. For data compression, it uses the aacPLUS codec from Coding Technologies.

An alternative vendor is Omnia, a division of Telos Systems. The Omnia-3net digital audio processor is designed especially for the webcaster and has AGC, limiting, and multiband processing.

Monitoring

It is vital that you monitor the results of any audio processing before the file is encoded. Although big monitor speakers will make the audio sound impressive, it is worth listening to some of the small speakers often used with desktop workstations – this is what your audience is probably using.

Summary

Noise is a killer for codecs. So before encoding, it makes sense to try and clean up as much of the noise as possible. That way you can ensure that you have the optimal encoding for a given stream bandwidth. This noise reduction applies equally to both video and audio.

The preprocessing products have a veritable toolbox of noise filters to deal with the different types of noise that you will encounter with different sources. The sparkle from a satellite link will need a different treatment from the tape noise from an analog VCR.

Video requires additional processing to remove some of the characteristics of the television system. This includes interlace scanning and the 3:2 cadence of content originally shot on film then transferred to video by a telecine. To cut down unnecessary data, the outside edge of a television picture usually can be cropped without losing relevant content. Television frame composition allows for over-scanning in the television receiver, not a problem with PCs. Some color correction also may be used; the rendering of color is different from the composite television systems.

The audio usually will benefit from dynamic range compression as well as noise reduction. The dynamics compression will make speech much easier to understand when it is played back on a PC's small speaker. The processors work in three areas: peaks are limited to avoid clipping, the general audio is compressed by an AGC, and then noise below a threshold is suppressed.

Last of all, do not forget to watch and listen to the stream after the selected treatments. It is the best way to judge the improvements that preprocessing can make to your streams.

11 Stream serving

Introduction

What happens once you successfully have encoded your multimedia content? Much like publishing a web page, the file is uploaded to the delivery server. That is where things diverge. A conventional web server simply downloads the media file. A streaming server has to manage the delivery rate of the stream to give real-time playback. In addition, the streaming server supports VCR-like control of the media clip.

When a browser requests a web page, the files are delivered as fast as the network connection allows. TCP manages an error-free transmission by retransmitting lost packets, but the download time depends upon the intervening bandwidth available. TCP starts at a low rate then ramps up to the maximum that can be achieved. An accurate delivery is ensured, but timely delivery cannot be guaranteed. Streaming media has opposite requirements: the delivery must be in real-time, but reasonable levels of transmission errors can be accepted.

Streaming servers can be proprietary to an architecture or designed to handle standard formats like MPEG-4. The system architecture can vary from a single machine serving a small corporate training site, to large distributed server farms, capable of serving hundreds of thousands of streams for live events like breaking news footage, fashion shows, and rock concerts.

Streaming can be delivered as a push or pull process. Push is used to stream live or prerecorded content as a webcast – this is the television model. Push streaming can be used for web channels or live events. Alternatively, the user can pull prerecorded content on-demand. This interactive experience is akin to using a CD-ROM or a web browser.

A webcast can be a mix of live and prerecorded content. With live events the server is acting as a distribution point, just echoing the stream onto the viewers. For the prerecorded content the server has two functions. The first is to recall the content from the local disk storage arrays and the second is to control the stream delivery rate.

In the case of interactive content the client or player is requesting the files from the server. With the simulated-live webcast, the server runs a playlist, which streams files at the scheduled time to the player.

Table 11.1 Web Server versus Streaming Server

	Web server	*Streaming server*
Advantages	Part of existing infrastructure No additional expertise or training for IT staff	Optimized media delivery Dynamic stream control Interactive media control Multicast support Improved server hardware utilization Supports live webcasting
Disadvantages	None of the streaming server advantages Only supports progressive download	Additional equipment required

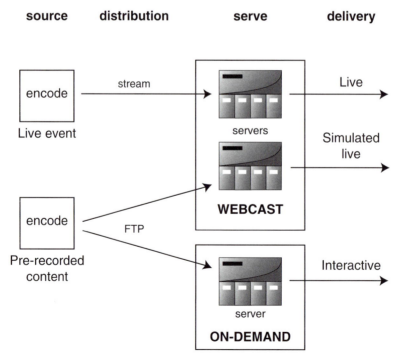

Figure 11.1 Webcasting and on-demand.

Streaming

What is a streaming server? The most-used server for the delivery of multimedia content is the web server, typified by Apache. Web servers use HTTP over TCP/IP to deliver HTML pages and their associated image files.

TCP/IP is used as the transport layer over the Internet. The files are downloaded to the web browser cache as fast as the system allows. TCP incorporates flow control to manage the download rate. There is no predetermined rate for delivery. TCP will increase the data rate until network packet loss indicates that the network is congested. At this point, the rate backs off. Another constraint is the receive buffer. TCP uses a sliding window of data in transit. The receiver processes packets as they arrive. If data arrives too fast, the receive buffer will overflow. The receiver sends messages to the transmitter to slow down, to stop the buffer from filling.

Suppose that you want to stream a stream encoded at 40 kbit/s. The TCP transmissions could start at 10 kbit/s. The transmitter then ramps up to 100 kbit/s, where network congestion sets the upper limit. Suppose other users come on to the network, and the transmission throttles back to 30 kbit/s. At no time has the data rate matched the data rate at which the stream was encoded.

Now consider if this clip lasts for 30 seconds, the complete file size is 150 kbytes. This is downloaded to the browser cache – not a great problem. Now suppose we move up to a 20-minute presentation encoded at 300 kbit/s. Now the file size is 45 Mbytes – very large for the cache. This has been the way that the Flash player handled video files, but Flash was limited to short clips.

When you stream content in real-time, the media packets are processed by the player as they arrive. There is no local caching, so the local storage issues are solved. This may not seem an issue to PC users, but many media players have very limited memory, for example set-top boxes and mobile devices. The problem with Flash also has gone, Macromedia now has developed the Flash player to support streaming of longform video, and the content is rendered then discarded.

There is still the rate control problem. If the stream is encoded at 40 kbit/s it must be delivered at that rate for satisfactory viewing. One of the functions of the transport layer protocol is to regulate the stream rate. But what happens in the example where the network is congested and the best rate is 30 kbit/s? The player runs out of data and stops, one of the main complaints about streaming.

There are ways around this, but the first is to encode at a rate below that which will suit the worst-case network conditions. That may be hard to predict, so there are more sophisticated ways; the usual is to encode at several rates, then automatically select the optimum rate for the propagation conditions. This switching between different rate files is another task for the server.

One of the great attractions of streaming is the interactivity. The user can navigate the clip with VCR controls. The server has to locate and serve the correct portions of the clip using an index.

From these examples, it can be seen that the streaming server has several additional functions over a standard web server:

- Real-time flow control
- Intelligent stream switching
- Interactive clip navigation

HTTP does not support any of this functionality, so new protocols were developed for streaming media. Under the auspices of the IETF several new protocols were developed for multimedia real-time file exchange: RTSP, RTP, and RTCP. There are also a number of proprietary protocols using similar principles. Windows Media originally used the Microsoft Media Server (MMS) for the delivery framework (but now supports RTSP); the stream is in Advanced System Format (ASF).

Real-Time Streaming Protocol (RTSP) is the framework that can be used for the interactive VCR-like control of the playback (Play, Pause, etc.). It is also used to retrieve the relevant media file from the disk storage array. RTSP also can be used to announce the availability of additional media streams in, for example, a live webcast. Real-Time Protocol (RTP) is used for the media data packets. The Real-Time Control Protocol (RTCP) provides feedback from the player to indicate the quality of the stream. It can report packet loss and out-of-order packets. The server can then react to congested network conditions by lowering the video frame rate or gear-shifting to a file encoded at a lower bit rate. The real-time media stream can be delivered by UDP or TCP over IP; the choice depends upon propagation conditions. The control protocols use TCP/IP for the bidirectional client–server connection.

Streaming file formats

To stream media files in real-time, they must be wrapped by one of the streaming formats. These formats have timing control information that can be used by the server to manage the flow rate. If the client is using interactive control, the file index aids the navigation.

The main formats are MPEG-4 (mp4), the Microsoft advanced system format (.wmv and .wma extensions if created by Windows Media codecs, .asf if not), RealNetworks (.rm and .ra), and QuickTime hinted movies (.mov extension).

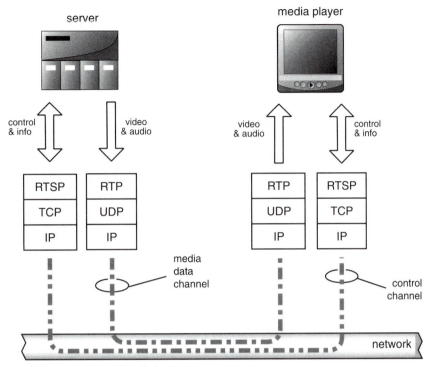

Figure 11.2 The streaming protocol stack.

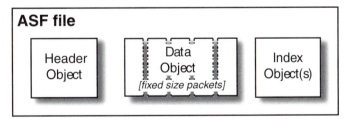

Figure 11.3 Typical streaming file format.

Web server and streaming server

If you already have a web site with web server capacity, and you stream only occasionally, it is possible to use that web server to deliver streaming files. The web server will use HTTP over TCP/IP. There will be no control of the stream delivery rate beyond buffer overflow in the TCP/IP stack.

Hint tracks

The MPEG-4 team has adopted the QuickTime concept of hint tracks for control of the stream delivery. A streaming file is called a movie. The movie file container contains tracks, which could be video, audio, or other clip data. The track consists of control information that references the media data (or objects) that constitute the track. This means that several different movie files could reference the same video media object. This can be very useful for rich media presentations. One video file can be repurposed into several different presentations – maybe multiple languages or a number of levels of detail (introduction, overview, and in-depth). A movie is not the video and audio media files; it is the metadata or instructions for a specific presentation of the media data. The files are flattened into a single file when the stream is encoded.

A streamable movie has a hint track in addition to the video and audio (MPEG-4 files are not limited streaming media applications). The hint track gives the server software pointers to the RTP information in order to serve the relevant media chunks. This information allows the server to deliver the correct video material in the sequence stipulated in the track file, and at the correct rate for the player display.

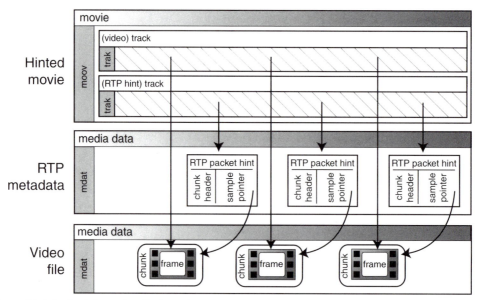

Figure 11.4 Typical streaming file format.

Adapting to network congestion

Both RealNetworks and Windows Media offer a way of changing the bit rate of a stream as network congestion varies. To get the best viewing experience we want to stream at the highest rate possible. But if the network slows down, rather than attempting to continue with a high bit rate, it makes sense to throttle back the bit rate. If the congestion eases then the bit rate can revert to a higher level. That way the viewer is not subject to stalling streams, just a graceful degradation in quality. These technologies work only with unicasting.

The Real-Time Protocol maintains the correct delivery rate over UDP/IP (or TCP/IP if bandwidth permits). The RTSP framework supports the client interaction with the stream, the VCR-like controls Play, Pause, and so on. The streaming server application can use RTCP reports from the player to measure network congestion and switch stream rates for multiple bit rate media files. The player can report lost and delayed packets, and the reception of out-of-sequence packets.

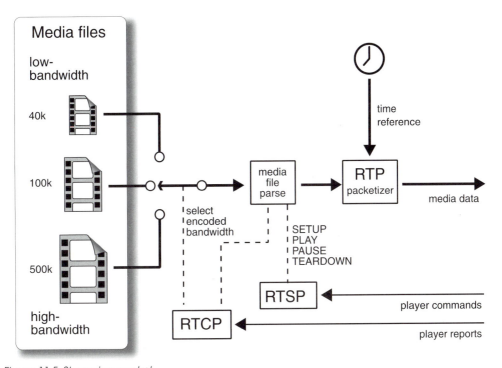

Figure 11.5 Streaming control.

RealNetworks SureStream

SureStream allows different encoding rates to be combined into a single media file. The streaming server will choose the appropriate data rate for the prevailing conditions by negotiating with the player. The lowest rate, called a duress stream, is a backstop, and will be streamed if congestion is very bad. When you are calculating the server disk space, a SureStream file takes the space of the sum of all the components. Because only the Helix Server can extract the correct component, a web server will serve the file in its entirety, including all the different rates.

Windows Media Intelligent Streaming

This is a similar feature, allowing multiple constant bit rate streams to be encoded and wrapped in a single file. The streaming server will then stream the best rate for the current network conditions. Windows Media Encoder comes with predefined multiple bit rate profiles, but the profiles also can be customized to suit your special requirements. If you want to multicast a file that has been coded at multiple bit rates, only the highest rate will be transmitted.

Drawbacks

If you want to serve at different rates, then better results can be obtained by encoding a small picture at low frame rates for low bit rate streams, and a larger picture for streams at higher rates. So you may want a 480 × 360 pixel frame at 30 fps for a 1 Mbits/s stream and 160 × 120 at 6 fps for an ISDN link. Multiple bit rate encoding has to use the same picture size, so that the player can switch seamlessly between the different rates. The automatic rate-shifters have their uses, but are not a complete answer to serving the same content over very different networks. The big advantage is that the process of changing bit rate is invisible to the user.

QuickTime and alternate movies

This is a less sophisticated method of offering different bit rates. You can encode a movie as several separate movies encoded at different bit rates, and maybe with different language audio tracks. These are the alternates: The player follows a pointer to the master movie, which then references the alternate movies. The player negotiates with the server to request the correct alternate file for the player settings.

MPEG-4 and scalable streams

The MPEG team has proposed a different way to cope with variable network bandwidth. The server transmits a basic low-resolution stream. Additional helper streams can carry more detail. If the bandwidth is available then these extra streams allow a better quality picture to be assembled by the player.

MPEG-4 also supports scalable encoding. This means that a basic player may decode only part of the stream to create the video, albeit at a lower quality than a more complex player, which can decode and display all the stream information.

Loading content

Whether you are using a managed service or doing your own serving, the first step is to deliver your content to the streaming servers. The encoding probably takes place near the video editing facility or, for a live webcast, at the venue. The servers have to be located close to an Internet backbone, unless you are streaming only over a local area. So in all probability the encoder and server are separated geographically. The simplest way to deliver the content is via a file transfer, using FTP. Some encoding systems have the ability to transfer a file automatically, immediately after the encoding has finished.

Live streaming

The file can, of course, be sent on a CD-ROM. If the content is a live broadcast, then neither of these methods is suitable; it has to be streamed. This is covered in the chapter on live webcasts.

The media encoder typically connects to the server using TCP for a bidirectional control link and a unidirectional media stream, using UDP. It is very important that the circuit used for this connection has more than sufficient bandwidth and a high QoS; that means low packet loss and timing jitter. Any data loss or corruption will be visible by all receivers of the webcast. This generally means using an uncontended circuit like T-1/E-1, rather than a domestic circuit like ADSL or a cable modem.

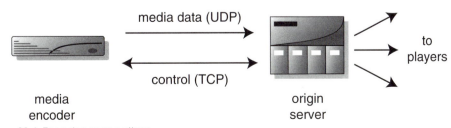

Figure 11.6 Encoder connections.

Announcing the content

The player usually locates streaming media by a hyperlink embedded in a web page. This link contains not only the URL for the content, but also the instructions to start the media player.

Web links

The usual way to announce streaming media files is by a hyperlink in a web page. The link points to a small file on the web server. Windows Media calls this the stream redirector, or ASX. Real uses the RealAudio Metafile or Ram file. Once the browser receives this file, using the MIME type, the metafile is passed to a streaming plug-in. The metafile has the full address and filename for the streaming content. The media player than transmits a request to the specified streaming server for the media file. This may use MMS or RTSP for communication rather than the HTTP used with the web server. If all goes well the correct clip is streamed to the player – success.

The metafiles can list several files to be played in sequence.

SMIL

If you are streaming rich media, then a number of different clips and images have to be synchronized for correct playback at the client. One way to do this is to use the Synchronized Multimedia Integration Language (SMIL) to write a control file.

SMIL is supported by the QuickTime, Real, and Windows Media architectures.

Webcasting

Webcasting can be live, prerecorded, or a mix of both. A webcast at its simplest can be just a single clip. If you want to play out a sequence of clips you can set up a playlist. Even if you are streaming a presentation, you may want an introductory promotional film, and possibly some follow-up material after the main presentation. The playlist controls the server to play the relevant clips at the specified time.

Splitting and relays

A streaming server can handle several hundred simultaneous clients. The only real way to establish how many clients would be by conducting load tests. To

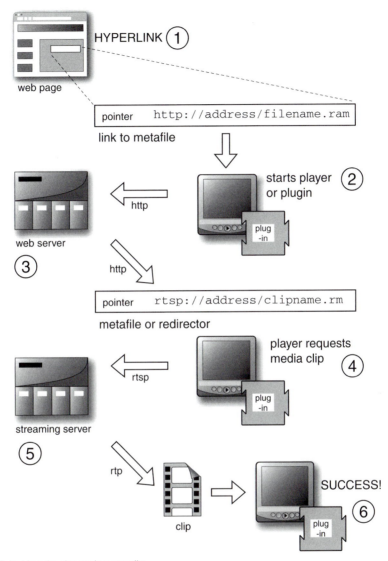

HYPERLINK ①

| pointer | http://address/filename.ram |

link to metafile

starts player ②
or plugin

web server

③

| pointer | rtsp://address/clipname.rm |

metafile or redirector

player requests
media clip ④

streaming server

⑤

SUCCESS!

⑥

clip

Figure 11.7 Linking to streaming media.

serve to a large number of clients, extra servers have to be used. For on-demand serving, they can be added in parallel, but for live streams a different architecture is used to save network resources. A relay server splits the live streams downstream, so what starts as a single live stream from the encoder fans out like the branches of a tree. Take the example of a CEO's webcast from the headquarters on the west coast to two other remote sites on the south and east coasts.

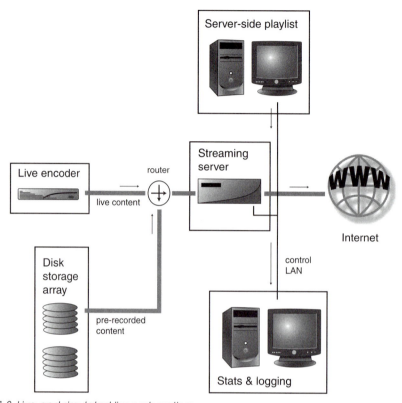

Figure 11.8 Live and simulated-live webcasting.

If only a few clients were watching at the remote sites, the streams could be delivered directly from the server at headquarters. But each client will be using bandwidth on the trunk networks, all carrying the same data. If a large number of clients at each site are watching the webcast, the server will be unable to handle the load. The alternative is to use local servers at the remote sites to receive a single stream, and then locally distribute it. This saves bandwidth on the long-distance circuits and reduces the load on the originating server.

You may be thinking that this is a really important broadcast, what happens if the link goes down? Companies like RealNetworks have come up with a number of solutions.

RealNetwork's Helix Universal Server includes the facility to set up backup links. You set up redundant transmitters, usually two servers in parallel. If the link from the designated transmitter breaks, the receiving server automatically falls back to the next available transmitting server. The clients will see the webcast has stopped; if they refresh the link, the stream will continue using the backup path.

Multicasting

If you are webcasting live to a large audience, a regular unicast establishes a separate network connection to each client. This uses considerable network resources, even though each client is watching exactly the same material. Multicasting offers a solution by serving a single stream. This is then routed to all the clients. So the network routers are doing the distribution rather than the streaming servers.

The drawback with multicasting is that you need to have control over the routers. First they have to be multicast enabled, which is not necessarily the case. There are different algorithms for setting up multicast routes: dense and sparse. If you are streaming over a corporate network within a single domain, multicasting has much to offer. It is when you want to multicast to the public Internet that problems can arise. The network of peer-to-peer connections that link a server to a client may not be multicast enabled, or the routers may not be set up to multicast across domains.

If you are multicasting you cannot use automatic rate changing. The server transmits a single stream and is not aware of the clients, so it cannot negotiate to serve at a certain rate. To get around this you may have to transmit three or four different rate streams from different server ports. The player connects to an appropriate port for the bandwidth available at their local end.

Multicast network

If you are setting up a multicast to several sites, and want to use Virtual Private Networks (VPN) for the intermediate connections across the corporate WAN, note that IPSec does not support multicasting. The way around this is to unicast to a splitter server at the remote site, then multicast locally. You will need to make sure that clients can see only one multicast server. Since the same IP address is used for the multicast, the client potentially could receive several duplicate packets. The player will not decode the stream correctly in these circumstances.

Announcing a multicast is different from retrieving on-demand content. With on-demand, the browser requests the media file. When the file is retrieved, the header carries information necessary for the player configuration. Once you join a multicast, there is no header. Instead, a small message file gives the browser/player the necessary information (like the port number to use). This message can use Session Description Protocol (SDP – RFC.2327); Microsoft uses the media station NSC file. The media station is analogous to a television station, so the station represents the channel and not the media streamed (programs transmitted) over the channel. The NSC configuration file will set up the player correctly to receive a multicast. The ASX file that announces a multicast points the player to the NSC file.

RealNetworks supports a form of multicasting with a control back-channel. This allows full statistics to be gathered from the clients, but has the advantage of multicasting the media data. It is best suited to small audiences; a very large multicast would have problems with the server capacity required to handle the unicast control traffic.

On-demand serving

On-demand serving is more like running a web server. The viewers choose their own content, and then a fast disk storage array delivers the content, as required, to the streaming servers. Each client has a unicast connection with the server, so the more viewers, the higher the server loading. A popular site will use many servers in parallel. The Internet traffic loading can be balanced across all the servers.

The server hardware does not need many facilities: a fast CPU, plenty of RAM, and at least two network-interface cards (NICs). If the server has very high loadings or there are network problems, you will need access by a separate network port for control messages, so always install at least two NICs. The system will be more reliable if the load is spread over several small servers, rather than one large multiple processor server. This also gives redundancy against hardware failure.

Inserting advertisements

If you are running a commercial site you will want to add advertisements to the content. They can be the same banner ads used on web pages. The alternative is to insert clips into the stream just like a regular television spot. This is called interstitial advertising.

The simplest way to place video advertising around an on-demand clip is to top-and-tail the content with preroll (gateway) and postroll ads (bumper) using an SMIL file (Synchronized Multimedia Integration Language) to play the clips serially. SMIL has a time container that can be programmed with a fixed sequence of media elements. The sequence command is used to place ads before and after clips. The player will run the playlist of content and advertisements as programmed. The viewer cannot step through the playlist manually to jump over the ads. An associated SMIL element, parallel, commands the group within the time container to run together. This ensures that the following clip is correctly prerolled to avoid any glitches as the playlist is running.

Windows Media Services offers two ways to deliver advertising and other interstitial material: with either a client playlist or the server-side playlist. The

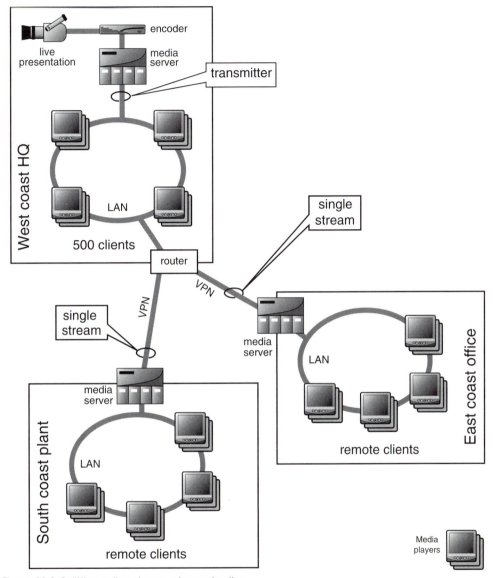

Figure 11.9 Splitting a live stream at remote sites.

client playlist cannot be changed once received, whereas the server-side allows dynamic changes to the playlist; for example, targeted ads. Windows Media use active server pages to generate dynamic playlists. RealServer can use a proprietary ad tag in the SMIL file (⟨RealAdInsert/⟩) to dynamically assign URLs to the advertisement clip. Since the advertisements may be changing hour to hour, this avoids the necessity to keep updating the SMIL file.

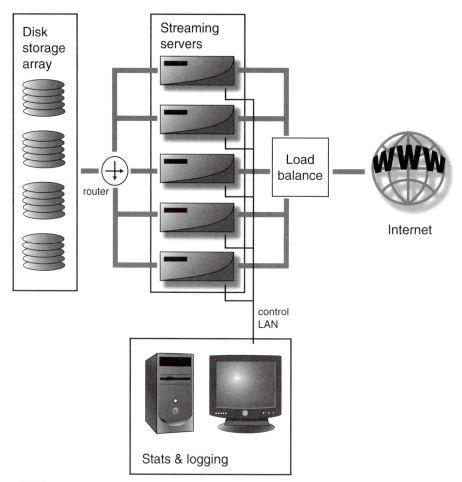

Figure 11.10 On-demand server farm.

In both cases the ad servers are linked to the streaming servers to generate the correct URLs. The ad servers often use solicited cookies to track users and ensure that targeted advertisements are used where possible. This means that a webcast, although streamed to a wide geographic area, can carry advertising that is local or relevant to the viewer.

Playlists

If you are streaming regular webcasts you will need a means of playing out clips to a prepared schedule. Just like a television station, clips can be put in playlists and streamed on cue. This means that corporate presentations and distance

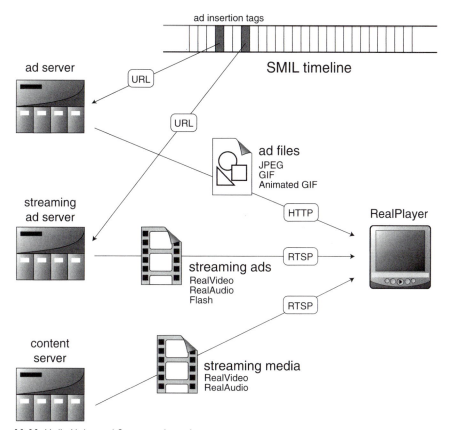

Figure 11.11 Helix Universal Server ad serving.

learning can be scheduled at fixed times. The viewer tunes in at the appropriate time to catch the required stream. Again SMIL can be used to program the playlist.

If you are using the Apple QuickTime Streaming Server, the administration terminal has a user interface for creating and editing playlists. This can be used for MPEG-4 or audio-only MP3 playlists.

Logging and statistics

So, you have set up a stream-serving infrastructure. But what is the return on the investment? With any system it is vital to monitor the traffic to the clients. This is partly to see who is watching what, and partly to find out the utilization of the servers and network elements. You will want to know who the clip's audience is, and perhaps more important, how many are watching the entire clips and how many watch only the first 10 seconds.

Playlist		duration
gateway	ident	00:30
program	segment 1	05:24
interstitial	spot 1	00:30
	spot 2	00:15
program	segment 2	09:37
bumper	closeout	00:15

Timeline

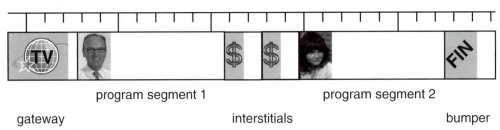

program segment 1   program segment 2

gateway   interstitials   bumper

Figure 11.12 Server playlists.

The monitoring can be performed at the client or at the server. The television model is to monitor activity at the receiver, like Nielson reporting. With streaming media, there is a back-channel from the player so server-side reporting also can be used.

Several companies have products that can collect server logs, and then process the data into reports. These include EnScaler, SyncCast, and Web-Trends. Arbitron specializes in audience measurement with their MeasureCast service. They use a combination of comprehensive server logging, and complement this with client-side statistics gathered from selected streaming media users. The client-side statistics can give more demographic information than the raw server data. The two are combined to provide comprehensive statistics for the webcasters.

The servers log can include basic information about the client such as client IP address, connection protocol (RTSP, HTTP), player version, operating system and version, language setting, and the CPU speed.

The logs also collect session information. This includes the time the request was logged and how long the stream was watched. You can see from the reports whether viewers watched all of a clip, or dropped out in the middle. It is also possible to see when user interactions were taken. So if an interactive presentation is being viewed, you can log whether the viewer has selected a hotspot link. It is possible to turn off this reporting on the players for users concerned about privacy.

More detailed information also can be collected about the transmission quality packet loss, number of resends, and how many packets arrived out of order, early or late.

This information for a single client is collated with other client access logs into viewing statistics for content producers and service quality for network administrators. Some of the statistics that can be collected are:

- Number of concurrent streams
- Number of hits
- Time spent viewing content
- Amount of content delivered
- Number of unique viewers

Logging software will collect information from unicasts, but if you are multicasting, the server will not be aware of the clients (unless you are using RealNetworks back-channel multicasting). The only way you can identify clients is when they first log in to request the stream redirector (ASX or RAM file) from a web server.

One very useful statistic is the type of player being used and the stream bit rates. This information can be used to justify (or otherwise) the number of formats to encode. You may be able to drop one of the architectures because it has a very small audience, which will save you the costs of both the encoding and serving.

A typical example of a reporting package is WebTrends. Logs from all the different servers are collected and collated at a central point. The results are stored in a database, from where any number of reports can be generated for the interested parties.

Proprietary server architectures

Windows Media Services 9 Series

Microsoft's streaming server is bundled with Windows Server 2003 as Windows Media Services. Windows Media Server supports several different delivery mechanisms in a process of rollover. This is so that the streams can be delivered through corporate firewalls. With the release of Windows Media 9, Microsoft added support for RTSP as well as their proprietary MMS (Microsoft Media Server) protocol.

RTSP and TCP

This is the streaming mode of choice. This gives full support for real-time delivery, fast cache, and client interactivity. The fast cache allows the player to use the player buffer as a data cache to help average out network bandwidth variations (only with TCP).

RTSP and UDP

This is the fallback mode if RTSP and TCP are not supported by the player. Some network administrators set up the firewall to block UDP traffic, so this protocol cannot always be used.

HTTP and TCP

This is an alternative for firewalls that will allow regular HTTP web traffic. The Windows Media Services still provides controls like fast forward, reverse, and so on. The stream will suffer from the TCP retransmissions and rate adaptation.

The server will attempt to connect by each protocol in turn until a satisfactory dialog is established. Windows Media Services also support multicasting over IP.

Versions of Windows Media player prior to version 9 do not support RTSP, so has a further sequence of rollover starting with MMS and UDP. If UDP traffic is blocked, then HTTP will be used.

RealNetworks Helix Universal Server

RealNetworks offers the Helix Universal server for the distribution of RealVideo and RealAudio. It can also be used to stream Windows Media, QuickTime, and MPEG-4, hence the universal tag. The Helix server can be deployed on Windows and UNIX platforms (AIX, FreeBSD, Linux, Solaris, HP-UX).

The mobile version of the server adds a feature set for the delivery of 3GPP content to wireless players.

RTSP and TCP

This is used for the control connection. It gives full client–server interactivity.

RTP and UDP

This is the optimum choice for streaming the media content.

RTP and TCP

This is second choice for streaming the media content if the firewall blocks UDP data.

HTTP and TCP

This can be used for progressive downloads if no other delivery is possible. The media file is wrapped with the HTTP format, a process called HTTP cloaking.
   RealServer supports SMIL for rich media presentations.

Apple QuickTime

QuickTime started as a CD-ROM format, and was developed for progressive downloads. True real-time streaming has been supported from QuickTime version 4. Apple adopted the RTP for streaming over UDP. If this is blocked by corporate firewalls the alternative is progressive download over HTTP. Apple has two solutions for streaming: one is the QuickTime 5 Streaming Server (QTSS) that is part of the Apple OS X Server, the other is the open source Darwin server.

Server deployment

Video server hardware

The streaming server has to read the media files from disk, packetize it, and deliver at the correct rate to give real-time playback. These tasks then have to be performed for multiple concurrent streams. The real-time requirement contrasts with the asynchronous operation in a regular office server application. In the latter case, at times of peak resource demand, file delivery is delayed. With a video stream this would result in stalling playback.
   As the performance of server components improves with time, it is becoming easier to meet the demands of streaming.
   The areas to focus upon include:

- Disk drive performance
- Network card performance; it can be advantageous to use multiple cards for streaming and control

- The system and I/O bus bandwidths
- Symmetrical multiprocessor CPUs
- The stripping out of unnecessary software services, leaving the resources for uninterrupted stream delivery
- System memory large enough to manage multiple high-speed streaming buffers

The basic configuration can be calculated from the bandwidths, but test and measurement will be required to determine the true capacity of a server configuration. To aid testing, Microsoft supplies a Load Simulator that can provide dummy loads during the server tests.

One way to get good performance is to scale wide, with many small servers, rather than one big multiprocessor server. This also makes the system more tolerant to faults; you can lose a single server from a cluster, without losing the whole site.

Once you have determined your available bandwidth, and how many users will connect to the system, you can then decide on a server design. You may want a separate staging server to test content before it is placed on the public server; alternatively, this could be a different directory.

Hosting

If you want high-performance streaming to large numbers of public clients you are going to need a fat pipe to the Internet backbone. If you do not want to install a T-3 line, the easiest way is to use a hosting facility or a content delivery network. The hosting providers usually are located at hubs of the Internet with intimate and very wide band connectivity to the backbone.

If you are running a web site, you already will have looked at the pros and cons of outsourcing the servers. Outsourcing has advantages from the point of view of physical security. The service providers usually are located in secure buildings, with standby power facilities, halon fire extinguisher systems, and multiple paths to the Internet backbone. If all the servers are remote from your corporate network, there are no issues with unauthorized access and firewall configurations. On the other hand, if your files contain confidential information you may want the servers on your own premises, managed by local staff. If you are using DRM with pre-encryption, this may not be so much of an issue.

The companies will offer a number of different services:

- Turnkey hosting
- Shared hosting
- Co-located hosting

Turnkey hosting is the simplest to implement; you upload your media files using FTP. Everything else is done for you.

Co-location gives you more control; you rent secure cages and install your own server plant. You get reliable power and connectivity. Your servers can be monitored by telnet from your own location.

Take care to study the service level agreement (SLA). Think carefully about the service you really need. Will your business suffer because of site outages? Can you work with more relaxed service reliability?

High availability

If you want to set up a system with high availability the system should be secure, reliable, and easy to maintain.

It may not be unusual for video servers to be called upon to serve up video content at any time, day or night, to anywhere on the globe. To achieve a higher level of system availability will require a fault-tolerant design. This may come in the form of redundant hardware such as power supplies, fans, or NICs, or in the form of redundant multiple server architectures. To minimize downtime, hot-pluggable components such as disk drives, power supplies, and fans are also desirable.

Security

Don't forget security when planning your systems. If you are streaming around the clock, and it becomes a core business service, then server outages could impact your business.

The security of your streaming provision is determined by many factors. There are the physical threats, like fire and theft. Redundant, mirrored server sites are a good way to deal with these issues. Then there are power outages – do you need uninterruptible power supplies?

If you are using a reputable hosting service, then most of these issues will be covered, but check the service level agreements.

The other threats come from hackers. If they can gain access to your servers they can wreak havoc. There are also the denial of service attacks. The best route is to call in a network security consultant to advise and audit your systems.

Authentication and authorization

Access to the origin server has to be restricted to authorized users. There are three types of users: the system administrators, the content creators uploading content, and the viewers of the content.

Authentication is used to verify the identity of a client. You may not want to know, in which case anonymous authentication can be used where no user name or password is required. Authorization then allows authenticated clients access to confidential information. A database can store lists of authorized users in the three categories. The users gain access by password.

If your media is of commercial value, or confidential, then some form of digital rights management provides much greater protection against unauthorized access to your content.

Summary

The streaming server is a type of content server that uses a special software application to deliver streaming media in real-time to the players. It differs from a normal web server in having constant flow control, rather than the rate-adaptive transmissions of TCP.

There are two types of transmission: live and on-demand. On-demand gives the interactivity that sets rich media applications apart from traditional video delivery systems. The user interaction is via an out-of-band bidirectional control channel.

The control channel can also control the streaming delivery rate to react to network congestion. By encoding material at several different rates, the server can select the appropriate stream for the prevalent conditions.

Streaming is usually over a one-to-one connection between the server and the client, called a unicast. The alternative option for a webcast is the multicast. The server transmits just one stream, and any number of clients can connect to the stream. This potentially saves network utilization, but has yet to be deployed universally across the Internet.

One of the most important aspects of managing a streaming system is the server logging. This is where you can measure the audience, and establish the return on your investment. It also provides vital information for the network administrators to tune the systems and identify possible bottlenecks.

The streaming server is an effective replacement for other means of delivering multimedia content that can offer lower costs, immediacy, and interactivity.

12 Live webcasting

Introduction

In some ways webcasting is no different from encoding back at the shop. The main issue is that you usually get only one shot at it, so everything must be carefully thought out in advance. There are some golden rules for webcasting:

- Capture clear audio.
- Minimize the camera movement.
- Check that the encoder CPUs are up to the task.
- Make sure the backhaul is secure.
- Make an archive copy.

And always take at least two of everything – just to make sure.

Most of the issues for live events relate to the available resources. Is there sufficient bandwidth to the publishing server? If you want to stream multiple formats at multiple bit rates, does the encoder have the necessary processing power? The codecs available have limits, but since CPU clock speeds have past 1 GHz, this is becoming less of an issue.

Planning a webcast

Perhaps the first thing to consider is: What is the requirement? Is it a single-format stream at one resolution, or will you need to produce several streams? This sets the requirements for the link. Once that is clear you can start planning the backhaul from the venue to the streaming servers.

The backhaul

If you are really lucky, it is a corporate presentation and everything is on a local network, right down to an Ethernet jack in the meeting room. If it is at a remote venue, that is when a site survey helps. Is there a T-1 line to the venue? Most convention centers and stadiums have very good telecommunications links, and their staff are well versed with hosting television crews and providing Internet access.

If you are webcasting from the middle of a field you may have to fall back on satellite backhaul. It is getting easier all the time to arrange this. Local television stations use them all the time for live news inserts. You have the advantage that you do not need the same bandwidth as broadcast television. There are services available from companies like DirecWay (Hughes Network Systems) for two-way IP connectivity. They use a VSAT (very small aperture terminal) dish to link up to the satellite. These antennae can be less than half a meter in diameter, so you do not have to call on a big uplink truck with a 4.5-meter C-band dish. The equipment is easy to use; the terminal equipment hooks up with a USB connector to the encoding PC.

If the webcast is very important it is best to have a backup, maybe a dual-ISDN line. A 56 kbit/s modem could suffice if it is an audio-only webcast. If you have the opportunity to use a cable modem, they do have drawbacks. The cable companies do not in general offer the same reliability as the telephone companies. The bandwidth is not guaranteed, as there could be contention at the node if there are a large number of other users on the same fiber.

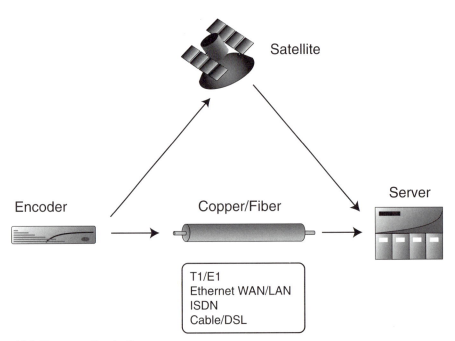

Figure 12.1 IP connection to the server.

Whatever you use, it is best to have a direct circuit to the server. If you use the Internet, you could get packet losses. That would distort the signal before it has even reached the distribution server.

You do not have to encode at the venue; you can backhaul the video and audio and encode back at base. It just needs more bandwidth to do it that way. If your event is being used for television, it would make sense to encode at base; the facilities are better and there is less to go wrong.

The rig

So you have planned what streams you want and how you are going to get them from the venue. The next step is planning the capture. For video you will need cameras and a video switcher. For audio, microphones and a mixing board. Plus there is ancillary equipment: video lighting, camera support (tripods), microphone stands, and lots of cable for power and for signals. Out in the field you will even need a generator.

Distribution and serving

Once the IP connection is established to the server, all you have to do is enter the IP address of the server, plus the port number and a log-in name and password.

If you are multicasting, have you got one of the special multicast addresses allocated? Did you check that the network supports multicasting? Do the expected clients support multicasting?

Publicity

Last of all, have you announced the webcast? Does the potential audience know where to link to the stream? If you sent out e-mails, were the data and time correct? Make sure the webmaster has the correct URL for the links, and then double-check on the day. You will not be popular if no one can find the webcast.

Logistics

Will you need to set up help-desk facilities to aid the viewers? They may have browser problems or connection difficulties. The networks have to be up to the task. If you are making corporate webcasts, the network may not have the capacity for multimedia traffic. If a wide-area network includes long-haul links, they may be running close to capacity. It may be necessary to use extra circuits to link directly to additional servers at remote sites.

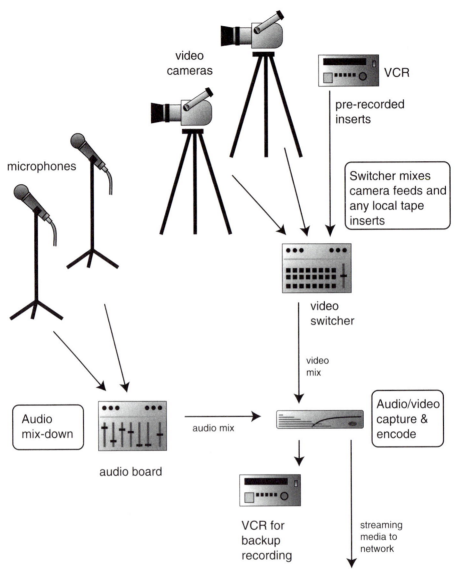

Figure 12.2 The live encode.

If the webcast includes e-mail feedback, you will need to set up the facilities to connect the encoding site into the net meeting.

Audio/video crew

Most of the set-up for a live webcast is all in a day's work for a technician from an audio/video facilities company. To employ such a company is probably the best way to undertake a big webcast. The only thing that is different from a normal live event or conference is managing the signal after the streaming encoder.

Video capture

If you are shooting for the Web, the production should reflect the final viewing experience. Just as the movie has panoramic shots and big sets, television is designed for a smaller screen, with close-ups and more domestic size sets. Webcasting has another set of rules. The images have to be simple and uncluttered. Keep close to the subject and avoid wide shots. The less motion there is, the better the encoding will be. Subject movement is difficult to avoid, but you can keep the camera still, very still. It is essential that the camera sit on a tripod wherever possible. If the camera has to move, use a dolly or a SteadiCam to keep the motion smooth. Try to avoid too many panning shots; the background smears into a blur at low bit rates. The more subject movement, the less spatial detail that can be transmitted.

The amount of movement is going to be dictated by the final bit rate. If the encoding is for distribution only over broadband circuits, then the camera operator is free to use more movement – it is, as always, a trade-off.

The camera

You may not be making a program for one of the networks, but a good camera will help with a clean signal. A three-chip CCD camera can be purchased at a very low price now, so there is no need to borrow the family's holiday camcorder. At the time of this publication, two good camcorders to consider are the Canon XL1S and the Sony DSR-PD170. Many camcorders have zoom lenses with built-in image stabilizers; these will take out the shakes from a hand-held shot. This can be very useful if you cannot use the camera on a tripod.

To connect the camera to the encoder there are several options. If the encoder is very close you can use an IEEE 1394 connection, but the cable length is limited to 4.5 meters. For longer distance you will have to use analog connections, ideally S-video, but as a last resort composite NTSC or PAL. If you are using professional cameras, you can opt for a digital hookup using the 270 Mbit/s SDI connection. This will not introduce any artifacts to the camera signal, and is the best choice if available.

Lighting

A camera will give a much better picture if the set is properly lit. I know that modern cameras can produce reasonable pictures by ambient domestic lighting, but you want the subject to stand out with some punch to the picture. The lighting should isolate the main subject from the background. A high light level will also avoid any camera noise intruding into the video picture.

So you should expect to use some video lighting equipment. Follow the usual rules of a key light to model the subject, a fill to limit the contrast, and background lighting for the rest of the scene.

Chroma key

If you are shooting a presenter against a blue screen so that they can be composited over a different background later, use the best tools. It is a very useful production technique, especially for a talking head. The Ultimatte products have long been the choice of videographers for this sort of work. You will need to take care with the lighting to get good results; it is best to use a crew who is used to the equipment.

Introductory splash

If viewers log in early to a webcast, maybe to check that everything is operating correctly, you will need some sort of splash screen so they can confirm that all is well. This can be a holding slide, or a short video clip. The encoder can be set up to stream this before switching on cue to the live webcast.

Graphics

If you want to add graphics to a streamed presentation they can conventionally be keyed into the video signal using a switcher. After they have been through the streaming codec they will be rather soft; at low bit rates they may be unreadable. An alternative is to deliver them as a separate synchronized stream. RealNetworks streams can carry synchronized text and Flash files. Windows Media can have a PowerPoint presentation synchronized to the video stream. These technologies will produce sharp, easily readable text to the viewer.

If you are going to use separate graphics files delivered from a web server, make sure it has the capacity if you are making the webcast to a large audience. Because the graphics are synchronized, all the players will request the file at the same instant.

Audio capture

You can watch poor quality video if the audio quality is good, but high-quality video with poor-quality audio is not acceptable. This is especially true for the talking head.

Mixing audio for the Web is a little different from mixing for music production or for television. For the Web, simple, clear sound is best. Background music might set the mood for a feature film, but for the Web it just gives the encoder more data to compress. We are used to listening to stereo audio, but for webcasting it is not usually important – it just uses bandwidth. It also eases the mixing if you have to produce only a mono signal.

If you are mixing a group of people you will have to ride the faders, shutting down the microphones for everyone except the current speaker. This will maximize the ratio of the speaker to background noise.

Microphone placement

The secret of a successful webcast is to aim for clear, intelligible sound throughout the presentation. The correct placement of microphones is critical in obtaining the optimum sound quality. No amount of equalization and dynamics processing is going to rescue a poor signal. The goal of microphone placement is to achieve the highest possible ratio of the level of speech to the ambient sound (background). Other factors may impede this goal – aesthetics may dictate microphone placement. How do they look from the camera?

The golden rule is, get as close as possible.

It is worthwhile buying expensive microphones. They are more rugged and have a much flatter frequency response. It is difficult to get a clean encode from the peaky response of a cheap microphone.

Microphones are categorized by their directional characteristics; some pick up sound equally, called omnidirectional, and others are biased to sound from one direction, called unidirectional or cardioid. You also can get microphones with a figure-eight or bidirectional pattern. The unidirectional are good for speakers, because they do not pick up the background noise from the audience.

Microphones come in many different styles:

Hand-held Some speakers like to hold the microphone, but it is more suited to the variety performer on television than the general presenter. You cannot use your hands for expression, to turn a script, to point at a slide.

Lavalier and clip-on These are good for standup speakers. They keep the microphone close to the mouth, yet are unobtrusive to the camera. They can pick up rustle from clothing if the speaker is moving around. The microphones have a special frequency response to compensate for the position on the chest; this can give an unnatural boom to the voice if not equalized.

Stand microphone These are good for speakers on a stage. Beware of the speaker who walks about; his or her voice will fade if he or she gets too far from the microphone.

Sportscasters' headsets They are unsightly in shot and really not suitable for most webcasts. They are a strictly practical choice for the sportscaster, so that they can hear the director's talkbalk over the roar of the crowd.

Rifle or shotgun These look impressive, but they are a last resort, when you cannot get close in. That's why they are used at ball games, to pick up the players.

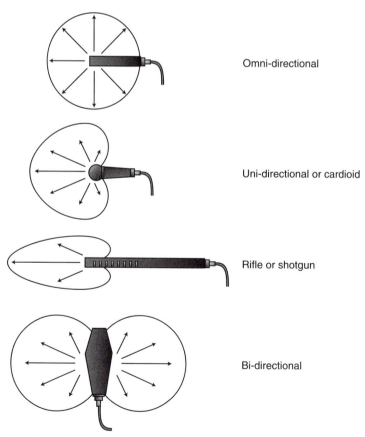

Omni-directional

Uni-directional or cardioid

Rifle or shotgun

Bi-directional

Figure 12.3 Directional characteristics of microphones.

There is no reason why you cannot use more than one microphone; in fact, this usually gives the best results. For example, use a tie-clip microphone and a stand mike, then mix the two to get the best sound.

One microphone to avoid at all costs is the camera-mounted mike. If you want to pick up the zoom lens motor, the tape transport, and the cameraman coughing they are just fine. They are meant for news-gatherers working in tight spots.

A windshield is often useful. If you are outdoors, they are obligatory to avoid wind noise.

Radio microphones

One problem with microphones is always the cables; they get in the way and they can get in view of the camera. The way around this is to use a radio microphone. This avoids the issues with trailing cables, but introduces a new set of problems. As a speaker moves around, the signal can fade or even disappear. The way around this is to use several receiving antennae. A special receiver, called a diversity receiver, picks out the best signal and uses that. This will give excellent results, albeit at a price.

Backup

Microphones and their cables get a lot of physical abuse, and as a result are prone to unexpected failure. So it makes sense to provide redundant equipment. For important webcasts, for example a company's quarterly call, the show is not going to wait while the sound crew fixes the equipment. Important speakers should have two microphones, and spares should always be on hand. A company president's time costs far more than a microphone.

Encoding

Live encoding is different from encoding back at the shop. It has to be real-time. Often if you want to encode to many different formats, the encoder can sit rendering the video until the streaming files emerge some time later. With a live webcast, you must have the horsepower in the CPUs to process the streams as they come out of the camera. If you are streaming multiple formats, make sure the equipment is up to it: do thorough testing before you get to the venue. Some low bit rate encoding can use more CPU resource than higher bit rates, so the processing power required is not directly related to the bandwidth. If the CPU utilization exceeds 75 percent you have no safety margin for the live encode. If you are encoding several streams, split the load between multiple encoders.

In the late 1990s, if you wanted to webcast you had to build your own encoder, with a desktop PC and video card. For road use at live venues what you need is a rugged rack mount box. Today there are several such products. A typical example is the Digital Rapids StreamZ.

Digital Rapids StreamZ

The StreamZ product family from Digital Rapids is a range of encoders that can be used for live streaming. The different models offer analogue and digital inputs, with input modules for IEEE 1394 DV signals and regular SDI digital video, and analog composite and S-video.

There is a choice of single processor, or dual processor for sufficient resources to encode Real and Windows Media streams simultaneously. The Digital Rapids media processing engine (MPE) optional dual-power supplies give redundancy. The StreamZ is especially suited to the demands of live encoding. The StreamZ supports most popular encoding formats including MPEG-1, MPEG-2, MPEG-4, and the proprietary streaming architectures Windows Media 9, Real Helix, Quicktime 5 and 6, and DivX.

Figure 12.4 Digital Rapids StreamZ encoder. © Digital Rapids Corporation.

One feature that makes it handy for webcasting is the Digital Rapids media processing engine (MPE). This relieves the CPUs of de-interlacing and noise reduction tasks and also provides comprehensive audio processing tools including a dynamic range processor and parametric equalization. The controller lets you set up preset configurations for rapid set-up on the road.

On-site file archive

A live stream can be archived to a local disk, for on-demand playback at a later date. A local copy of the streaming file also provides security against failure of the outgoing telecommunications circuit, perhaps the greatest risk during a live event. A second backup can be a conventional videotape of the encoder feed.

Summary

Streaming offers a new way to distribute a live presentation to remote viewers. The previous alternative was to rent a satellite transponder for a live television hookup. Only the larger enterprise had the budget for this technology. Now any business with an IP network can distribute live audio and video for a modest outlay.

With a live webcast you get only one shot, so good planning is essential. Make sure that the network is up to it. If you are using a corporate network, check in advance for potential bottlenecks. If you want to multicast, check that the network routers and the clients support multicasting. If you need to stream several different formats, it would be prudent to test the encoder capabilities before the event. And do not forget, it takes only one vital cable to be missing, and the show does not go to air (or to the Web).

Just because an event is live does not mean production standards should be relaxed. To get the best quality webcast, you need to capture stable pictures and clear audio.

Much of what I have said in this chapter will come as second nature to the experienced event organizer. It is no different from providing video and sound reinforcement facilities for a rock concert or a product launch.

13 Media players

Introduction

The media player is the public face of streaming media, the equivalent of the television receiver. The original media player was a software application for the PC, to be used like a Web browser. Now streaming has become a popular way to deliver multimedia content; we see players in mobile devices and in home entertainment products like the set-top box. In these devices, the player even may be embedded on silicon chips.

The personal computer users could have three or more players installed to provide support for different codecs. Apart from the odd software update to get the latest version, we are unaware of the mechanics of the players.

For the content creator the player may be the simplest part of the end-to-end chain, but without it your content cannot be seen. This is where streaming departs from television. We expect our television to display all broadcasts, but imagine if you transmitted NTSC in Europe. Your audience would be zero. To distribute content by streaming, you have to deal with the problem that there is no universal player. Potential viewers may be unable to view your streams. MPEG-4 promises to deliver a universal delivery mechanism, but the safest way to ensure the widest audience is to encode for different players. A corporate intranet may have the luxury of a single player on every desk, but webcasting to the public must deal with diversity.

The designers of the architectures have made their players robust, and fool-proof to deploy. You rarely will have to be concerned about the set-up of a player, except perhaps setting configurations to transmit streams through corporate firewalls.

To make sure that you have the largest possible audiences for your streams, it must be easy for viewers to install the player. By its very nature, the player should not intrude between the content and the viewer. The ideal player should have the following characteristics:

- Free of charge
- Automatic installation
- Compact software executable
- No configuration
- Invisible software upgrades
- Modest use of processor resources

In general, a proprietary architecture needs a proprietary player. This naturally has limited the number of streaming formats, weeding out all but a few. Nobody wants his or her PC cluttered with 10 different players; ideally we would want to install only one.

The leaders have been Real, as the pioneers of the technology, and Microsoft, with a huge installed OS base. QuickTime also has very wide usage. It has been tough for other players to compete against the brutal realities of the marketplace. MPEG-4 is gaining ground, especially for mobile devices.

The players are available in different versions for different operating systems, but if you are running Linux, for example, you may be excluded from viewing streams created by the proprietary architectures.

Portals, players, and plug-ins

Players can be used in three different ways: as a content portal, a player, or a plug-in to a Web browser. Real and Windows Media players can be used as portals to streaming media content.

The player can be used as a basic player – just open the file and play. The third way is to use the player as a plug-in to a Web browser. The streaming is then treated as an integral part of a synchronized rich media experience. The plug-in is the method of choice for rich media. Text and graphics can be combined seamlessly with the video stream into a unified presentation using SMIL (Synchronized Multimedia Integration Language) to synchronize the elements.

The new international standard, MPEG-4, has changed the status quo. We now can see a universal architecture that can be applied to any number of media viewers from the cell phone up to high-definition video displays.

Typical player

Players share a number of features, although the exact details vary from vendor to vendor. First there is a video display area. This can be resized, using interpolation to scale up pictures if a large screen size is set. The VCR-style controls enable viewer interactivity. Hot spots on the display area can also be used – much like a web page – to link to alternative content. A status display shows

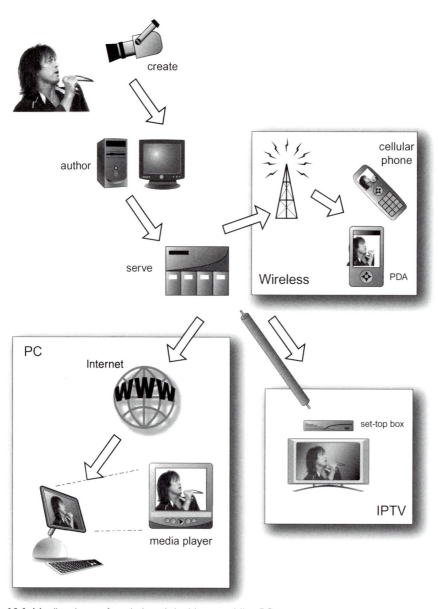

Figure 13.1 Media players for wireless, television, and the PC.

Figure 13.2 Windows Media player with the integrated media guide. Screen shot reprinted by permission from Microsoft Corporation.

Figure 13.3 Media player and plug-in to web browser.

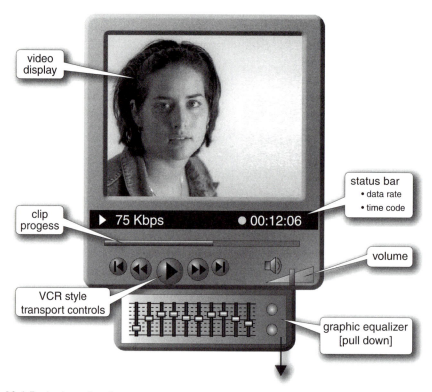

Figure 13.4 Typical media player.

time code and data stream rate. The players may have additional controls for the audio (graphic equalizer) and video (brightness, contrast, color).

Players and plug-ins

A player can be used standalone or as a plug-in for a browser; each has its merits. The browser-based approach is suited to rich media application. Just as a browser renders images and text into a unified display, the media player plug-in makes video just another component in the display.

The player is called with an HTML<embed> command or as an ActiveX object. The control line launches the plug-in. Parameters can control the size and appearance; you want just the video display, or you may want to embed the full player in the page. If you are using the straight rectangular video display the transport controls (Play, Pause) also can be embedded.

Against this approach is the checkered history of browsers. Authoring content that has the same layout and functionality on all the different browsers and different operating systems has proved quite a challenge. This has been a consequence of the development of HTML. The standard was the language. The MPEG-4 standard has taken the opposite approach, by specifying the player. That route guarantees a consistent look for content.

The standalone player treats a stream more like a CD-ROM or a DVD. The player is dedicated solely to the playback of streams. Rich media is still possible; the Real player can render Flash vector graphics, text, and pictures.

MPEG-4 players

The MPEG-4 player potentially can offer the content creator much greater flexibility in the formats it can handle. Whereas a conventional media player is limited to streaming audio and video, and possibly still images and Flash animation, the MPEG-4 player can render a wide variety of two- and three-dimensional objects. The object can be natural (like rectangular video objects) or synthetic (like avatars).

The incoming media files are decompressed as audio-visual objects. The objects are layered in the correct order as specified in the scene descriptor. The MPEG-4 player then processes the video objects into two-dimensional representations appropriate to the player's point of view. This representation is then rendered to the video display. A similar process applies to the audio objects, the only difference being that the objects are mixed rather than layered. The

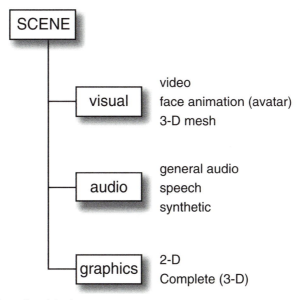

Figure 13.5 MPEG-4 media objects.

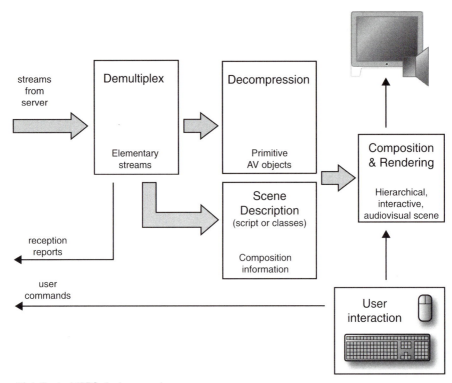

Figure 13.6 Basic MPEG-4 player system.

standard supports the ability to change the viewpoint of three-dimensional objects, although existing players do not offer this facility.

Proprietary players

The majority of players in use today are part of a proprietary architecture. The players are multipurpose in that they can function as a media portal, a stand-alone player, or a plug-in to a web browser. The players can all play files from the local storage, hard drive, or CD-ROM, or from a stream. Some suppliers sell a version of the player with extended facilities (the basic version being a free download). Typical extras include an audio graphic equalizer and controls for the video display, like contrast and brightness. In the case of QuickTime, the Pro version adds authoring capability.

QuickTime

Apple QuickTime player has been enhanced beyond its original functionality for playing CD-ROMs. It now has full support for streaming media. The player

video object

graphic object

navigation objects

info

buy

graphic object

video objects

composite scene
rendered by player

info

buy

Figure 13.7 MPEG-4 player rendering video objects.

Apple
QuickTime™ player
version 6.5

Microsoft
Windows Media™ player
version 9

RealNetworks
RealOne Player™
version 9

Figure 13.8 Popular media players: QuickTime 6, Real One player, and Windows Media 9.

installs with a Picture Viewer that can display still images. The QuickTime Pro version can save movies, create slide shows, and add soundtracks.

RealPlayer

The RealPlayer has changed from a straight player to media portal. RealPlayer 8 was superseded by the version 9 RealOne Player. This player also can be used as a music store and to listen to Internet radio through the subscription-funded RadioPass. CD-burning is supported, as are downloads to portable music players.

Earlier players supported most operating systems. The RealOne player is aimed at the consumer, and is available in two versions for Windows and Mac OS X. UNIX and Linux users can use the legacy RealPlayers with RealVideo codec upgrade. When it is finished, the open source Helix player will provide support for the Real formats including RealVideo 10 for UNIX and Linux users.

Real also supply players for mobile users, with support for Symbian OS, Palm OS 5, and PocketPC for PDAs. The RealPlayer also can be used with some Nokia cell phones.

Windows Media player

The Windows Media 9 player is available as a stand-alone player, but its true strengths come when it is integrated into a web browser. The player then

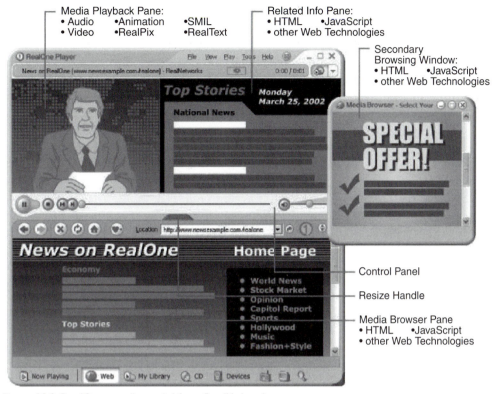

Media Playback Pane:
• Audio   •Animation   •SMIL
• Video   •RealPix   •RealText

Related Info Pane:
• HTML   •JavaScript
• other Web Technologies

Secondary
Browsing Window:
• HTML   •JavaScript
• other Web Technologies

Control Panel

Resize Handle

Media Browser Pane
• HTML   •JavaScript
• other Web Technologies

Figure 13.9 RealOne media portal from RealNetworks.

becomes the rendering engine for video content referenced from an HTML file. So the emphasis here is on rich media, linking video and audio, with conventional web text and images, and also with PowerPoint presentations.

Java players

A number of companies have developed players based on lightweight Java applets, sometimes called 'playerless' players. One, HotMedia, is part of IBM's WebSphere product. Clipstream Video from Clipstream Technologies is another typical example of a Java solution.

Television set-top boxes

Streaming is not just for PCs. New designs for set-top boxes now can display an IP stream as well as conventional cable and satellite television channels on a regular television receiver. Such boxes support MPEG-1, MPEG-2, and MPEG-4, and proprietary formats like Windows Media 9 and On2. Video over IP is a simple way to set up a video-on-demand system and offers an alternative to conventional RF cable systems. Video over IP can be used to deliver video over DSL or cable television systems, or can be used for closed networks. It means that businesses like hotels can deliver video and data services direct to the room using low-cost Ethernet cabling.

On2

On2 Technologies has focused on high-end streaming. Rather than follow the rich-media vein of the three main architectures, On2 has developed codecs aimed at the broadband VOD market. Their codecs can be used with embedded chipsets as well as the PC.

The VP6 codecs can be used with HD video resolutions up to 1920 × 1080 pixels. VP6 is the first On2 encoder to offer different profiles. This allows content to be optimized for the target device, whether it is a low-cost embedded processor, a high-quality set-top box, or low bit-rate for mobile applications.

The On2 codecs potentially open the VOD market to DSL and cable modems. By using set-top boxes for playback, streamed movies can be displayed on the television rather than the PC for the shared experience of television viewing, as opposed to the lone and interactive PC user.

Figure 13.10 TrueCast Player from On2 Technologies.

Wireless and portable devices

Now that we are familiar with streaming to PCs, we want the same access to information while out on the road. The third generation of wireless devices offer wider bandwidths than the early cellular phones, with the ability to display pictures and video, and, using integral cameras, to transmit.

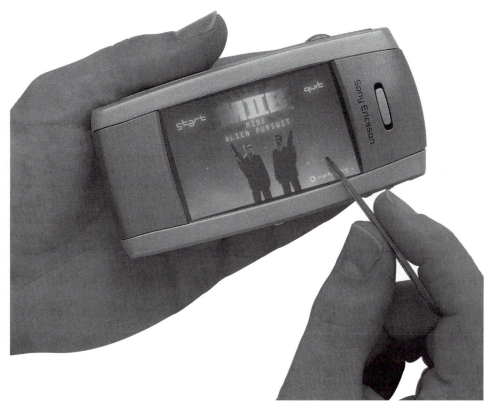

Figure 13.11 P800 phone from Sony Ericsson.

The MPEG-4 standard has many features that make it particularly suited to wireless delivery. Now such devices have color displays with sizes of 320×240, they are large enough to watch video. Companies like PacketVideo and Emblaze have end-to-end solutions for encoding and serving streaming media to hand-held devices. The connection could be to a third-generation cell phone or, via wireless networking, to a Personal Digital Assistant (PDA).

The streaming client usually is embedded to give the small footprint demanded by these devices. For example, the client application, pvPlayer, from the PacketVideo product line can decode streamed media for viewing on mobile devices at data rates ranging from as low as 9.6 kbit/s to more than 768 kbit/s. It is optimized for embedding into cell phones, PDAs, laptops, and other mobile devices with varied display sizes and constraints on the power usage and consequent battery life. To give bandwidth-efficient wireless distribution, the pvPlayer has error detection and concealment. This masks data loss in poor wireless propagation conditions, while supporting true MPEG-4 compliant scalability.

Audio players

Audio-only players were the first to become popular, spurred on by the huge demand from music lovers to download tracks over the Internet. Many do not support true streaming, but can download and play MP3 files. They act as a jukebox inside the PC, with the ability to rip CDs, store MP3 files on the hard drive, and download to portable music players like the iPod. Some form of library management is included to find tracks and set up playlists. A typical example is Nullsoft's WinAmp. The major operating systems offer similar products with iTunes from Apple and integral music facilities in the Windows Media player. Music download is now a feature of third-generation cellular phones.

The lack of video has led many of the players to offer a number of visual features. One that is popular is the ability to change the look or chrome of the player by reskinning with any number of different designs. Another is the visualization, where random colored patterns change in time to the music.

Digital Rights Management

Several players have integrated Digital Rights Management (DRM) clients. Determined hackers can extract the media data when it is in the clear between the DRM client and the media player. Most of the clients have means to detect tampering, and to report this back to the rights server and shut down the streams. Microsoft has taken this a step further by integrating the decryption into the operating system kernel. By these means a secure audio path to the sound card can be ensured. You could still extract the video data, but what use is a movie without a soundtrack?

MPEG-4 Intellectual Property Management and Protection

MPEG-4 has accepted the principle that one-size-fits-all is not wholly appropriate for DRM. Instead, the level of complexity and the security offered is left to the application developer. In other words, the complexity can scale with the cost. This reflects the different demands for DRM: it may be to protect confidential information, or it could be to encrypt pay-per-view movies. The MPEG-4 Intellectual Property Management and Protection (IPMP) framework leaves the details open to different DRM system vendors.

A group of leading providers, the Internet Streaming Media Alliance (ISMA), have cooperated to create the ISMA Encryption and Authentication Specification based on the IPMP framework. Such specifications promote interoperability, a feature lacking in proprietary DRM schemes used with other architectures.

Summary

This has been a brief chapter, but players have to be simple to gain general acceptance by users. Many proprietary players have come and gone. The installed base is dominated by the three main streaming architectures, Microsoft, Real, and Apple. These players can be used as media portals, as players, or as plug-ins to a web browser, and all have similar feature sets. New players were emerging in 2004 to view MPEG-4 compliant streams. One issue with MPEG-4 is that there are many possible profiles and levels. Most players are designed for specific applications – mobile, VOD, IP-TV – and support only the relevant set of profiles. The majority support the Visual Simple Profile and AAC LC audio. Beyond that, you will need to check the supplier's specifications.

The choice of player is largely personal; they all produce a roughly equivalent video and audio quality. New codecs are released at regular intervals, so the quality improves year after year. Many users are happy to install all; some may want only the pre-installed codec that comes with the operating system.

All the main architectures offer fully featured portals, but for many applications the chrome is a distraction from the content; compare them with digital interactive television, simple navigation, and discrete packaging. The portal is useful for locating content, but can be replaced by a browser plug-in for display of the wanted content. Perhaps the audio player is the exception, where the portal provides visual stimulation and information to accompany the music.

A core component of the player is protection of intellectual content, or digital rights management. This enables content vendors to successfully monetize their content by protection of their intellectual property.

The player has broken free of the reins of the PC, and is finding its way into everything from hand-held wireless devices to the television set-top box.

Section 3

Associated Technologies and Applications

14 Rights management

Introduction

The Internet is a public network and open to all. Owners of content who want to distribute over the Internet may want to restrict access to their intellectual property. It may be confidential corporate information, or it could be entertainment media sold through an e-commerce site. Unfortunately, content with value is also of interest to unauthorized users. It could be the piracy of digital entertainment: music, movies, or games. Some Internet piracy is in the domain of the lone hacker, who treats unauthorized access as a challenge. A bigger problem is piracy for commercial gain. Therefore, digital assets have to be wrapped securely to prevent access to all but authorized users that have been properly authenticated.

File security and digital rights management becomes more of an issue when content is delivered over the public Internet. If a system is deployed entirely within the corporate firewall the risks will be lower and easier to police.

Digital rights management offers systems that can control access and aid the successful monetization of streaming media. Like many other issues related to streaming, there are numerous choices to consider when buying a digital rights management system. In choosing a system, you will have to judge the level of threat; the more secure a system, the more it will cost. With increased security, authorized users will find it more difficult to access the required content. So there is a trade-off between cost, security, and ease of use. Even the most secure systems can be cracked: One clear copy can be distributed in a flash all around the world.

There are two main facets to rights management. The first is the maintenance of artists and producers' contracts and royalty payments. The second is the secure delivery. The latter commonly is referred to as Digital Rights Management (DRM). It is the technology that allows owners, distributors, and providers of content to deliver content securely to consumers. The rights management also can control who has access to content; for example, restrictions to geographic areas. DRM also can be used standalone, to protect confidential information.

There is a certain amount of controversy around digital rights systems. Perhaps the medium with the longest history of rights is the printed book. It is recognized that the intellectual property of the author is protected against unauthorized imprints. But there is also the concept of fair use, without which the public library would not exist. To make a copy of a book using a photocopier is expensive and the result usually lacks an adequate binding, so it is easier to buy a new book. As we migrate to the electronic medium, a digital clone can be made simply at no cost (ignoring the disk space). So fair use – with the attendant risks of illegal copying – becomes difficult to police.

E-commerce systems already exist to protect the integrity of financial transactions when ordering goods. Traditionally these goods are physical, and the online transaction merely replaces mail order or telephone order. The goods then are delivered by mail or parcel service. When the goods are streamed media, not only does the transaction have to be secure, but the goods also have to be protected against unauthorized access.

Authentication and trust

Consider a person going to the local store to make a purchase. The storeowner will recognize that person by their gait as they walk in, their physical appearance, and their voice. They already have authenticated the customer as a trusted customer. The customer pays by check; the storeowner hands over the goods. The key words here are authentication and trust.

The same customer now travels to an out-of-town store. The checkout clerk does not know the customer, so refuses the check. The customer has the option of paying by charge or credit card. The card is authenticated, then the transaction is authorized by the terminal. The store trusts the credit card company to pay them for the goods. The customer walks out of the store with the goods – everyone is happy.

As retail transactions become globalized, the opportunities for fraud escalate. The mail order/telephone order sector has procedures in place to authenticate customers. Most will ship goods only to the address where the payment card is registered. Card suppliers have added extra digits to the card number that are not printed as part of the embossed number, or carried in the magnetic strip. This can be used during a phone transaction to confirm that the purchaser has the actual card in their possession, not an impression.

The usage contract

Digital commerce is based on the usage contract. The content provider and the user agree to a contract, possibly involving the payment of fees. Then the user receives the right to use the content.

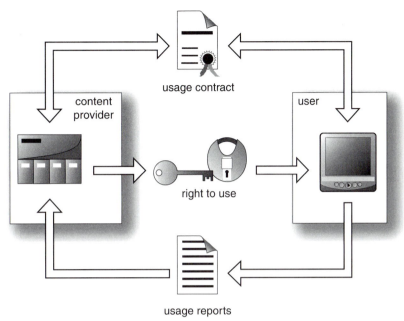

Figure 14.1 Usage contract.

As the user views the content, usage reports are returned to the content provider.

Conditional access – the television model

Television is funded by advertising, subscription or, in the case of state-controlled networks, from government taxation (in some countries independence of the state networks from government interference is provided by the use of a license rather than an income from taxation). A limited number of channels also offer pay-per-view, primarily for movies and for major sporting events. Channels funded by advertising, sponsorship, or taxation can be broadcast free-to- air, or 'open.' Subscription-based channels and pay-per-view use encryption to protect content against unauthorized viewing – conditional access.

Advertising and sponsorship

When corporations first started to use the Internet, funding for the web site came from either the marketing budget or from advertising. The subscription model is starting to become popular, especially for sites providing information. This is partly because consumer resistance to banner advertising is increasing, and also as a result of the often-limited revenues generated from advertising. The page-based Internet media (HTML) mainly has used the banner, with pop-ups also being popular. Streaming media offers the possibility of following the television model, with interstitial spots or breaks as well as banners.

Conditional access

Television broadcasters have chosen closed systems of conditional access to protect subscription and pay-per-view channels. The receivers or set-top boxes use smart cards and possibly a phone back-channel as part of the authorization procedures.

Streamed media often is viewed on PCs. These users have great resistance to add-ons, software dongles, and other additional hardware, so other methods have to be used to authenticate consumers.

The value chain

Content and payment form a cycle. The content is delivered to the consumer for use and the consumer then pays the intellectual property owner (through intermediaries) for the content.

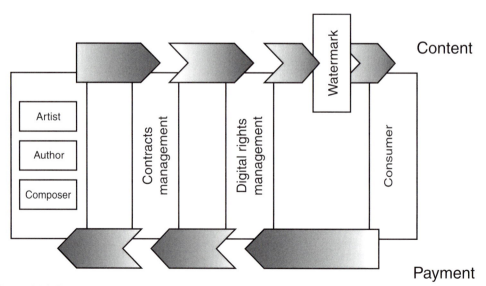

Figure 14.2 The payment cycle.

The Digital Rights Management system ensures secure delivery of the content in accordance with business rules defined by the contracts. The monies collected then are apportioned by the contracts management payment to the relevant parties.

Content distribution

Although an artist may want to sell work directly to the consumer, most content is sold though a conventional distribution chain. A DRM system should support the classic supply chain: content creator, publisher, aggregator or portal, distributor, retailer, and finally, the consumer.

The DRM also should support traditional product marketing tools like promotional offers and viral marketing. Finally, the methods of payment have to be flexible, all the way from subscriptions to micro-payments and electronic purses.

Digital Rights Management

Digital Rights Management is the use of computer technology to regulate the authorized use of digital media content, and to manage the consequences of such use; for example, a payment.

A Digital Rights Management (DRM) system encrypts the content so that distribution can be controlled in accordance with the agreed rights and their terms and conditions. To this end, it wraps prices and business rules around the content to enable the payment transaction.

For the transaction, the DRM is tightly integrated with the chosen e-commerce systems. Streaming media is representative of the many formats that an Internet content provider may want to manage, deliver, and sell. The digital information also could be electronic books, research reports, or graphic images like still photographs. Most DRM systems are designed to protect some or all of these different media formats. The initial developments in DRM were for text files. Not all these systems can handle streaming media. Encryption tends to be at file level. For a streamed file the encryption has to be implemented at packet level, otherwise the media playback cannot start immediately.

This, plus the intimate connection required to the player, has led naturally to many DRM solutions being proprietary to the codec format. The MPEG-4 format has a standard intellectual property management protection (IPMP) interface, so potentially will offer a more open environment.

Why do we need DRM?

Digital content is subject to many forms of piracy:

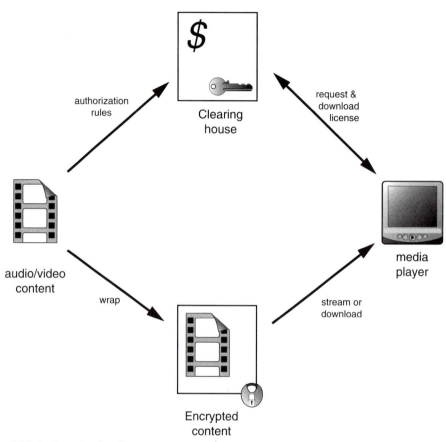

Figure 14.3 Exchanging the license.

- Illegal copying
- Loss of data integrity – tampering with content
- Peer-to-peer distribution

Perhaps the best example of peer-to-peer distribution was the case of Napster. If there is a secure DRM, then e-commerce can be used for online content. This electronic distribution removes the manufacturing costs of physical media and can simplify distribution. Within the corporate networks it can protect valuable and confidential information. For a distance-learning project it ensures protection of intellectual property.

Piracy protection

Two methods are used to fight piracy: one is *encryption* and the other is *watermarking*. Encryption gives the primary protection. Should the encryption be compromised, watermarking enables the tracing of the possible sources of the piracy.

Business models

The DRM has to be very flexible to accommodate the many different ways a consumer can purchase the content. There are many business models for monetizing online content.

Usage

There are several ways to sell content. There is rental or outright sale. The rental may have qualifiers applied; it could be for a fixed period or for a certain number of plays. Then there is the video-on-demand model, where a payment is required for each viewing of the clip.

Delivery

The delivery of content can be as a download or stream. The download might be for music files to be used by a portable player or a PDA. Streaming could be for ephemeral content that is watched only once. A third possibility is to archive the file, while it is streaming, for repeat viewing. If it is possible to download content to portable players, security is potentially compromised. Microsoft has developed an interface that allows content to be downloaded securely from the Windows Media Player to portable audio devices that support the SDMI (Secure Digital Music Initiative) standard.

Promotion

DRM enables many forms of product promotion. The first is to let the viewer see a preview. This may be the edited highlights or the first few minutes of the clip. The preview may be at a lower resolution than the main clip. Other forms of promotion may be special offers such as 'pass this on to five friends and get a free play'.

Payment

The traditional method for mail order payment is by credit or charge card. This is not a good method for very small transactions; it may cost only 10 cents to listen to a single music track. So other methods have to be used that have a lower cost overhead for such low-value transactions.

Subscriptions, long popular with print media, are another method of collecting payments. They are more suited to a service rather than pay-per-view. Subscriptions usually are prepaid. An alternative for business-to-business transactions would be to bill in retrospect. Account payments can support a fixed rate service or pay-per-view.

For the business selling content to the consumer, the prepaid purse or micro-payments are the alternative. With the purse, the customer buys credit from the clearinghouse. This credit is stored securely in the DRM client. The value is decremented as content is viewed. Micro-payments are aggregated by the clearinghouse into larger transactions, perhaps made at monthly intervals.

Business rules

The business model will dictate a set of business rules. The DRM client uses the rules to gain access to the content. The terms and conditions can change with time so the license issuer must be able to change the rules or revoke a license. This may be necessary for legal or business reasons, or the content may become outdated or inappropriate. A good DRM system should allow the revocation of content even after it has been downloaded.

Wrapping

This is the process of securing the content and associating with the content the business rules to enable unwrapping by the media player. The processes are not necessarily concurrent. Encrypting may be performed while the media is encoded, and the business rules added later.

There are two different points where content files can be encrypted. The first is before media is placed on the content server. The second is to encrypt on-the-fly, as the content is streamed to the media player. The latter is the model that conditional access systems have used for pay-per-view television.

Pre-encryption and on-the-fly

Pre-encryption systems usually package the clip file as a whole, rather than packet by packet. For live use this is not an option; for webcasts the encryption has to be on-the-fly. To meet this need, a different form of encryption has been developed, where the processing takes place at the point of delivery. This on-the-fly encryption has a second advantage that a new key is generated for each stream. Pre-encryption generates a single key for the file at the time of wrapping. So if the key is compromised, all copies of the file can be opened.

On-the-fly encryption can be an additional application running on the streaming server, but this will lower the number of streams a given server can deliver,

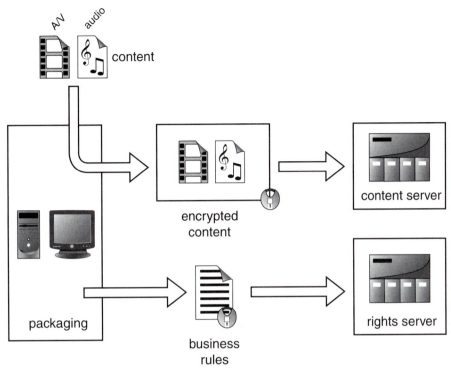

Figure 14.4 Wrapping the content.

Table 14.1 Pros and Cons of the Pre-Encryption and On-the-Fly Methods

	Pros	*Cons*
Pre-encryption	Content is secure on the server No serving overheads	Not suited to live streaming Single key per file
On-the-fly	Can be used for live webcasts New key per stream	Additional server-side processing Content can be compromised on the streaming server

typically by 30 percent. The alternative is to use a bridge or router at the output port of the streaming server that can perform the encryption. This allows the use of a standard media server.

Unwrapping

The final user or the consumer wants to view and listen to the content. To decrypt the content, first the user has to obtain authorization. This authorization, suitably modified by the business rules, then initiates the decryption of the content.

The DRM client follows this typical sequence:

1. Send a request for the content and, if necessary, undertake a financial transaction.
2. If the client has credit, the commerce server transmits the authorization key.
3. The DRM client requests the business rules from the rights server and the media file from the content server.
4. The rights server forwards the business rules.
5. The content server streams the media.
6. The DRM client allows access to the media according to the business rules.

The exact sequence varies from product to product. Note that the business rules can be downloaded each time and are separate from the content. This allows the content owner to change the rules at any time without having to reencrypt the media file. A movie initially might be available on a pay-per-view basis, then at a later date released for outright sale. The publisher may want to add or withdraw special offers.

This division between the product and the promotional wrapper gives the retailer of virtual products greater freedom than the vendor of physical merchandise (where the offer could be printed on the packaging). It also allows pricing to be changed in real-time, much like the street vendor or an airline trying to fill empty seats at the last minute.

The authorization can be issued in several ways. It could be from a subscriber management system (long used by pay TV) or it could be an e-commerce system.

The rights management parties

There are several parties in any content transaction. Each is looking for a different set of features in a DRM system. The final choice has to satisfy all parties if the commercial model is to be successful.

Content creators/publishers

Content can take many forms. The first focus was on music distribution, a consequence of the Napster debacle. The distribution of video content is very much tied to satisfactory security, much like the delayed release of the DVD. Live events are an area where pay-per-view could be applied.

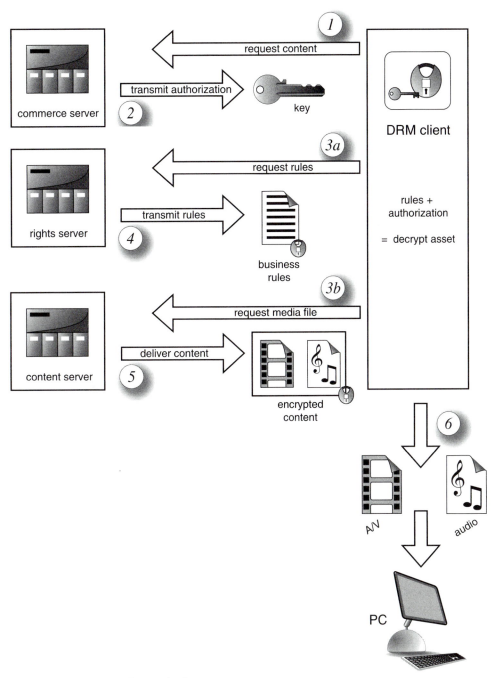

Figure 14.5 Unwrapping the content.

The target devices for streaming are not just PCs; they could be wireless PDAs or portable music players. Content will have to be repurposed for the requirements of each device. Content for the PDA requires careful design to be compelling within the limits of a small display area.

Compatibility with media players

Which player do you choose? Corporate users can choose a single system. B2B and B2C suppliers may want to offer the user a choice. Two of the popular streaming architectures already include DRM systems (Real and Windows Media). If you want to support several architectures you may end up having to interface with three different DRM systems.

Commerce

When you are selecting a DRM system, you need to look at the features on offer. Does it support cross-selling? An important factor is the transaction costs for micro-payments. Can you make retrospective changes to the business rules? This allows price changes for downloaded content that already resides on the customer's PC. Is it possible to revoke access to content?

Reseller

The reseller could be a retail web store or a content portal, aggregating content from several suppliers. The content could be sold through several stages before the final purchase by the end-consumer. A distributor may buy content from many creators and sell to the consumer. Distributors will want to set up the business rules for the trading of content, and may want to add further rules, add their own margin, and then add special offers.

So the DRM systems should support modification and additions to the business rules by trusted partners in the value chain.

Consumer/user

The end-user first gains authorization from the clearing house or data center. Then he or she is free to open and view the encrypted content. Now a consumer may want to preview content before making the decision to buy. This purchase may be outright, or could be for a fixed period rental. Consumers are often encouraged to forward media to friends – a process known as viral marketing. The DRM system has to support secure super-distribution for this personal recommendation to operate.

Payment and usage information is passed back to the clearinghouse. An electronic purse can store a small cache of credit within the media player. This avoids the need to clear every transaction. DRM systems should have means to silently report tampering back to the data center.

Super-distribution

Super-distribution commonly is used in viral marketing. This is where customers pass content to friends, perhaps in the belief that it is a shared secret. Content that is passed from user to user has to have persistent protection after copying. Each user must make an individual transaction to gain authorization to use the content.

Issues for the user

So far I have considered the providers' issues. The choice of DRM is also an issue for the consumer. If the system is too complex, there are thousands of other web sites out there, only a click away. Another major issue is payment security. Customers have to trust the supplier with their credit card details. The consequence of this fear is that reputable traders can lose potential business. There are steps being taken to counteract these fears, where trusted third parties act as brokers for online transactions.

A good DRM system should be transparent to the end-users. The acquisition of the software executables should be automatic and not require manual intervention from the user. Browsers now include rights management preinstalled. The second is that the financial transactions must be simple and secure.

Most DRM systems allocate the license to a node and not the user. Some attributes of the PC are used as part of the key; for example, the file may be locked to an IP address. If you want to move protected media between a desktop PC and a laptop this may require a nodeless DRM. Note that this is not copying; the content is moved to the portable machine and then moved back to the desktop.

Clearing houses

Subscriptions could be managed by a web site database. All that is required is secure authorization and usage statistics. If the consumer pays for content the clearinghouses will process the micro-payments from consumers and pass payments to the content providers. An electronic purse may hold a small local cache of credit.

Financial clearing house A facility that receives financial transaction records, resolves the transactions, and makes the required payments to the value chain participants and value chain delegates.

Usage clearing house A facility that gathers reports and statistics of how DRM protected media is used by consumers and by other participants in the value chain. It resolves the requirements for usage reporting and provides reports to specified recipients.

Third-party revenues The DRM supplier has two possible sources of revenue: a fee for each transaction or a license for a fixed period (typically annual). The clearing houses usually charge per transaction.

System integration

A large system is going to require many disparate software systems to be integrated. Is middleware required to ease the integration of DRM with back-office systems? These include e-commerce systems, contracts management, digital asset management, and the clearinghouse.

Contracts management

Most DRM systems produce comprehensive statistics and reports of consumer use. To apportion payments to the relevant parties the DRM operator may well need other software products, specifically a contracts management package. These products are outside the scope of this book. Good examples can be found in *System 7* from Jaguar Consulting and *iRights* from Ness. These products have modules for the following functions:

- To manage contracts with artists
- To acquire content from production companies
- To track the usage of content
- To distribute royalties to artists

The contracts management application often sits at the hub of the business. Gateways link to the DRM, and to the digital asset management system that may be used as the content library or vault.

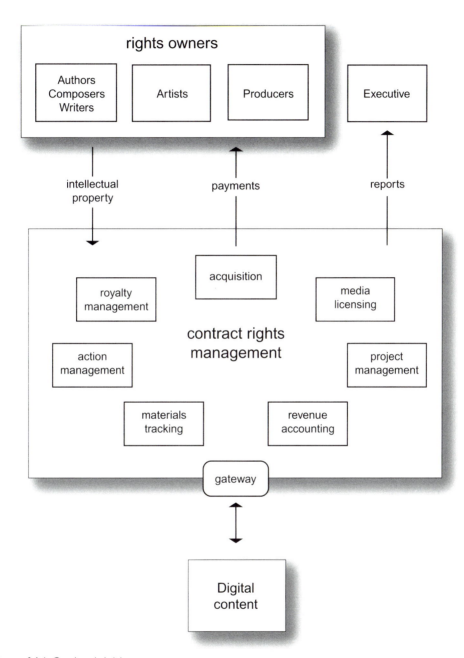

Figure 14.6 Contract rights.

Encryption

Cryptography has two uses within DRM. The first is to encrypt content for confidentiality or protection of the owner's rights. The second is for the protection of the certificates that are used for authentication and for access control (authorization).

There are two families of cryptography: shared secret and public/private key. A shared secret key (also called a symmetric) uses the same key to encrypt the content and then to decrypt it at the receiving end. In cryptography the clear file is called *plaintext* and the encrypted version is called *ciphertext*. The scrambled ciphertext feasibly can be decoded only with the key. One way to crack the encryption is to try many different keys until you chance upon the correct one. The more characters in the key, the longer it will take, on average, to find the key. This cracking can be made more difficult by changing the key at certain intervals. Shared key encryption is efficient and suited to large files – just like media files. An example of a shared secret is a personal identification number (PIN) used to withdraw cash with an automated teller machine. The PIN is used to verify the physical credit card. The PIN is a secret shared by the bank computer and the authorized holder of the card.

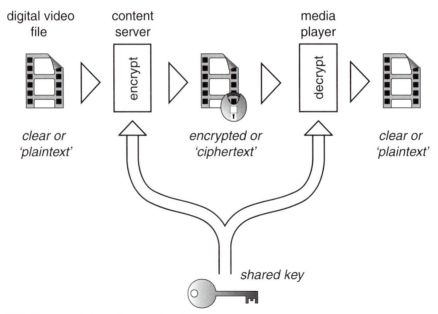

Figure 14.7 The secret shared encryption key.

The standard for shared secret cryptography is the DES algorithm (Data Encryption Standard).

The problem with a secret key is the secure distribution from one party to the other. Different methods can be used to deliver the key. One is the secure courier. Another is the telephone callback. One party phones the other, and says 'call me back.' The other party calls back to an unlisted phone number; now the original party has authenticated they have the wanted party and can divulge the key.

The courier is not a viable option for e-commerce systems. Pay-per-view conditional access uses a smart-card in the set-top box, plus a phone link to connect to the box. Each box is uniquely accessible, so can be shut down by the subscriber management center. The media player in a PC is a much more open system than the proprietary hardware in the set-top box. There is also consumer resistance to the use of a smart-card, although such systems exist.

The alternative is an electronic version of the telephone callback. This uses the digital signature security standard (DSS). Once the rights server has authenticated the client from the digital signature, the secret key can be exchanged.

One algorithm that has proved popular is the Diffie–Hellman key exchange. It starts with two publicly available integers, P and G. Each party, the rights server and the client, generate private keys, X and Y. The Diffie–Hellman algorithm then is used to generate public keys, E and F, which the two parties exchange. Each party then uses the other's public key, their own private key, and the public number P to generate a common number. This common number K is now a secret shared by both parties. Note that at no time has this shared secret key been exchanged over the Internet. This shared key then can be used to encrypt the media file.

This description is somewhat simplified; the full description can be found in the IETF RFC 2631: Diffie–Hellman Key Agreement Method.

Note that the Diffie–Hellman key agreement can be intercepted by a man-in-the-middle attack, because there is no authentication between the two parties. Such authentication could involve the prior exchange of digital signatures.

Watermarking

In the digital domain, watermarking embeds a persistent signature that identifies the source of the content or the client copy. The latter is often called fingerprinting. For a content provider to trace the sources of piracy, two clues are necessary. The first is a means of identifying the owner of the stolen content, and the second is a trace of the client that compromised the security. These clues can be introduced as a watermark to identify the owner of the stolen content and as a fingerprint to identify the instance that was copied. The

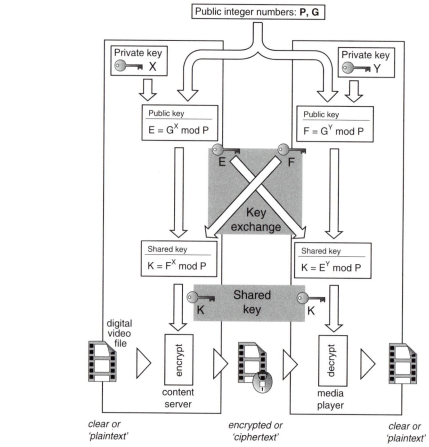

Figure 14.8 The Diffie–Hellman key agreement.

fingerprint is akin to the serial number of the copy. If a clear copy is found, the fingerprint identifies the copy that was compromised.

Originally, a watermark was a faint imprint from the mould used to make high quality paper. We are all familiar with the use of watermarks in bank notes. In this application, the watermark is part of a number of measures used to indicate that the note is genuine rather than a counterfeit, to authenticate the note.

A watermark can be highly visible, like an embossed logo. This often is used for preview copies of still images or video, where its role is partly to brand the content. Something subtler is needed for the full-resolution content, just like the watermark on a piece of paper or bill. An invisible identifier can be hidden in the video files, using the techniques of steganography (from the Greek, meaning hidden writing). The identifier can be extracted or detected by a software agent. Watermarking does not have to be a visual; there are schemes that embed a watermark in an audio file. This uses similar auditory masking processes to those exploited by audio compression schemes.

Automatic web spiders continuously can search the web looking for open (unencrypted) content that carries invisible watermarks. A typical example is the MarcSpider from DigiMarc.

Persistent watermarks usually should be able to survive copying to be effective. The copies may be compressed using codecs like JPEG or MPEG. There may be intermediate analogue copies. The watermark should survive all this signal processing. There are other watermarking schemes where the mark deliberately is made very fragile. It should not survive the copying process, so if it is missing, that content can be identified as a copy. This is very much the analogue of the bank note. The lack of the watermark would indicate a counterfeit.

Unlike data encryption, watermarks can be embedded in the waveform rather than the data. This can be used for images, audio, and video. Spread spectrum techniques can be used to add data in the time domain. These can be thought of as time-delayed echoes. These can be recovered by cepstrum analysis. If video and audio are compressed by a codec like MPEG, the coding thresholds can be modulated with the watermark data.

Watermarks are no panacea. They can be defeated, just as encryption can be broken. They form part of an environment where the theft of digital assets is made more difficult and the culprits can be traced more easily.

Security

Before setting up a secure media distribution system, it is a good idea to look at your goals. What are you trying to protect and how much do you want to spend on security? The security analysis splits into three areas:

1. The content
2. The monetary transaction
3. The server infrastructure

DRM gives protection of the content and often includes the monetary transaction. The transaction can use mature technologies from the e-commerce arena. The third area, the server infrastructure, is covered by normal enterprise level computer security (outside the scope of this book). The infrastructure should be protected for several reasons. One is the value of the content asset library; another is that attack could compromise the brand of the publisher, aggregator, or retailer. This attack could be from denial of service or loss of data integrity.

Hackers present many threats to a business. It could be through unauthorized access to confidential information or loss of data integrity, where the hacker alters the content, possibly to embarrass the content owner by substituting inappropriate material.

The threats

Although cracking the encryption may appear to be a common threat, it is difficult and can take a very long time. The more usual threat is theft of the keys.

Some licenses are valid for a short time period; one method that has been employed to fool such licenses is to change the computer's date and time. A good DRM plug-in should be resistant to such manipulation.

Video and audio content can be copied once in the analog domain. The wires to the loud speakers and the VGA connections to the computer monitor are both easy access points to make analog copies of audio/video content. It is difficult to prevent such attacks, just as it is difficult to stop somebody sitting in a movie theatre with a camcorder.

Third-party audit

Before investing a considerable sum in a DRM product, find out how secure it really is. Ask to see third-party audits, or instigate your own.

Caveats

No encryption is proof against determined efforts to crack.

- DRM makes piracy difficult, but does not prevent it.
- Other methods of defense of property rights will be necessary.
- Watermarking aids tracing of stolen content.
- Some level of theft is inevitable and should be included in the cost of sales.

XrML

As streamed media is handled by a number of applications during the processes and workflows of authoring and distribution, there is a need to express the content rights and the rules for access in a portable format through the content lifecycle. That means that information can be passed from one application to another without the need to develop custom interfaces. The Extensible rights markup language (XrML) is one such grammar.

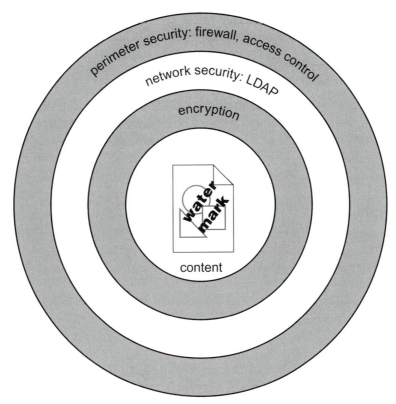

Figure 14.9 Security shells.

XrML was developed at the Xerox Palo Alto Research Center in the late 1990s as the Digital Rights Property language. The original meta-language was changed to XML in 1999 and renamed. It has now been adopted by leading software developers and publishing houses as a common rights language for digital resources, both content and services.

The core concepts of XrML are as follows:

- Principal
- Right
- License
- Grant
- Resource
- Condition

The principal is the party who is granting or exercising the rights. The rights detail what action a principal may undertake using a resource. As an example, you may be granted the right to view a movie once only, or you may be given the right to print an electronic document.

The license is a set of grants and it identifies the principal who issued the license. The grant gives the authorization upon a principal. The rights expression is authenticated by a digital signature. A resource can be digital content: an e-book, a digital image file, or a video clip. It can also be a service like an e-commerce service or a piece of information like an address that is owned by a principal. The condition specifies the terms and conditions of the license. This could be a rental agreement or the terms for outright purchase.

XrML has been used for the basis of the MPEG Rights Expression Language, part of the MPEG-21 standard.

Examples of DRM products

Microsoft

In recent years, Microsoft has devoted much attention to security. Their initial focus was on solutions to protect digital entertainment in the form of audio and video files, although they since have added document security. The Windows Media Rights Manager can protect audio-visual content encoded in the Windows Media streaming format. In 2003, Microsoft announced Windows Rights Management Services. Much like Windows Media, a central rights management server stores licenses that control access to protected files. Windows 2000 and XP both offer flexible file security and access control, but only on the corporate network. There is always the constant problem of staff burning copies of files to CD-ROM. Network security and access control lists cannot protect files outside the corporate firewall.

Windows Media Rights Manager 9

Microsoft's Windows Media Rights Manager provides a secure end to digital media e-commerce solution for Windows Media. This solution enables both application service providers and Internet content providers to manage, deliver, and sell streaming media. It supports download-and-play and conventional streaming.

The Windows Media Rights Manager system is designed to work with third-party credit card software that is compatible with MS Site Server 3.0. The Windows Media Rights Manager allows the publisher to set up the rules for the transaction. The player then uses these rules to open the encrypted content.

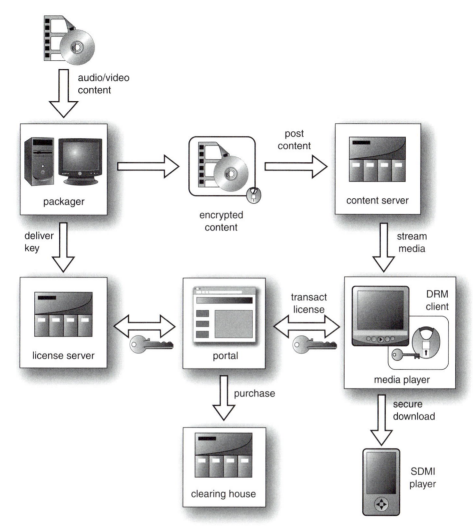

Figure 14.10 Windows Media Rights Manager.

Flexible Business Models

New licensing rights have been introduced with Windows Media Rights Manager 9 to help enhance the creation of new, innovative business models.

Licenses are issued independently of the actual media files. This provides flexibility for the business model and allows wider distribution of content. The Rights Manager checks for the consumer's license every time a media clip is played. If the user does not have a valid license, they are directed back to the registration web page. Because licenses and media files are stored separately from the media, the licensing terms can be changed without the need to encrypt the media file again and then redistribute to the client.

Windows Media Rights Manager supports rental or subscription business models. Limited play previews allow the potential purchasers to look before they buy. Windows Media Rights Manager can predeliver licenses. This helps to remove the consumers' resistance to the acquisition and playing of secure media files. One feature is silent licensing, which means that a content provider may 'silently' deliver the license to the consumer, without the need for the consumer to intervene.

Secure Audio Path

One area where content can be stolen is within the user's PC. If the clear audio data passing between the DRM client and the sound card driver is intercepted, then the content easily can be diverted and saved to the disk. To prevent this, Windows Media has a feature called the Secure Audio Path (supported by Windows ME and XP). The DRM is embedded in the OS kernel. Before decryption, the DRM kernel component verifies that the path to the sound card driver is valid and authenticated. If any unauthorized plug-ins exist, then the decryption is barred. This prevents plug-ins on the sound card from copying the audio data. Microsoft certifies valid drivers for security.

Controlled Transfer to SDMI Portable Devices

Windows Media Device Manager permits the secure transfer of protected media files to Secure Digital Music Initiative (SDMI) portable devices or the removable media for those devices.

SyncCast

One of Microsoft's partners is SyncCast. They have a suite of products that allow Windows Media content to be distributed as streams or on CD/DVD-ROMs over intranets or the Internet. To sell content, SyncCast partnered with iBill, a supplier of turnkey e-commerce solutions.

Their SyncPack DRM packager is a client application that permits content creators, authors, and distributors to encrypt Windows Media files. SyncCast has adopted the .NET infrastructure to allow the remote administration of content licenses. The digital rights are managed from the Web browser-based DRM Dashboard. From this the administrator can view usage reports, change business rules, add new products, and control users.

The business rules and licenses are stored on SyncCast's centralized DRM servers.

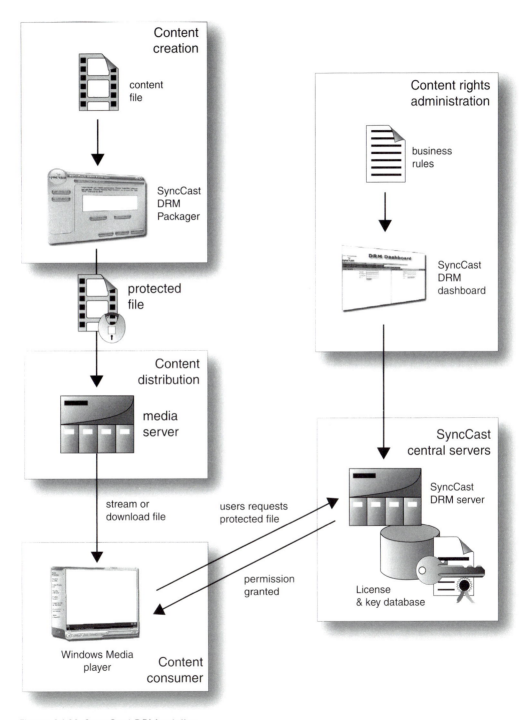

Figure 14.11 SyncCast DRM solution.

RealNetworks Media Commerce Suite

RealNetworks has developed a fully integrated DRM system for the Real architecture under the Helix name. The Helix DRM 10 Suite comprises three components:

Helix DRM Packager A set of tools for content providers to securely package streaming media files.

Helix DRM License Server An HTTP server that generates licenses for access to secured media. They are issued in response to a request from the player client.

Helix DRM Client Allows the media player to decrypt protected content in a trusted and tamper-resistant environment.

Real also provides support for consumer electric device manufacturers who want to design secure native support for the Helix DRM platform. These components interact with existing content delivery mechanisms, a retail web server, and a back-end database.

The Helix DRM supports the Real codecs, MP3 and H.263. Once the licensing issues are resolved, MPEG-4 codecs will be added.

Widevine Cypher

Widevine Cypher is an on-the-fly encryption product. It is architecture agnostic and supports Windows Media, RealVideo, and QuickTime. A normal streaming media server is deployed for the appropriate architecture. The output streams then are passed through the Cypher network bridge. The bridge negotiates the keys then performs the real-time encryption.

A shim decrypts the stream at the client. The shim also monitors the media player for tampering and reports any such actions back to the rights server. The normal interactive play controls pass back through the shim and bridge to the streaming server.

As the Cypher encrypts streaming media on-the-fly, it can be used to protect live webcasts. The primary focus for Widevine is the protection of content streamed over VOD networks to set-top boxes. A virtual smartcard is used to enable the set-top box.

MPEG-4

The design of DRM solutions to protect MPEG-4 content has lagged behind the development of the audio and video codecs. Under the auspices of the Internet Streaming Media Alliance (ISMA), a specification for content protection has been drawn up. This will enable encoders, servers, and players from different vendors to exchange encrypted content. The specification supports both file download and streaming. It is independent of device or operating system. It uses the AES 128-bit encryption algorithm as a default, but stronger encryption can be used. The specification has simple interfaces for support of codecs like MPEG-2 and AVC.

Summary

If you want to monetise content, that content has to be protected against theft. For media producers, the Internet has become the Home Shoplifting Network. Certain groups look upon music as a free commodity. You may have confidential corporate information to protect. Digital rights management can provide you with solutions, but can be expensive to license and operate. You need to define your goals for content protection and identify possible threats. A cost-benefit analysis would be very sensible.

The level of security that you use is very much a compromise. Strong security does not come cheap. You need to balance the potential loss of revenue against the cost of the DRM solution.

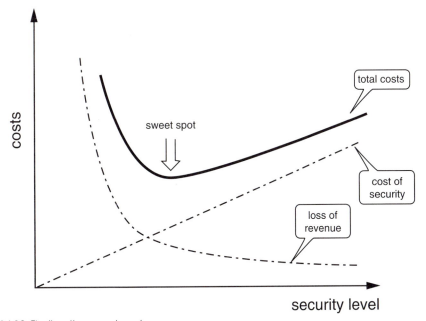

Figure 14.12 Finding the sweet spot.

Traditional text file DRM packages the entire file into a secure container. To stream, the encryption has to be in chunks, so that the player can render the file immediately. Securing the client is quite a challenge, so most DRM systems have a means of identifying tampering that could compromise the security. Live webcasting requires an on-the-fly encryption system, rather than the pre-encryption employed in the majority of systems.

The best systems employ a number of means to protect content against unauthorized access. When content is on the media servers, it can be protected by physical means like access control for the building. Once in the building, the standard network security provides password-controlled authentication. Once logged into the network, the files can be encrypted with a DRM product to provide further protection. If an unauthorized user penetrates these three layers, then the watermark can be used for forensic tracing of the leak.

If streaming media files are accessed remotely, or are sold, rented, or syndicated, then the physical and network security are stripped away. Encryption and watermarking become the primary means to discourage theft.

A successful rights management deployment will require constant vigilance against efforts to compromise the system. To justify the expense of DRM, proper auditing and monitoring is required. Never take the word of a vendor that their system cannot be cracked. There is a large community constantly probing for weaknesses in asset protection systems.

15 Content distribution

Introduction

Efficient content distribution is vital to the publisher of streaming media. As early as 1997 codec development had reached a point where a reasonable video quality could be achieved at bit rates as low as 100 kbit/s, but the viewing experience did not live up to the potential offered by the codecs.

Watching a stream as it stalled and hiccupped led many of the potential adopters of video content to stick with animated vector graphics. The streaming infrastructure is shared with the general Internet, which offers only best-effort delivery. Streaming video often passes over 20 routers between the media server and the viewer. The routes switch as traffic varies, leading to varying latencies. If the network is congested, the routers can drop packets.

Contrast this with television. The signal leaves the master control suite at the television station and then travels over a dedicated microwave link (the studio-transmitter link or STL) to the tower. The viewer sees the picture a fraction of a second after it leaves master control. Alternatively, the signal passes through the cable-operator's head-end then fans out through dedicated fibers to the set-top box. Both delivery channels have a fixed (and very short) propagation delay. They also have bandwidth dedicated exclusively to the channel. It is not surprising that they both exhibit a high quality of service. The cable operator owns and operates the entire infrastructure right through to the set-top box in the home. This gives complete control over service quality.

As viewers become accustomed to the quality offered by high-definition television and the DVD, their expectations are raised. For streaming video to be accepted universally as a means of delivering media, the service quality has to approach broadcast television. Without that, the business of monetizing entertainment content delivered over the Web can be tough.

There are many facets to distribution: improving the utilization of the Internet, delivering to the edge, and alternative carriers to the switched Internet. Much

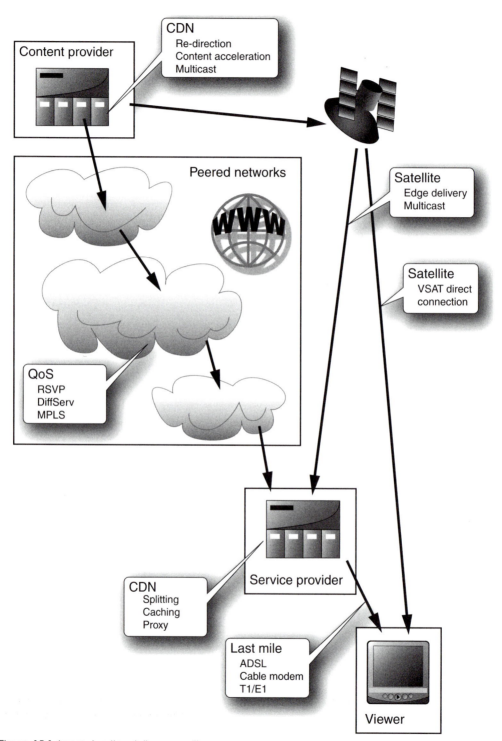

Figure 15.1 Improving the delivery quality.

of the technology focus for streaming, apart from codec development, has been to address these distribution issues. There are a number of pinch-points that can make streaming a less than satisfying experience. The first is the network-to-network peering points. The next is the backbone of a network, and the third is the last mile to the consumer. For live events the encoder-to-origin server link also can present problems. More and more fiber is being laid to augment the bandwidth of the backbone, but as ever, demand exceeds capacity. Just look at web sites. An index page used to be under 50 kbytes. Now many have well over 200 kbytes of Flash graphics. As the public takes up more broadband connections for the last mile, although it removes a bottleneck, it also creates more demand for higher bit-rate streams.

One family of solutions is the Content Delivery Network (CDN). These were first developed for the delivery of conventional HTML pages and file downloads. The CDN also can be used to improve the streaming experience, while giving more efficient utilization of the intervening network. With a CDN the viewer should see less of the stalled streams that mark the delivery of content over long-haul networks. The service provider also benefits, as less bandwidth is required to connect to the Internet backbone.

Content delivery networks

The basic premises of the CDN are to serve content closer to the user rather than across the Internet and to intelligently direct the routes taken by the data packets that make up the stream. The former is called edge serving. If you are not using a CDN to view streaming media, a request for content traverses the Internet from network to network; it can pass through as many as 20 routers. The content data then returns, possibly along a different path through another 20 routers. At each stage packets can be lost or delayed, but streaming requires a regular data delivery rate to the player. Any congestion is going to result in the often-seen picture freezes and loss of the soundtrack.

The CDN avoids the effects of this transit congestion by serving the content from the user's point-of-presence (POP), at the edge of the Internet. The CDN places special edge servers at the ISP providing your local point-of-presence. The CDN then uses a control network overlaid on the Internet to respond to requests for clips and to manage the delivery of clips from the origin server to the edge servers.

The CDN has four main components to help provide high-quality streams local to the user:

- Intelligent routing
- Edge caching of content

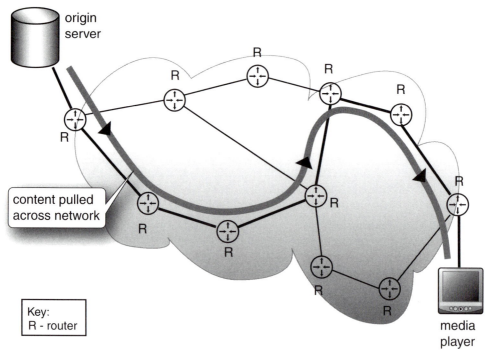

Figure 15.2 Serving from the origin.

- Proxy serving
- Splitting of live webcasts

Intelligent or smart routing is an overlay above the regular Internet routing. Requests to the origin server for media clips are intercepted and redirected to the nearest available edge server. The smart routing also delivers content from the origin server to the edge server by the best route, bypassing congested links.

The downside is the cost of the provision of the edge servers. So the ROI for the deployment of the CDN depends partly on the saving in bandwidth costs that can be achieved.

Another problem stems from the open structure of the Internet. It is not a network, but a federation of interconnected networks linked through peering agreements. In the United States alone, there are thousands of networks. It is unlikely that one network alone will handle a request. In all likelihood, a connection will pass through several peering points between different networks. Typically, an ISP will offer a service level agreement (SLA) for connections within its network. This complex network of interconnections makes it difficult to guarantee an end-to-end service once the data leaves the service provider's own network.

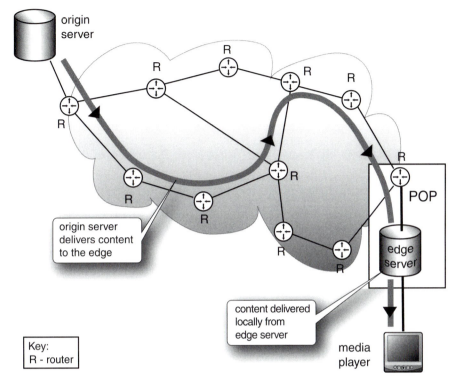

origin
server

R

R

R

R

R

R

R

R

origin server
delivers content
to the edge

R

R

R

R

POP

edge
server

content delivered
locally from
edge server

Key:
R - router

media
player

Figure 15.3 Serving from the edge with a CDN.

If you are setting up media streaming over a corporate wide-area intranet, the situation is simpler. You most likely are using a single network provider, so a closed CDN system can be installed over the corporate network.

If you are serving content to the public, you will have less control over the quality of delivery. This is the enigma. The end-user's ISP receives their revenue from that end-user. If the user has opted for a low-cost service, there is little incentive for the service provider to invest in edge servers. So, although a content provider may have partnered with a high-performance CDN, there is no guarantee that this performance extends all the way to the final end-user. Clearly there is a case for the content providers to educate the users – there is no free lunch. The user of rich media will have to choose an ISP with much more care than simply surfing web pages if they want a reasonable viewing experience.

An ISP is very unlikely to install a range of different proprietary edge servers. To provide servers for many different CDN products is not a satisfactory business proposition. For the corporate user, serving content over corporate networks, there is the freedom to choose a single system for in-house use.

These realities limit the number of successful CDNs operating within the public Web. If you want high-quality delivery to the public the simplest route is to approach the large CDNs like Akamai, Speedera, Globix, and Mirror Image. In 2004 Akamai had over 15,000 servers deployed around the Internet. These global networks have the resources to handle very large numbers of media streams as well as conventional HTML files.

Overlay network

To provide high-quality delivery some intelligence is needed to control the transmission of multimedia streams. The Content Delivery Networks use a control layer overlaid on the Internet. This layer can capture requests for files, and then manage the delivery by the most efficient way to give a high quality of service at the media player.

The CDNs aim to improve the streaming experience by three main processes: splitting, caching, and proxy serving.

Local proxy

This is the basic edge server. The delivery from origin to user is split into two hops. The first is from the origin to the edge, and the second is from the edge to the client. If streams are delivered locally to the client, the RTSP and RTCP control messages are exchanged locally rather than across the network. This cuts down control latencies and the network traffic to provide a better stream-

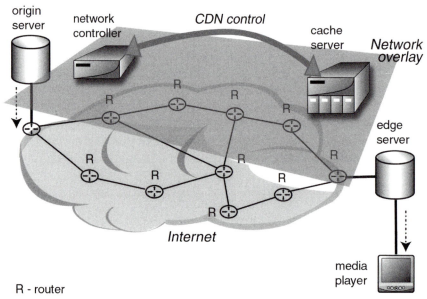

Figure 15.4 The overlay control network.

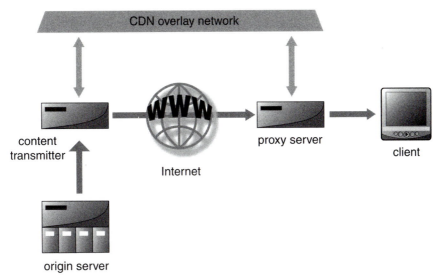

content transmitter

origin server

proxy server

client

Internet

Figure 15.5 Proxy edge server.

ing experience. It also makes interactive applications much more responsive to the user. The CDN feeds the content to the edge server through content accelerators.

Edge splitting

The local proxy offers another opportunity to make more efficient use of the network. If more than one client logs in to a live webcast at the same point-of-presence, a single stream is hauled to the POP. Cache servers then split the content and serve directly to the multiple clients. This has two advantages. The first is the reduction in network traffic; only one stream crosses the backbone. The second is that the clients are receiving the stream from a local server, rather than a long-distance negotiation through 20 or so routers.

Local caching

If a client requests content on-demand, that content is cached at the POP as it is streamed. If a second user requests the same file, then it is served from the cache, not the origin server. Caching has long been used for static web content. It greatly improves performance for popular pages, and also saves capacity on the main Internet backbone by serving content locally to the user. One potential issue with a cache is stale material. Some content is very dynamic, for example news sites, and changes from hour to hour. It is important that the CDN keeps the cache synchronized with the origin server. Cache servers

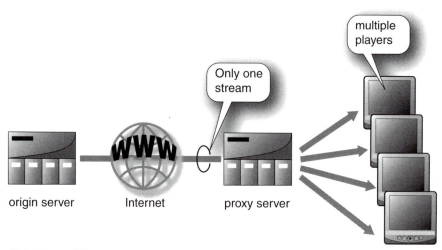

Figure 15.6 Edge splitting server.

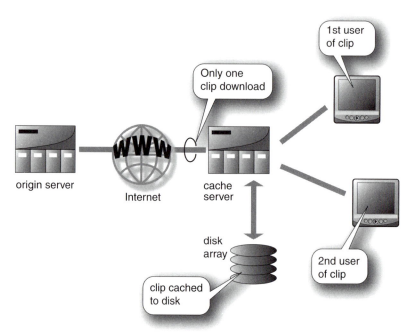

Figure 15.7 Edge cache server.

originally were developed for the speedy serving of graphic content for web sites. But the file sizes are usually under 1 Mbyte. Although caching can be used for streaming, it does not promise the same return as conventional web page caching. Streaming files are just too large to cache anything but the most frequently accessed files.

The alternative is to provide a quick response to a request for streaming content. The wait for the first frame of video is the crucial period; that is when you can lose the impatient viewer. If the first 30 seconds of a clip could be cached, the remainder can be streamed on-demand from the origin server to the edge server. To the viewer, this process can be made transparent by assembling the two halves in a playlist.

Reporting

The cache server provides full reporting data back to the origin server. This means that the origin server can collect the same usage statistics as if the content were being served directly to the client, and not via a proxy server.

Network controller

The core of the CDN is the network controller. This can intercept requests for streams and redirect the player to the nearest cache server. So the DNS server, rather than using a single IP address for an URL, will return the IP address of the correct edge server for the current conditions. This redirection can take into account network congestion and server utilization.

Referring to Figure 15.8, when the media player receives the metafile from the web server (4), the URL addresses the CDN controller (5). The controller then redirects the request to the optimum edge server (6) and the content is streamed to the player (7). The redirection can load-balance requests across a number of server clusters.

Akamai

Akamai has one of the most extensive CDNs with their FreeFlow streaming network. Akamai has become very popular for the rapid delivery of web content from distributed caches dispersed around POPs. Web sites use Akamai for widely accessed content and banner advertisements.

If you have your content 'akamized,' the reference tag uses an ARL or Akamai Resource Locator instead of an URL. The Akamai CDN uses this ARL to divert the browser request for a streaming file to the optimum edge server to retrieve the content.

Globix

Globix has tier-one fiber network linking major data centers in Santa Clara, New York, Atlanta, and London. This gives high performance coverage of North

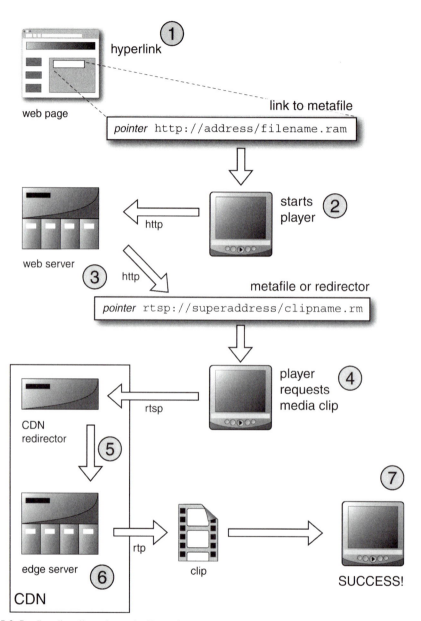

Figure 15.8 Redirecting the player to the edge server.

America and Western Europe, especially for live events. Globix uses caching for streaming media as well as web content. Their EarthCache CDN uses a minimum of 1 Tbyte at each cache node with wide-band connections to the Internet backbone. The caching enables media servers to cope with peaky traffic demands, without unduly stressing the origin servers.

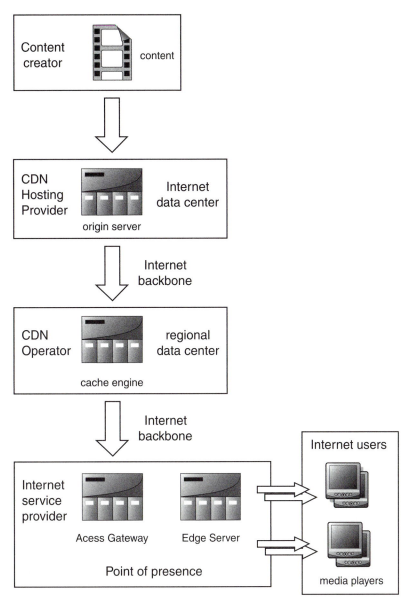

Figure 15.9 Content network.

The Globix network has continuous monitoring to ensure that media players are directed to the optimum connect points to receive their stream. The routing control keeps content on the Globix network where possible, rather than packets roaming around peered networks. This direct routing gives the high QoS that streaming demands.

Speedera

Speedera uses a network of edge servers to deliver content close to the viewer's POP. The viewer is directed to the best edge server by the Speedera DNS Server. This provides intelligent routing, derived from a network of probes that collect data about the QoS of the network and the load status of the Speedera server network. Content distributors can view viewer statistics and monitor live events with the SpeedEye interface.

The Speedera network extends across North America, Europe, and the Asia Pacific region. Speedera supports Windows Media and Real architectures and, using the open-source Darwin server, QuickTime and MPEG-4.

Corporate intranets

The corporate network has a different set of requirements from the public media viewer. An enterprise may want to use streaming for corporate communications, sales presentations, and distance learning.

Planning

Within an enterprise there will be conflicting demands. The different user departments – training and marketing – will want the flexibility to schedule webcasts at times to suit themselves. They will want a high QoS whatever the network load.

Conversely the IT department will want to maximize utilization of the network by the proper scheduling of high network demands. IT will have to keep important services like transaction processing and mail running reliably, whatever the streaming load. The solution here is for the network to be content-aware, so that the service provision can be controlled for the different applications.

Return of investment

You must have a top-down strategy to fund the network resources properly to provide for the agreed levels of use for streaming media. When scoping the ROI for the additional network cabling, router, and switches, remember the legacy costs. These include duplication costs for VHS tapes and CD-ROMs, plus their distribution costs. Another cost is travel time and expenses for meetings with regional and branch offices.

The corporation probably wants restrictions on the content that can be accessed. This is partly to stop the viewing of inappropriate content in working time; the other reason is to manage the bandwidth requirements for the wide-area circuits (to lower costs). Many companies rely on streaming for financial news and other corporate information. So controlled access to the Internet is becoming a necessity.

Firewall

The corporate network already will have a firewall to protect the internal networks from unauthorized access. The firewall listens to network traffic passing between the corporate network and the external Internet. Most firewalls are set up to block all incoming traffic and to restrict outgoing traffic. The outgoing traffic allowed is most likely TCP and HTTP. All UDP traffic is blocked, but that is the optimum network transport layer for streaming video. Streaming can pass through if it is cloaked as HTTP traffic or streamed over TCP. Neither provides the best streaming experience, especially if you want interactivity and the best control over the streaming delivery rate.

The firewall has two ports: one on the corporate side, the other in a so-called demilitarized zone (DMZ). The DMZ is where equipment that has to be accessed from the Internet is located. This will include Internet and extranet web servers.

If you want to provide staff with access to streaming media from the Internet, rather than passing the files through the firewall, a separate proxy streaming server can be used. The proxy allows your network administrators to set up access control rules, but does not allow external access to the internal network.

There is a potential issue with cached content – it may be that you need authorization to view a file. If the file is sitting on a cache it easily could be copied. RealServer Proxy gets around this by encrypting the file and the file name. The only way to access the file is to stream it. Material is retrieved from the cache and decrypted for streaming after an accounting connection is established to the origin server. This way, full usage reporting is maintained.

The Real player can be configured to point at the proxy server rather than trying to connect directly to the origin server. This would be the normal set-up in a corporate application.

The CDN and managing bandwidth

The proxy server can be used as a cache to sensibly manage the delivery of large files over external links. Suppose that you have a remote office connected by a T-1 line (1.5 Mbit/s). The link originally was leased for transaction data to the company databases and/or e-mail traffic. Both applications use relatively small files, so a T-1 has the capacity for a mid-sized office.

Now you want to start streaming internal presentations across the link. A high-quality encode (at say, 1 Mbit/s) is going to use almost the entire capacity of

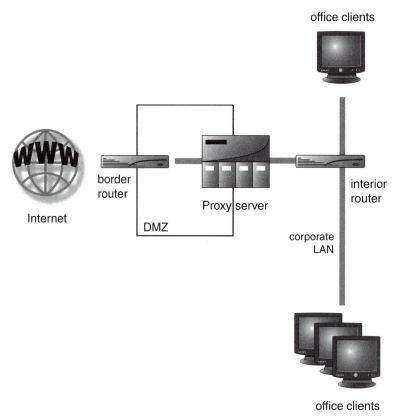

office clients

office clients

Figure 15.10 Corporate intranet with proxy server.

the link, clearly not a viable option. One way around this is to place a proxy server at the remote site. This can be preloaded with the presentation overnight, and then viewed from the cache during office hours. So during the day the T-1 line is left free for the regular data traffic.

A second solution would be to segregate traffic. Existing transaction processing, e-mail, and other data traffic can use the T-1 line, and media traffic can utilize a VPN (virtual private network) over the Internet via a POP close to the remote office.

The solution with the proxy server is *pushing* content. Most CDNs rely on a request from a player before content is delivered. This is called *pull* delivery. It has advantages in that the cache does not waste disk space by storing unwanted material. The disadvantage is that the first user to request a clip has to wait for delivery. Later users of the same clip will get a prompt response to their request.

The advantage of pushing is that the administrators have more control over wide-area network utilization, but this is to be balanced against the previously mentioned storage costs.

Running a reliable webcast

Computer equipment and software is not known for 100 percent reliability. Fiber cables can get severed. So if you are planning to host important webcasts, it is worth considering what would happen if the webcast went down. Even if you have taken great care in selection of equipment with a long mean time before failure ratings, the unexpected can always happen. So for a highly available system, it is best to assume that things will go wrong, and accordingly plan systems that are fault tolerant.

As an enterprise uses streaming more and more, then the requirements for high availability increase. Once streaming is core to corporate communications, the expectations of the systems approach those of the phone system. Conventional splitters are single points-of-failure in the delivery network. Real's Helix servers lets you design in redundancy to improve the QoS of the corporate network.

Helix platform

RealNetworks RealSystem iQ has been replaced by the Helix Universal Server and Gateway. One of the features of the system is support for redundant paths from the encoder or origin server to the media player. This means that if any part of the network is no longer available, the content delivery will fail-over to another path, thus ensuring the continuous delivery of the stream. Where the redundant streams reconverge at a Helix edge server, the server accepts the first packet and ignores any other packets that duplicate the same media data.

A peer-to-peer network can be set up so that servers can act as transmitters or receivers. This means that live content can be injected anywhere in the network.

The distribution can be push or pull. The push system transmits content to all the receivers that it has been configured to feed. Pull awaits a request from the player for content. The receiver feeding the player then requests content from the origin server. The push distribution can use forward error correction to correct for packet loss. This allows a unidirectional stream to be transmitted to edge servers, with no requirement for a back-channel. This can be very useful for satellite distribution by multicast. The level of error correction is configurable to suit the network conditions. Different paths can be set up separately, so, for example, a satellite link that already may use error correction could be set to a

push initiation

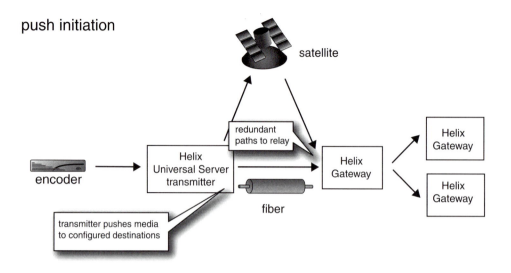

pull initiation

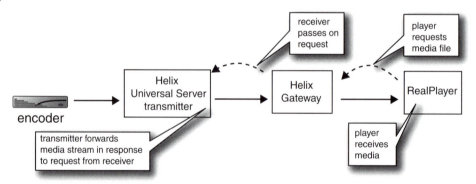

Figure 15.11 Push and pull with Helix server.

low value, and a high value set for a congested Internet connection. If a backchannel exists, the receiver can request resends of corrupted packets; this can be used in combination with, or instead of, forward error correction.

Improving the QoS

Alongside edge serving many strides are being taken to improve the QoS of the Internet. Two initiatives are resource reservation and multiprotocol label switching. The IP layer of the Internet uses best-effort delivery. The complexity to ensure error-free delivery is located at the server and client using a protocol like TCP. IP works very well; it uses a simple network system. But as the traffic grows to the point of router congestion, then packets are dropped. This causes delays and jitter. This is not a problem for general data traffic, but is an issue with real-time applications like multimedia and voice-over IP.

Even if you opt for a CDN, improving the intermediate network can only help. The challenge to improve the quality of service is to implement improvements without increasing complexity at the core of the network. Some technologies can be employed on closed systems like intranets, but rolling out developments to the public Internet is not as easy.

RSVP

Resource Reservation Protocol allows a client (the media player) to request a guaranteed network resource for unicast and multicast data flows. Resource Reservation is complex and too much of an overhead to be used generally across the Internet, but it can be deployed usefully at the edge. Potentially it delivers the best QoS delivery for packets.

MPLS

Multiprotocol Label Switching (MPLS) has emerged as a step on the road to photonic networks. It is used not just for IP (hence the qualifier multi-), but also other packet-switching protocols like frame relay. The label contains layer 3 routing information to indicate the next router hop. This means that the routers simply can switch the packet, using the data in the label. The data takes the label-switched path rather than using the usual router paths. This means that the labels can be assigned to allow control over the network traffic, hence providing potential routes around congestion.

Diffserv

Differentiated services or Diffserv allows coarse information about the service requirements of a packet to be coded in the IP header. It replaces the type-of-service or traffic class field in the header and determines the priority within the router. Diffserv marks traffic at the input to a network and is unmarked when the packet leaves that network. To operate, Diffserv requires a service level agreement at network peering points.

There is no holy grail for improving the quality of service for media streams crossing the Internet. There are a number of solutions that deployed together can improve the streaming experience, without requiring a complete swap-out of the network infrastructure. Diffserv can assign packet priorities, MPLS allows control over traffic, and RSVP can reserve resources at the edge. None of these protocols can make bandwidth available if the network is overloaded, so they are not a substitute for proper traffic engineering.

Satellite delivery

Some people are looking up to the sky for the answer to Internet congestion. Satellite communication can be used in two ways. One is to supplement the Internet backbone; the other is for direct connection to the user. Satellites are particularly useful for handling peak demands for popular webcasts. The satellite hops can completely bypass the backbone, by streaming multicasts to the edge of the Web. The Internet can be used for the back-channel to gather usage statistics and manage authorizations. The main bandwidth-hungry content data travels via the satellite circuit.

Multicast

Satellites are an efficient way to distribute multicasts to widely dispersed audiences. Any POP within the footprint of the downlink potentially can receive a multicast feed, without all the intermediate routers that a fiber connection would entail.

Satellite to the user

So what about the person who has had enough of the city and heads for a cabin in the hills? Technologies like ADSL are limited to a range of about 5,000 meters from the central office. One solution for remote sites is to use satellite delivery of broadband content. Satellites are also a good way to multicast a single stream to large audiences. They do not have the capacity for on-demand streaming to the very large numbers that the terrestrial circuit can offer, but are more suited to the burst transmissions of general web page downloads, where many users can share the same bandwidth.

Satellite can be one-way or two-way. One-way uses a regular telco backchannel, for example, through a dial-up circuit. This is an asymmetric configuration, but for the average user, the much lower bandwidth of the back-channel would be no more of an issue than that experienced by the ADSL user. Note that in some countries the regulatory authorities do not allow private uplinks, stemming from paranoia about security and state control.

VSAT

The use of very small aperture terminals has revolutionized satellite communications. The 4–5 meter diameter dishes common with C-band have been supplanted with compact Ku-band antennae, less than 1 meter in diameter. Typical capacities of a geo-stationary satellite (in the year 2000) were in the region of 108 Mbit/s of bandwidth per cell. A cell is about 640 km in diameter.

Hughes Network Systems have a system called DirecWay. This satellite distribution offers several advantages for the multicasting of live events. Only one stream is sent up to the satellite, and then any authorized user within the antenna footprint can participate in the webcast.

The Ka-band now is being used in the search for more free space in the RF spectrum. This band uses a compact dish with small beam width, but does suffer attenuation if there is rain in the path of the beam.

Summary

A compelling viewing experience demands a media stream that does not stall, that does not lose the audio. To achieve this goal, the bottlenecks that slow down the data packets have to be eliminated. As a clip is transferred from a live encoder or an origin server, the first impediment may be the link to the backbone. This is often a problem for live webcasts. The capacity of the available existing circuits may not be sufficient. Satellite back-haul may be an option.

The next step is to cross the backbone. Improvement in capacity has been assisted by the ever-increasing bandwidth of the fiber backbones, but the capacity of the last mile has not kept pace. Many incumbent utilities are burdened with an historic infrastructure designed for the plain old telephone service. The investment required to bring fiber to the curb is staggering, with a long payback time. This is an area where the television broadcaster wins hands down. They have a fixed cost for transmission. It makes no difference if there are a hundred or a million receivers within range of the tower.

Even if the end-to-end connection could be established satisfactorily, it is unlikely that all the remaining components are going to have excess capacity. Traffic always expands to fill the excess. So how can the traffic cross the Internet without suffering delays?

Content Delivery Networks (CDNs) mean that files no longer have to be served right across the Internet. Instead, content is delivered from servers placed at the edge of the Internet in your local point-of-presence. This edge serving makes for a much better viewing experience, without all the problems that packet loss and delays can cause as clips transit the Internet routers.

Edge serving by CDNs has been very successfully applied to static web content. To extend this to streaming is not trivial; the demands for disk space at the caches are large, but disk prices are always falling. The method can be applied successfully within a closed system, where a sensible booking system can be used for space. This could be a corporate network or a campus-wide system.

On the public Internet it is possible for special events with very large audiences to use caching effectively. The alternative is a hybrid approach – a prefix of the media clip could be cached to give a rapid start to the stream. The remainder of the stream then is pulled from the origin to the edge. The CDNs are content-aware and can apply smart routing algorithms to avoid traffic bottlenecks in the Internet, potentially lowering packet loss and delay. A big advantage with the CDN is that a live webcast can be split at the POP. This replaces a stream per client with a single stream from the origin server. The final goal would be the ability to multicast across disparate networks; this offers the best potential to reduce network congestion for live webcasts. The on-demand user is a more difficult customer to satisfy with high-quality delivery. If content is little used there is no advantage in caching; there are going to be different standards for popular content, which possibly could be dispersed to the edge, and content that is used very occasionally. To expect otherwise would need a CDN with a capacity that would not make economic sense.

When selecting a CDN to deliver to the public, size counts. If the CDN owns the fiber, has control over as much of the routing as possible, and has edge caches, then the stream is going to arrive in better shape than if it is launched into an unknown number of peered networks before arriving at the viewer's ISP.

As the bottlenecks are removed and the performance of streaming improves, more companies will want to use rich media, so the traffic will grow and congestion will increase. The improvements will have to continue at a pace to keep up with ever-increasing demand; it is just like building a highway network – traffic expands to meet the capacity and is regulated only by congestion.

16 Applications for streaming media

Introduction

In a period of ten years, streaming has evolved to become a primary medium for the delivery of video and audio content. It sits beside television for use in applications where the audience is too small or dispersed to warrant conventional broadcasting.

Other communications media now are finding that the codecs developed for Internet streaming have many other applications. Streaming demands highly efficient compression for the limited bandwidth available. These efficient codecs also can be used to reduce very high data rates – high-definition television – or for the very low data rates of mobile wireless applications. We see MPEG-4 and Windows Media being adopted for high-definition DVD coding, and MPEG-4 forms a key part of third-generation wireless standards.

This chapter explores some of the applications of streaming. Although streaming can be used standalone to deliver audio and video content, it is often deployed as a component in a wider system – often called rich media.

The advent of SMIL (Synchronized Multimedia Integration Language), has given content producers the tools to seamlessly assemble video, audio, animated vector graphics, and stills into the compelling and interactive experience that is rich media. At a simple level, one of the most-used styles is a combination of PowerPoint slides with accompanying audio and video. Such multimedia presentations can be used for sales promotions, distance learning, and product launches. It adds another component to the marketing mix, one that has the immediacy of video and the interactivity of the CD-ROM.

MPEG-4 offers new ways to create interactive applications, with features previously found in the DVD and CD-ROM. MPEG-4 was conceived to support object-based interactivity. Objects are not just video and audio, but many different types of content including 2- and 3D objects, animation, graphics, and text. The many objects are all delivered as parts of the stream. The viewer can use hotspots on the screen to switch objects at will; alternately, one object can trigger another object. MPEG-4 supports both client-side and server-side interactivity. Basic support uses the binary format for scenes (BIFS), which provides interaction between scene objects. JavaScript and Java provide more sophisticated functionality.

Applications for streaming include:

- Training
- Entertainment (Internet radio and VOD)
- Corporate communications
- Marketing
- Advertising

Some applications use streaming as the primary focus, others use streaming as a tool. A typical example of the latter is the use of streaming media as a proxy for broadcast quality content in digital asset management systems. Another use is for the rapid approval of clips, often needed when making commercials. The video production industry needs to exchange dailies (rushes) of clips to interested parties to preview the production processes. These parties could be in another city or even another continent. For such applications streaming media is an ideal vehicle.

Rich media

Rich media used to be the preserve of the CD-ROM. Tools like QuickTime allowed a combination of text, graphics, and video to be combined into an interactive presentation. In contrast, web content was limited to text and still images. The later development of Flash allowed content creators to enliven their static web pages with compelling vector graphics. Streaming media now allows regular video to be added to web pages, so the same mix of formats that was once restricted to the CD-ROM now can be delivered in real-time as a stream.

Before embarking on a rich media project, it's best to sit back and think, 'What and how am I trying to communicate?' If you want to webcast, use it because of its strengths; if you are using it as a substitute for a different medium your results may be less than optimum. Above all, it must hold the attention of the audience. That dictates the maintenance of high production values.

Whatever the codec designers may claim for video quality, the results can be less than satisfying once the stream has been distributed over the Internet. If you want the viewer to enjoy the experience, you should always plan the content for worst-case delivery quality, possibly offering alternative streams for narrow- and broadband users.

Many examples of rich media have indicated a complete lack of appreciation of the experience gained by the producers from other media formats. Some of the results of best communicators can be seen in regular television programs.

They use a combination of video and graphics that has been developed over a period of 50 years to produce content that is compelling to follow and easy to understand.

You will notice that there is a strict limit on the amount of information presented. A television program rarely will convey more than six key facts in 30 minutes, a long time for a webcast. The graphics are kept simple. As web developers have discovered, people will not read vast amounts of text on a screen. Often they graze the text, linking rapidly from one page to another.

The next point is to deliver a good quality image; that means restricting the aggregate data rate to sensible levels. The well-known saying is that the viewer will not wait. After a few seconds waiting for a download most viewers will click away to another site.

Another rule gained from the CD-ROM is to make it interesting by involving the viewer. Interactivity is the answer here. To reinforce the experience, make it immersive.

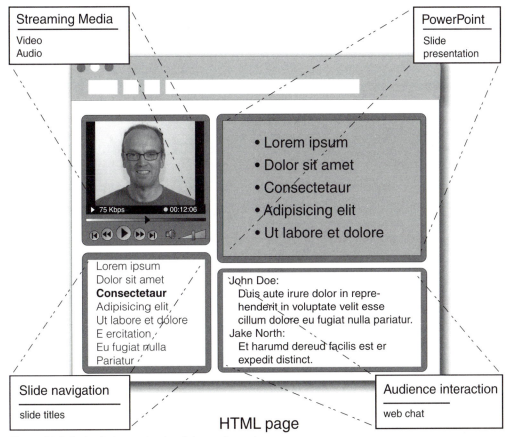

Figure 16.1 Typical elements of a rich media web page.

Typical presentations combine streaming media, PowerPoint slides, text transcripts, and interactive facilities like web chats.

Training

Streaming adds a new dimension to distance learning. The learner now can see and hear the lecturer, and interact with forums and chats. The same technology also can be used with corporate networks and the metropolitan area networks used by college campuses.

Most training solutions employ the conventional synchronized rich media model, often backed with linked documents in PDF format for background reading. The tools for creating content have become easier to use and lower in cost than initial product offerings.

Training can be a live webcast, or lectures called up on demand from an archive. The learner now can be separated in time or space from the lecturer, yet still feel the bond of the video communication.

Traditional text-based distance learning was plagued with high drop-out rates. The addition of audio and video adds immeasurably to the bonds of communication.

Entertainment

The streaming of legally obtained entertainment has had a slow start. The content providers have to see a return. The poor quality of early distribution networks meant that the public was unwilling to pay – plus they could get content from peer-to-peer networks, albeit by the theft of intellectual property. The advent of DRM and better content delivery networks means that content owners now are prepared to sell content via the Internet.

Internet radio

The webcasting of audio began in 1993 with Internet Talk Radio. It is now possible to listen to thousands of streamed radio stations from all around the globe. All genres are covered, and the technology has reached maturity. The bandwidth demands are reasonable compared with video streaming, and the audio quality can be very good.

Mobile

As third generation (3G) cellular wireless networks roll out their coverage, it has become feasible to deliver video to mobile devices. Early services have chosen to offer short clips by download and play, but streaming also can be used. Content can be encoded using MPEG-4 codecs, or can use proprietary codecs like Oplayo. This uses a lightweight player that can run on Java and Symbian platforms. The Oplayo technology also can run on GPRS network, so allowed service providers to offer video services prior to 3G network availability. The minimum bandwidth requirement is 10 kbit/s and it integrates with standard WAP and Web servers.

One advantage of the cell phone is the existing systems for billing for premium services. An equivalent did not exist for delivery to the desktop PCs via the Web.

Figure 16.2 Oplayer media player for mobile applications from Oplayo.

Video-on-demand (VOD)

Video-on-demand (VOD) has presented a challenge to many operators over the past 20 years. Ever since analog cable systems offered a gateway to the home, companies have strived to construct systems to deliver content on demand. Various schemes have been tried, including fiber to the home. Until this century, there has never been a return on investment. The VHS (and later DVD) rental outlets set the benchmark for price and picture quality – even though you had to drive to the nearest mall.

Conventional television required expensive storage and distribution systems to deliver unicast content. The advent of video compression and the ever-lowering costs of storage and servers now make cost-effective VOD services a reality.

The early systems were adopted by the closed networks like hotel movie channels. The hotels could charge premium prices for the captive customer. To provide such a service to the public requires a different scale of infrastructure. There are two ways to deliver content, over cable television circuits, and using broadband phone connections (ADSL). In countries that are deploying new cable television networks, there is the opportunity to supply IP set-top boxes so that VOD can be streamed, then displayed on a regular television receiver. In countries with an installed base of older boxes, support for such services awaits the replacement cycle for the installed base of boxes.

Many CDN networks now offer VOD, including Real, MSN, and Akamai.

Corporate communications

The corporate webcast has become an integral part of the quarterly earnings call, but streaming is not just for investors. Most departments can use streaming, either to replace meetings or to convey information – product training, conveying HR policies, and general corporate messages – the possibilities are immense. Streaming becomes vital for corporations with many remote sites, or to communicate to distributors, agents, and resellers.

Staff training

Staff training is a prime user of multimedia technology. Staff training can be expensive. It is costly to travel to a dedicated training center. CD-ROMs have been popular, but the production costs are high if interactive presentations are used. Rich media allows the typical stand-up with slides to be used, without the extra production costs. PowerPoint alone lacks the presence of the speaker.

A presentation can be prepared offline with simple products like Microsoft Producer. What about the live presentation? Anystream has created a product,

Apreso, which can capture a live presentation. The presentation is encoded as a video and audio file, and the slides are captured as they change. The live stream also is archived so viewers can watch on-demand at a time that may be more convenient than viewing the live stream. Virage's VS Webcasting adds the facility of interactivity with the audience, to answer questions, conduct polls, and collect viewing statistics. Products like Apreso and VS Webcasting make it very easy to share information with remote offices or foreign clients.

The news site

One of the most successful applications for streaming has been the financial news site. The big agencies like Bloomberg and Reuters have television channels, streaming stories around the clock. The traders have an insatiable demand for content, plus they have broadband access to the Internet. Rich media allows interviews to be combined with text stories generated from the agency feeds. Unlike television, there is more freedom in the use of text. The screen resolution of the typical computer display is higher than a standard-definition interlaced television receiver; so more background information can be given in text form.

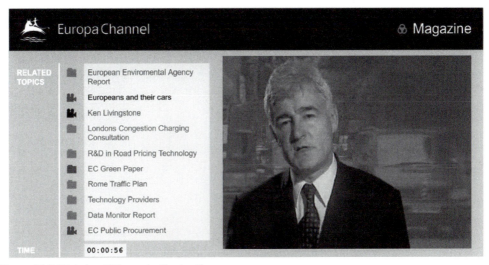

Figure 16.3 Webzine © Tornado Productions.

Marketing

Streaming can be used as part of the marketing mix to inform sales personnel and customers about new products. The interactive nature of streaming lends it to applications like product launches.

Product launches

Conventional product launches usually mean gathering at a venue for a live event. With remote offices, this is not always possible. Rich media means that part of the experience can be shared with any viewer that has a connection to the Internet.

Music promotion

The web has a long association with music, stemming from the use of the Internet to download MP3 audio files. So it is natural to use the Web to promote and retail music. This site was designed for a broadband service provider. It has clips of the band performing, backstage interviews, and other content of special interest to fans of the band. Two versions were created, one broadband for delivery at 250 kbit/s and a simpler version for delivery at 28 kbit/s. Many younger people – the potential audience – may not have broadband access, so it is important not to exclude them. By offering alternative low bit-rate content, perhaps audio-only, they can use low-cost dial-up modems to access similar content to broadband connection.

The style is very different from the average web page; it is more akin to television or the CD-ROM. Note that the small size of the video playback area does not detract from the overall design. Relevant graphics merge with the video into seamless tableaux.

The media player has been embedded into the background image, so the player surround does not impinge upon the overall graphic design. Some of the usual Web design conventions are used for familiarity; note the drop-down menu to select other pages on the site. The site is designed to display full-screen.

Advertising

When streaming first started, proponents imagined TV-style advertising on web sites. As broadcast television had demonstrated, video is a compelling format to deliver the marketing message. The reality was that brands were unwilling to deliver their message as a stalling, postage-stamp size video. As broadband usage has risen, and CDNs can offer a higher quality of service, streamed video advertisements are gaining acceptance. The pop-up ad and the banner have proved unpopular with viewers, and advertisers are looking for different ways to deliver a message. The auto manufacturers pioneered the medium, but now it is used by fast-moving consumer goods.

The early users have adopted Macromedia's Flash. It is almost ubiquitous in Web browsers, and is very easy to upgrade as new versions are released.

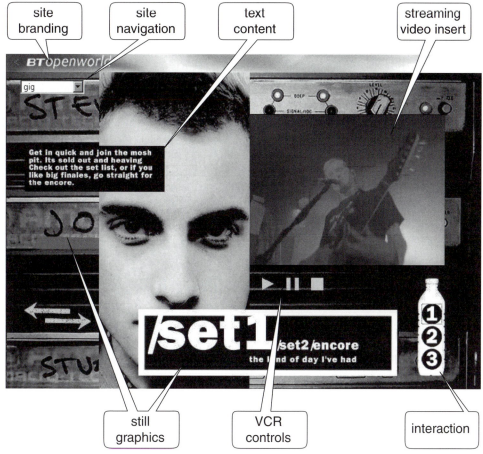

Figure 16.4 Music promotion site. © BT Openworld, produced by Tornado Productions Ltd.

Advertisers would be reluctant to place technical barriers in the way of potential viewers of their messages.

There are many outlets for advertising beyond the Web; video can be streamed over dedicated circuits to digital signage for live commercials at the point of sale.

Producing rich media

A skilled multimedia developer will have no problems adding interactive video and audio into existing rich media web pages, but a certain amount of hand scripting is bound to be needed. For the less skilled, there are a number of tools to ease the creation of presentations.

Microsoft Producer 2003

Microsoft Producer is a product for creating synchronized multimedia presentations for viewing in a web browser. Audio and video tracks, PowerPoint slides, and images can all be linked together on an interactive time line. As the user navigates back and forth through the presentation, the slides change in synchronism with the video track. In this way it is very easy for the viewer to step through different parts of a presentation.

The tool is an adjunct to Microsoft PowerPoint. It is aimed at the internal communications staff of a corporation, so presentations can be prepared in-house, without the need to outsource to a production company.

The production process starts with a PowerPoint presentation. As the presentation is run through, the slide changes are recorded on a time line. Audio and video tracks can then be synchronized to the same time line. At its simplest, you can make a voice-over to accompany a PowerPoint presentation. For a more compelling presentation, a video clip of the presenter can be added.

Other elements can be incorporated, like still photographs and links, and placed into an HTML page for delivery. Microsoft supplies a number of templates for the page layout, much like a word processor. The final integrated presentation is a web page; the Internet Explorer browser can be used to play the final presentation. The audio and video content is carried by Windows Media, embedded in the pages.

The advantage of Producer is that it is simple to use; any PowerPoint user could soon learn to use the extra facilities. Note that the output does not have to be streamed; it can also be distributed via FTP or CD-ROM.

Discreet Cleaner

Many nonlinear editing applications can directly output a limited set of streaming formats. If you need flexibility and additional control, then Discreet Cleaner is a stand-alone encoding platform. This very popular authoring application is available for both Windows and Mac platforms (Cleaner XL and Cleaner 6, respectively). Cleaner supports over 60 streaming codecs including the lesser used like the Kinoma (for Palm PDAs). It also can be used to code MPEG-2 for DVDs. Cleaner has a facility for programming synchronized events, called Event-Stream. This lets you create interactive rich media applications. All of the main streaming architectures offer some level of interactive features. Cleaner lets you add stream navigation, synchronize HTML to streaming media, embed links, and add interactive hotspots. Cleaner is agnostic toward the streaming architecture, so you can author once and then encode many times to support several streaming architectures.

Figure 16.5 Microsoft Producer output on a web browser. Screen shot reprinted by permission from Microsoft Corporation.

Digital asset management

Streaming provides a vital tool for digital asset management systems. These are the systems used for the management of multimedia content for the workgroup or enterprise. Traditionally video content has been distributed by U-matic or VHS tape, or more recently, the DVD. Using streaming, video content can be viewed with a desktop computer without the need for a VCR and video monitor. This enables access to video content by anyone with a network connection. Although the full advantages will be most evident in media businesses, corporate-wide access to video can be useful to many other businesses. Content could be television news clips with relevance for the corporation, the archive of television commercials for the company's products, or past corporate addresses.

Digital asset management provides the tools to search for relevant content, browse the streaming proxies, and order broadcast resolution copies as required.

Many businesses have libraries of video material, and not just broadcasters. Advertising agencies and large corporations both can have extensive archives of commercials and training material. As you build up a library of video clips, gradually a problem becomes evident. How do you find the clip you want? With text documents, you can search for a string of characters to locate relevant material. With video and audio you do not have this luxury. Traditional libraries of tapes on shelves often have either simple card indices or a computer database.

The initial use of asset management was for television news archives to give journalists and program researchers full access to the vault. Asset management is not limited to internal use; it also can be used as an aid to the marketing of video content to the consumer or for sales to other program makers.

A typical example would be a health information provider that wants to sell videos. The use of a powerful video search engine helps potential customers to find the right product for their needs – a useful adjunct to the selling process. The potential purchaser can preview material, find the right video, then order a DVD or, alternatively, watch a stream. Video libraries also can be used in higher education. A university can record lectures as streams and make the files available on-demand to students. Again, the asset management makes the lecture archive searchable.

There are several issues to overcome with an asset library:

- How do you access the library from remote or dispersed sites?
- How do you find material that you want?
- How do you preview the material?
- How do you distribute the material?

The obvious way to offer access is through a web browser. That way the user can use a conventional search GUI, and the media can be viewed with a player plug-in. The drawback is that the library material may be on analog tape – Betacam, U-Matic, or VHS – or for more recent material, Digital Betacam or DV. Clearly you cannot deliver video over the corporate network; it has to be in a format that can be carried over IP. Streaming formats provide the answer. Once the video is encoded it can be viewed from a desktop computer, rather than requiring a dedicated video player and monitor.

The solution to efficient network utilization is to use a hierarchy of lower resolution proxies. That way you start with lightweight downloads, and as you narrow the search, larger resolution media files can be viewed. That way the speed of search and the network utilization are optimized.

The initial search is text only; the results set may be 10 or 100 possible clips. You then can view thumbnails to help identify the required clip. Once a likely file has been located, then you can view a low-resolution stream, maybe 30 kbit/s. Once you have confirmed that you have found the correct file, you then can view a high-resolution stream, perhaps at 500 kbit/s. The alternative would be to order a dub of the master tape.

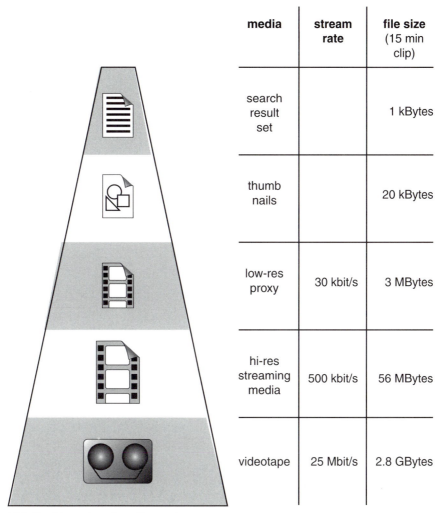

media	stream rate	file size (15 min clip)
search result set		1 kBytes
thumb nails		20 kBytes
low-res proxy	30 kbit/s	3 MBytes
hi-res streaming media	500 kbit/s	56 MBytes
videotape	25 Mbit/s	2.8 GBytes

Figure 16.6 The hierarchy of media proxies.

Streaming media is used as a core technology for the location of the relevant content and then for subsequent viewing of the media library. You can find an in-depth study of digital asset management technology in the book by David Austerberry (2004), *Digital Asset Management*, Focal Press, ISBN 0240519248.

Remote content production

If content can be viewed as proxies, why not edit the content using the proxies? This would allow an editor remote from an event to view the content and edit it into a finished program. This frees the editorial processes from traditional linear videotape editing or the dedicated nonlinear workstation.

TWIinteractive has developed a digital asset management solution called the Interactive Content Factory (ICF). This provides an end-to-end solution for the acquisition, production, and distribution of video content to a wide range of delivery channels including television and wireless applications. ICF has much simplified the delivery and syndication of live sports programming and the associated highlights packages using a number of new technologies.

One component of the ICF solution is NetEdit, a desktop editing product. This leverages the power of streaming video, and specifically new features of the Windows Media 9 Series to provide increased functionality for the remote user.

Most digital asset management products give the ability to view proxies of video assets. ICF takes this a step further. NetEdit is a browser-based interface that can be used to edit archive files, or even live video feeds. The operator can perform frame-accurate edits with transitions and effects, and record a voice-over. The result can be exported as an edit decision list (EDL) for a craft editor to refine the rough cut. Alternately, the ICF video server can use the EDL to automatically implement the edits on the broadcast resolution material (a process called auto-conform).

ICF has developed a way to burn running time code into a live feed encoded as Windows media format. Conventionally the time index object for the streaming file is generated when the file is closed. The ICF video server embeds the time code, so that live content can be edited whilst being captured. For sports coverage, this means that highlights can be packaged during play as fast as the editor can mark the in and out points. As an example, a goal could be delivered to viewers as a short clip less than a minute after the event.

NetEdit has a familiar timeline interface, with all the functions needed for simple editing, but requires only Internet Explorer installed on the workstation and a broadband connection with an IP connection to the media server.

Summary

The last 100 years have seen a steady evolution of new media channels. The first mass communication media, print, was joined by radio. Alongside the development of radio the telephone opened up personal communication. Then came television. At each stage the new medium originally was treated as a variant of its predecessor. Some of the first radio news broadcasts used the anchor to read the newspaper headlines. Early television was like a radio broadcast with pictures. Gradually the creators of content learned how to exploit the new medium in a way that broke from the stereotypes of its forerunners.

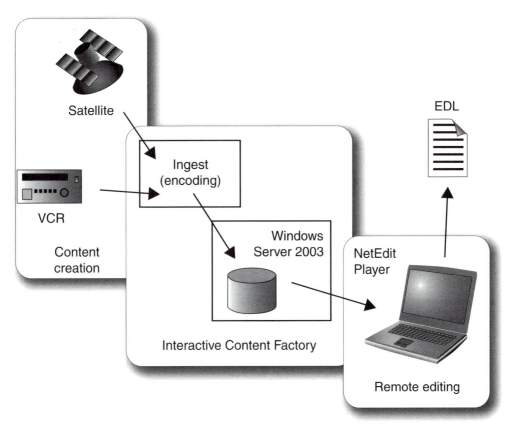

Figure 16.7 Interactive Content Factory data flow. TWIinteractive Ltd.

The barriers between the electronic media are becoming blurred. Interactive television can combine web content with off-air television. Telephones and radios can display text and graphics. Web browsers have audio and video.

The old paradigm of a handful of major television networks being the prime source of video programming has long gone. Cable and satellite can deliver several hundred channels to the home, but television is still mass media – 200 channels for a population of millions is hardly bespoke programming. Streaming adds a new and high-capacity delivery vehicle for video content that can be personalized for each viewer. It may be special content or targeted ads.

The quality delivered to the viewer has increased steadily since the mid-1990s, with improvements in codecs and broadband access for the last mile, and in 2002, it could rival VHS, with many quality improvements in the offing.

Figure 16.8 Interactive Content Factory NetEdit desktop editor from TWIinteractive Ltd.

QuickTime dominated multimedia production. RealNetworks pioneered the introduction of streaming to the Internet community. Now Windows Media have joined the fray with the integration into the operating system. MPEG-4 promises to open up streaming beyond the environment of the PC. Breaking away from the bounds of the rectangular video picture offers new possibilities for immersive and interactive experiences. The player could be a cellular phone, a PDA, a games console, or a high-definition television receiver.

There is no doubt that the first streaming pictures were less than satisfying, but AM radio in the 1920s and television in the monochrome days both provided a great source of entertainment. The advances in delivery technologies, including broadband and CDNs, are offering both the consumer and the corporate user a whole new way to communicate. It is a very flexible medium, offering everything from live webcasts, distance learning, and the whole gamut of corporate communications.

It is important that suitable content is selected for the medium. Take the movie industry. The realistic limit for the last mile is going to be 1 Mbit/s for the next decade. Will an on-demand movie streamed at that rate compete with the consumers' expectations of DVD quality? This quality gap will stretch further when the high-definition DVD becomes available. The DVD supports a higher data

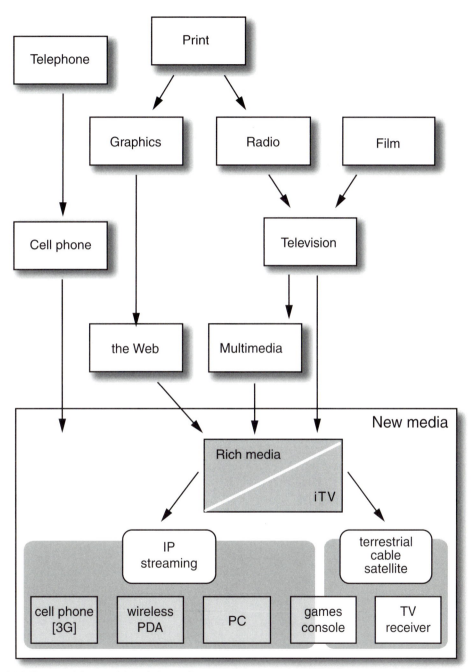

Figure 16.9 The road from print to rich media.

transfer rate than the last mile and the players are low cost, so perhaps streamed movies are not a good application for webcasting.

Many corporate applications of streaming replace the face-to-face presentation, saving on traveling costs and time. Other applications offer entertainment and information to the public.

And finally

Webcasting has finally broken the bounds of the PC. Content can be streamed to many different types of appliances, from mobile phones to television set-top boxes. The monetization of webcasting has proved more difficult than many people thought. There are many reasons for this, but the facts must be faced – much content has been of poor technical quality with indifferent production values. Consumers are happy to pay for good quality – look at the sales of CDs, DVDs, and games. As the quality issues of distribution are resolved and digital rights management becomes widely used, there are many indications that content will be sold very successfully.

The killer apps will have to exploit the strengths of the medium: the immediacy, the interactivity, the ability to personalize content, the rich media, and, through the Internet, the global reach.

Glossary

3GPP Third Generation Partnership Project. A collaborative agreement between telecomms standards bodies to produce specifications for 3G mobile systems based on GSM networks.

3GPP2 A parallel project to 3GPP set up to produce specifications for CDMA2000 networks.

4CIF Picture source format with 704 × 576 pixels for luminance and 352 × 288 pixels for chrominance.

16CIF Picture source format with 1408 × 1152 pixels for luminance and 704 × 576 pixels for chrominance.

Agnostic A system that can handle different streaming architectures.

Asynchronous Two devices, typically a transmitter and receiver of data, that are not synchronized. The receiver uses a buffer to store incoming data, and processes at its own rate. Usually feedback to the transmitter will indicate buffer overflow.

Broadband There is no rigorous definition, but this is usually taken to mean connections that can carry data at rates higher than 100 Kbit/s.

Browser A client-side application used to view HTML files, usually from the Web, but can be served over a LAN from a local server. Typical examples are Microsoft Explorer and Netscape Navigator. The streaming player usually is used as a plug-in to the browser.

CIF The common intermediate format of the H.261 video conferencing standard: 352 × 288 pixels for luminance and 176 × 144 pixels for chrominance.

Caching The temporary storage of often-used content in a proxy or edge server.

Capture The conversion of content from regular audio and video to a computer format.

Codec A compression and decompressor algorithm. The encoder will use the codec to compress the media file, which is decompressed by the media player.

DCT Discrete cosine transform; the basis of the spatial compression used by the MPEG standards.

DSL Digital subscriber line. A broadband connection that can carry voice or data traffic. The asymmetric DSL (ADSL) uses a legacy copper pair to provide high-speed downloads to the client alongside the analog telephone service.

Encoding The compression and packetization of video and audio to a streaming format.

Frame 1. A single television picture, the result of a scanned raster. An interlaced frame comprises two fields. 2. A packet of data used in telecomms circuits.

H.261 ITU video-conferencing standard.

H.263 Development of H.261 for low bit-rate applications like video phones.

Huffman coding A variable-length coding scheme where the most-used characters have a shorter code than the lesser-used characters.

Indexing The generation of a content catalog index by the extraction of metadata from the content.

Interlace scan The odd then even lines of a television frame are scanned alternately.

Intranet A private network for sharing similar content formats to that available over the public Internet, but for corporate use only.

JPEG Joint Photographic Experts Group. A compression standard for continuous-tone still images.

JPEG2000 A compression standard for continuous-tone still images using wavelet compression.

MDCT Modified Discrete cosine transform. A perfect reconstruction cosine modulated filter bank. It has the property of time-domain aliasing cancellation.

Metadata Attributes of data, or "data about data."

MPEG Moving Picture Experts Group. A working group of the ISO/IEC that develop standards for digital video and audio coding.

MPEG-1 Audio and video compression for CD-ROMs.

MPEG-2 Television and DVD compression standard.

MPEG-4 Rich media object coding standard for fixed and mobile use.

MPEG-7 Metadata framework for multimedia.

MPEG-21 Framework for integrating multimedia resources and to facilitate value exchange.

MP3 The audio codec for MPEG-1, layer 3.

Multicast A means of live webcasting to a large audience that requires a single stream to be transmitted by the server, rather than one per client. Each viewer connects to the multicast, so the network routers send copies of each datagram of the stream to all the clients participating in the multicast. Potentially can save network resources, but is not well supported on the WWW.

Narrowband A dial-up connection to the Internet, typically using a 28K or 56K analog modem over a regular telephone line.

NTSC The U.S. analog color television standard. The National Television Standards Committee devised a system that was backward-compatible with the RS-170 monochrome system. It has a field rate of 60 Hz and 525 lines. It has since been supplanted by the ATSC standards for high-definition digital television.

PAL Phase Alternating Line, the color television standard used in most of Europe (France used SECAM). It has a field rate of 50 Hz and 625 lines.

Plug-in A small software application that plugs into a web browser and renders file formats that are not supported by the browser. These include Flash vector graphics and streaming audio and video decompressors.

Progressive scan A television frame is scanned top-to-bottom on one pass.

QCIF Quarter-size CIF image format: 176×144 pixels for luminance and 88×72 pixels for chrominance.

Rich Media A combination of audio, video, graphics, and text, in a synchronized and possibly interactive presentation.

SIF The standard image format of MPEG-1 encoding: 352×240 pixels, 30 fps for NTSC; 352×288 pixels, 25 fps for PAL.

Telecine A device used to transfer movie film to a television format where it can be stored on videotape. To match the film rate of 24 frames per second to television at 30 frames per second every fourth field is repeated, called the 3:2 sequence.

Unicast A one-to-one stream from a media server to a client player.

VC-9 The SMPTE standard for the video compression codec based on Windows Media 9 technology.

Abbreviations

3G	Third Generation
3GPP	Third Generation Partnership Project
AAC	Advanced Audio Coding
AAL	ATM Adaptation Layer
ACE	Advanced Coding Efficiency (Profile)
ACELP	Algebraic Code-Excited Linear Prediction
ADC	analog-to-digital converter
ADSL	Asymmetric Digital Subscriber Line
AES	Audio Engineering Society
AIFF	Audio Interchange File Format
AMR	Adaptive Multirate
API	Application Programming Interface
ASF	Advanced System Format (Microsoft)
ATM	Asynchronous Transfer Mode
ATSC	Advanced Television Systems Committee
AVC	Advanced Video Codec (H.264, MPEG-4 Pt. 10)
AVI	Audio-Video Interleaved
BIFS	Binary Format for Scenes
CBR	Constant bit rate
CCD	Charge-coupled Device
CDMA	Code Division Multiple Access
CDN	Content Delivery Network
CELP	Code-Excited Linear Prediction
CIDR	Classless Inter-Domain Routing
CIE	Commission Internationale d'Eclairage
CIF	Common Intermediate Format
CPU	central processing unit
CRT	cathode ray tube
DAI	DMIF-Application Interface
DARPA	Defense Advanced Research Projects Agency

DCT	Discrete Cosine Transform
DMA	Direct Memory Access
DAT	Digital Audio Tape
DES	Data Encryption Standard (algorithm)
DMIF	Delivery Multimedia Integration Framework
DRM	Digital Rights Management
DS	DMIF signaling
DSL	digital subscriber line
DTP	desktop publishing
DV	Digital Video
DVB	Digital Video Broadcasting
DVMRP	Distance Vector Multicast Routing Protocol (used by MBone)
EDL	Edit Decision List
ETSI	Europe Telecommunications Standards Institute
FTTC	Fiber to the Curb
GIF	Graphic Interchange Format
GMPLS	Generalized Multiprotocol Label Switching
GPRS	General Packet Radio Service
GSM	Global System for Mobile Communications
HD	high-definition (television)
HFC	Hybrid Fiber Coax
HTTP	HyperText Transfer Protocol
HVXC	Harmonic Vector Excitation Coding
IEC	International Electrotechnical Commission
IETF	Internet Engineering Task Force
IGMP	Internet Group-Membership Protocol
IP	Internet Protocol, Intellectual Property
IPMP	Intellectual Property Management and Protection
ISDN	Integrated Service Digital Network
ISMA	Internet Streaming Media Alliance
ISO	International Standards Organization
JPEG	Joint Photographic Experts Group
LAN	local area network
LPC	Linear Predictive Coding
MBone	Multicast Backbone
MDCT	Modified discrete cosine transform
MIME	Multipurpose Internet Mail Extension
MMS	Microsoft Media Server
MOSPF	Multicast Open Shortest Path First protocol
MP3	MPEG-1, layer 3, audio codec
MPEG	Moving Picture Experts Group
MPLS	Multiprotocol Label Switching

MSBD	Media Streaming Broadcast Distribution
NFS	Network File System (UNIX)
NIC	network interface card
NTFS	NT File Systems (Microsoft Windows)
NTSC	National Television Standards Committee (USA)
PAL	Phase-Alternation Line
PCI	Peripheral Component Interconnect
PCM	Pulse Code Modulation
PDA	Personal Digital Assistant
PDF	Portable Document Format (Adobe)
PDH	Plesiochronous Digital Hierarchy
PNA	Progressive Networks Audio
PNG	Portable Network Graphics
POP	Point-of-Presence
PQMF	Pseudo-Quadrature Mirror Filter (MPEG-1 audio)
OD	Object Descriptor
QCIF	Quarter Common Intermediate Format
QoS	Quality of Service
RFC	Request for Comment (IETF)
RTCP	Real-Time Control Protocol
RTTP	Real-Time Transport Protocol
RTSP	Real-Time Streaming Protocol
SCSI	Small Computer Serial Interface
SD	standard-definition (television)
SDH	Synchronous Digital Hierarchy
SDI	Serial Digital Interface
SDK	Software Development Kit
SDMI	Secure Digital Music Initiative
SDP	Session Description Protocol
SECAM	Séquentiel Couleur avec Mémoire
SIF	Source or Standard Input Format
SLA	Service Level Agreement
SMIL	Synchronized Multimedia Integration Language
SMPTE	Society of Motion Picture and Television Engineers
SONET	Synchronous Optical Network (SDH)
S/PDIF	Sony/Philips Digital Interface
SVG	Scalable Vector Graphics
TCP	Transmission Control Protocol
UDP	User Datagram Protocol
UID	Unique Identifier
URL	uniform resource locator
USB	Universal Serial Bus

VBR	Variable bit rate
VC-9	Video Codec 9
VLC	variable-length coding
VOD	video-on-demand
VOP	Video Object Plane
VPN	Virtual Private Network
VRML	Virtual Reality Modeling Language
VSAT	Very Small Aperture Terminal
WAN	wide area network
XrML	Extensible rights markup language

Index